# "FICTION DISTORTING FACT"

# "FICTION DISTORTING FACT"

## The Prison Life,
## Annotated by Jefferson Davis

"It is important . . . to know just how far the various statements in the [*Prison Life*] are true and are based on contemporary notes and diaries. Unless that is known the book can necessarily have small value as a historical document."

—*Current Literature*, 1905.

EDWARD K. ECKERT

•MERCER•

ISBN 0-86554-201-5

The paper used in this publication meets
the minimum requirements of American National Standard
for Information Services—Permanence of Paper
for Printed Library Materials, ANSI Z39.48-1984.

*Library of Congress Cataloging-in-Publication Data*
Craven, John Joseph, 1822-1893.
    "Fiction distorting fact."

    Annotated ed. of: Prison life of Jefferson Davis,
by John J. Craven.
    Bibliography: p. 151
    Includes index.
    1. Davis, Jefferson, 1808-1889. 2. Statesmen—
United States—Biography. 3. Craven, John Joseph,
1822-1893. I. Davis, Jefferson, 1808-1889.
II. Eckert, Edward K., 1943–      . III. Title.
E467.1.D26C89    1986    973.7'13'0924    [B]    86-23746
ISBN 0-86554-201-5 (alk. paper)

# ·CONTENTS·

The impetus for this new edition of the *Prison Life of Jefferson Davis* stemmed from my research into the Confederate president's life for a projected biography. The more I read and reflected upon Davis, the more convinced I became that his life is obscured by a tangle of myths and concealed by the vines of symbolism that he himself fostered in his later years. It was clear to me that Davis had undergone metamorphoses at two critical periods in his life. In the first, after the death of his young wife, Sarah Knox Taylor, Davis entered a prolonged period of self-imposed exile during which he studied historical and constitutional works to prepare himself for a career in Southern politics. Formerly a carefree youth who had lived much of his early life in the North, Davis emerged from this trauma as the mature embodiment of a Southern planter-politician.

The second transformation occurred during Davis's forced imprisonment following the Civil War. Once again, with time to read and to contemplate, he redefined the meaning of his life. He consciously began to conform himself to the new cultural myths being devised to find meaning for the Confederate defeat. Jefferson Davis became the enduring symbol of the "Lost Cause."

As I researched Davis's life, I grew more aware that no one had fully appreciated the full significance of these two periods. I also realized that I was far from writing a biography of Davis, for I too had merely scratched the surface of his rich mind. A full understanding of Jefferson Davis involves reading the same works he read and discussed with his brother Joseph at the family plantation on Davis Bend, and exploring his thoughts while he was imprisoned at Fort Monroe.

Traditionally historians have relied on the *Prison Life of Jefferson Davis* for information on the latter period. This "memoir," attributed to his prison physician John J. Craven, graphically described the first six months of Davis's term. Written in a romantic style, it made an aloof statesman into a folk hero. Anyone who has spent time researching Jefferson Davis, however, should have realized that much of the book does not ring true. Yet because it is so convenient and so often quoted, and since it reinforces what people *want* to believe, it has become the accepted version of what happened while Davis was in prison.

After he had read the *Prison Life,* Davis angrily described a portion of it as "fiction distorting fact." Still the Confederate ex-president realized the importance of that account of his prison years. So despite his harsh criticisms of the *Prison Life* in the margins of his own copy, Davis never publicly disclaimed either Craven or the work, and he rarely mentioned them in private correspondence.

Davis had lost almost everything in the war. Furthermore, many Southerners attributed their personal losses to Davis's stubbornness. Is it surprising, then, that the book, which had so pointedly described his suffering for the "Lost Cause," was never publicly denounced by the man it had elevated to a hero?

Significantly, in his published writings Davis skipped over the imprisonment almost entirely. He voiced strong opinions about most other accounts of his life, and he and Mrs. Davis quickly challenged negative works about him. One can only conclude from their silence re-

garding the *Prison Life* that Davis preferred to permit this false account to stand as the approved source; denying its validity would have belittled the magnitude of his sufferings and
martyrdom. After all, in Davis's mind, while the details were incorrect, sometimes making
him appear less dignified than he really was, or wanted to be, his suffering was real.

The volume and variety of the letters Jefferson Davis wrote during his long life overwhelm
researchers and writers. The *Prison Life,* on the other hand, is a convenient, colorful description of the man's imprisonment, so Davis biographers have relied upon it to bridge the stormy
war years and the last two decades of the ex-president's life.

The authenticity of the *Prison Life* has been most actively promoted by those whose livelihood depends upon perpetuating the memory of Jefferson Davis. These persons have been
more aware than scholars that a large part of Davis's favorable postwar image rested upon
this memoir. These dedicated souls have carefully tended the everlasting flame of the "Lost
Cause."

This new study of the *Prison Life* places the work and these two years in proper perspective.
Davis was imprisoned and Craven was assigned to be his physician. Not much more than
that should be accepted as fact from the "memoir." This edition of the *Prison Life* reproduces
Davis's comments in the margins of his copy of the book, along with editorial notes and ex-
planations. The introduction provides a clear, objective description of Davis's life at Fort
Monroe, based on a careful sifting of the evidence, especially Davis's own letters from prison.
The introduction also explains the origins and importance of the *Prison Life*. Finally, the appendix is an account of Davis's imprisonment by General Nelson A. Miles, commandant of
Fort Monroe during the first fifteen months of Davis's incarceration. Now future historians
and biographers who wish to know what really happened to Jefferson Davis behind the walls
of Fort Monroe will have a standard reference text.

# ·ACKNOWLEDGMENTS·

I am indebted to Professor of History William Hanchett, San Diego State University, who first located and studied the marginal comments in Jefferson Davis's own copy of the *Prison Life*. Clearly the work contained more fiction than fact. Professor Hanchett early recognized the significance of my work and urged me to pursue it.

My thanks go to my wife, Linda Corroum Eckert, and my boys, Greg, Chris, and Dan, who accompanied me on two trips to Mississippi and Louisiana to research the physical and literary remains of Davis's own life. With little complaint they traveled the dirt country roads with me to locate homes and graves. My wife also corrected the entire introduction, made constructive suggestions, and accompanied me to Tulane and Transylvania universities to transcribe Davis's prison letters; she never lost faith in me or the work.

To St. Bonaventure University goes my gratitude for generous grants and a sabbatical leave that enabled me to pursue the research. St. Bonaventure also provided a publication grant that helped defer some necessary expenses.

Special thanks are due to three of my colleagues at St. Bonaventure who read the entire manuscript, taking time from their vacations to comment upon and to correct my work. To Steven J. Brown, Patrick K. Dooley, and Thomas J. Schaeper, my appreciation for your encouragement and gentle-but-valued criticism.

I thank Cy Courtney, Esq. of New Orleans, a foremost graphographer who spent hours researching Jefferson Davis's handwriting and verifying that the marginal comments in the Tulane University copy of the *Prison Life of Jefferson Davis* were written by Davis.

I also extend gratitude to the staff at the Special Collections Division of the Howard-Tilton Memorial Library at Tulane University, especially Wilbur E. Meneray; Carolyn Palmgreen, Special Collections Librarian, Transylvania University; and Theresa Covley, Interlibrary Loan Librarian, St. Bonaventure University.

To the editorial staff of Mercer University Press, my regards for working with my manuscript, that is, dismantling and reconstructing it so that my ideas and words flow more freely and accurately. Their labor has made this work far better than it was upon submission.

My sincere thanks to all these fine people and to the many others who aided my research or who offered me advice and criticism. Of course, the responsibility for errors of fact and interpretation is mine alone.

This publication was made possible in part by a grant from the Watson-Brown Foundation, Atlanta, Georgia.

*Edward K. Eckert*
*St. Bonaventure, New York*
*January 1986*

For my mother,
in memory of my father

## THE LOST CAUSE

The South stands in epic contrast to the rest of the United States. Both share a common history, but many of the most important national events have affected the South uniquely. America's history, mankind's great experiment in human freedom and material well-being, stands in stark contrast to Southern slavery, poverty, and military defeat. History alone cannot convey the depth of meaning that a distinct American past has had on the South. Myths arose, in part, to provide meaning for historical facts. The great Southern writer Robert Penn Warren once observed that "there are two kinds of memory. One is narrative, the unspooling in the head of what has happened, like a movie film with no voices. The other is symbolic."[1]

History—narrative memory—is only able to tell what has occurred. Bound by their evidence, historians may be able to relate why something happened and describe its effects, but history alone cannot recreate emotions or the meaning of events to those who have experienced them. Myth—symbolic memory—is better able than history to convey feelings and values. Myth is a tale, a story, sometimes based on actual events, but emphasizing the essence rather than fact. Any good storyteller knows that facts are less important than the point being made.

A myth is aimed at the mind through the heart. It is better able than history to provide philosophical values for inherently contradictory events. "Legendary myths are not told for entertainment," argues classicist G. S. Kirk, but to "glorify famous leaders and tribal history by telling of wars and victories, . . . or disguised contradictions between national ideals and actuality."[2] The appearance, duration, systemization, and acceptance of a myth is evidence enough that it has a necessary cultural function. Myths are neither fairy tales nor untruths; they are complex explanations for events that reach into the core of human understanding to provide meaning for life's essential contradictions. One expert on myth has defined it as "*a traditional tale with secondary partial reference to something of a collective importance.*"[3]

Myth always deals with serious, sometimes sacred, subjects important to a people's collective experience; myths are told not only for enjoyment but also for a broader purpose. French anthropologist Claude Lévi-Strauss believes that "history has replaced mythology and fulfills the same function, that for societies without writing and without archives the aim of my-

---

[1]Robert Penn Warren, *Jefferson Davis Gets His Citizenship Back* (Lexington: University Press of Kentucky, 1980) 1.

[2]G. S. Kirk, *Myth, Its Meaning and Function in Ancient and Other Cultures* (Cambridge: Cambridge University Press, 1970) 254. The subject of myth is one that has intrigued classical scholars, anthropologists, and philosophers. Excellent studies of myth include Walter Burkert, *Structure and History in Greek Mythology and Ritual* (Berkeley: University of California Press, 1979), Ernest Cassirer, *The Philosophy of Symbolic Forms* (New Haven: Yale University Press, 1955), and Claude Lévi-Strauss, *Myth and Meaning* (New York: Schocken Books, 1978).

[3]Burkert, *Structure and History,* 23.

thology is to insure that as closely as possible—complete closeness is obviously impossible—the future will remain faithful to the present and to the past."[4]

No region of the United States has confused myth and history more than the South. George B. Tindall broke important ground in his essay, "Mythology: A New Frontier in Southern History," which cautioned his fellow historians that "myth itself becomes one of the realities of history."[5] Myth, rather than history, more accurately fulfilled the South's need to understand itself. Before the Civil War—the great epic that split antebellum myths from the myths of the New South—there were myths of paternalism, racism, and benevolent slavery, all summed up in the Plantation Myth. Historian Paul M. Gaston believed it was due to the inherent contradiction between the ideas of the early Republic and the actuality of life in the South that myth rather than history was used to make "some sense and order out of the complex, ambivalent patterns of Southern experience."[6] Slavery stood in stark contrast to the ideals of Thomas Jefferson, and it forced the South to create its myth of agrarianism: that life on the Southern plantation for whites and blacks was more natural and virtuous than life in the cities or the factories of the North. A code of honor set rules so the mythical planter kingdom could flourish.[7]

The Plantation Myth was shattered by the Civil War. The virtuous South had been vanquished by Yankee power, and little remained of that once-glorious land called "Dixie." The antebellum South became more than fact; it was transformed into legend and remembered as a Garden of Eden, a noble culture, a benevolent way that had been struck down by Yankee materialism and overwhelming numbers. The war had not been fought to protect slavery, Southerners maintained, but to preserve the Southern way and its "peculiar institution." Yet slavery was gone—no other nation in the Western world had been willing to support the South on that embarrassing issue—and with it went the plantation system. What was left was a misty-eyed dream of a way that never was, a life lived less nobly than it had been portrayed. Only ghosts remained.

But even these spirits were Southern; outsiders would hear of them and laugh, but the ghosts were not of their making. In William Faulkner's *Absalom, Absalom,* Mississippian Quentin Compson's Canadian roommate asks,

> "I just want to understand it if I can and I don't know how to say it better. Because it's something my people haven't got. Or if we have got it, it all happened long ago across the water and so now there aint anything to look at every day to remind us of it. We don't live among defeated grandfathers and freed slaves (or have I got it backwards and was it your folks that are free and the niggers that lost?) and bullets in the dining room table and such, to be always reminding us to never forget.

---

[4]Lévi-Strauss, *Myth and Meaning,* 43.

[5]George B. Tindall, "Mythology: A New Frontier in Southern History," in Patrick Gerster and Nicholas Cords, eds., *Myth and Southern History* (Chicago: Rand McNally College Publishing Co., 1974) 2. Tindall's article originally appeared in Frank E. Vandiver, ed., *The Idea of the South: Pursuit of a Central Theme* (Chicago: University of Chicago Press, 1964). It has been republished many times.

[6]Paul M. Gaston, *The New South Creed: A Study in Southern Mythmaking* (New York: Knopf, 1970) 8.

[7]See Bertram Wyatt-Brown, *Southern Honor, Ethics and Behavior in the Old South* (New York: Oxford University Press, 1982), for a brilliant examination of how honor supported the antebellum South. William R. Taylor's pivotal study *Cavalier and Yankee* (New York: George Braziller, Inc., 1957) clearly showed that Northerners, especially abolitionists, were as influential in creating and perpetuating the Plantation Myth as were Southerners.

What is it? something you live and breathe in like air? a kind of vacuum
filled with wraithlike and indomitable anger and pride and glory at and
in happenings that occurred and ceased 50 years ago? a kind of entailed
birthright father and son and father and son of never forgiving general
Sherman, so that forevermore as long as your children's children produce children you wont be anything but a descendant of a long line of
colonels killed in Pickett's charge at Manassas?"

"Gettysburg," Quentin said, "You cant understand it. You would have
to be born there."[8]

On the surface it did not appear that Jefferson Davis had the right stuff for legends. Davis
was above all extremely human, more remembered for his shortcomings than his successes.
Robert E. Lee was the better material for marble statues, but events soon outdistanced Davis.
His fate was different from the deified Lincoln's or the adored Lee's, but he too would become legendary. Due to Northern stupidity his life soon became the proper medium for myth.

During the war Davis had been harshly criticized. In the spring of 1865, he personally embodied the Confederate failure. Many Southerners blamed his obstinacy for prolonging the
war. Robert Toombs, former Confederate secretary of state, had called Davis a "scoundrel."
Other Southerners had called him worse.[9] Davis was a sad figure—symbol of the secessionist
leaders who had brought on the war with all its suffering and loss.

A recent historian of Southern background quipped that to reach amateur status as a true
neo-Confederate, a believer not only has to "cry during *Gone with the Wind*" and "have a great-
grandmother who buried silver under the smokehouse," he also needs to "hate Jefferson Davis."[10] Davis's contemporaries blamed him for many of the Confederacy's problems. In January 1865 the Virginia legislature politely but firmly requested Davis and his Cabinet to
resign.[11] Three months later a prominent Maryland journalist and Confederate sympathizer
called Davis "pigheaded."[12] An unsigned letter from the private secretary of a Confederate
Cabinet member appeared in the *New York Times*. Dated Richmond, 15 May, the letter called
Davis a man "whose faults of temper and intellect would have ruined a far stronger cause
than that of the South."[13]

Similar opinions were offered by wartime critics. John B. Jones, the "rebel war clerk," noted
in his diary on New Year's Day, 1865, that while Davis was "a man of ability" who would be
"eminently qualified to preside over the Confederate States" in peacetime, he lacked the "broad
intellect" and was too prejudiced and obstinate to overcome "such a crisis."[14] William Wilkins
Glenn, a Maryland editor whose Southern sympathies had caused him to be imprisoned by
federal authorities in Baltimore early in the war, kept a journal from 1861 to 1869. Near the

[8]William Faulkner, *Absalom, Absalom!* (New York: Modern Library Edition, 1964) 361.

[9]Toombs's quote is taken from Grady McWhiney, "Jefferson Davis—the Unforgiven," *Journal of Mississippi History* 42 (May 1980): 113.

[10]Thomas L. Connelly, *Will Success Spoil Jeff Davis?* (New York: McGraw-Hill Book Co., 1963) 13.

[11]C. Vann Woodward, ed., *Mary Chesnut's Civil War* (New Haven: Yale University Press, 1981) 706.

[12]William Wilkins Glenn, *Between North and South: A Maryland Journalist Views the Civil War*, ed. Bayly Ellen Marks and Mark Norton Schatz (Rutherford NJ: Fairleigh Dickinson University Press, 1976) 202.

[13]*New York Times*, 19 May 1865, 4-5.

[14]John B. Jones, *A Rebel War Clerk's Diary at the Confederate States' Capital*, 2 vols. (Philadelphia: J. B. Lippincott & Co., 1866) 2:372.

end of the war, Glenn called Davis "a gentleman" and "a man of high tone" who would have been an excellent choice for the presidency of a peacetime Confederacy. "But Davis unfortunately is a man [of] quick temper, strong attachments and bitter prejudices."[15] Davis's obstinacy and temper, said Edward A. Pollard, editor of the *Daily Richmond Examiner* and wartime critic, blinded him to his own faults. According to Pollard, Davis "was sustained by a powerful self-conceit, and a sanguine temperament; and he went down to ruin with the fillet of vanity upon his eyes."[16]

Modern historians have agreed with these contemporary estimates of Davis. They admit that he was fiercely loyal and devoted to his family and friends and that he was a successful bureaucrat. There are few who doubt that he would have been the right man to head the Confederacy in peacetime—hardly anyone in the South was as well prepared through education and experience to assume the office of first president. Yet they also acknowledge that prejudice often blinded Davis. Convinced of his self-righteousness and exaggerating his own abilities, he was unable to delegate work to subordinates. Bell Irvin Wiley concluded a brilliant sketch of Davis: "To the historian who attempts to judge him in the perspective of time both the virtues and the faults are apparent, but his record as President leaves more to condemn than to praise."[17]

Non-Southerners have even more extreme opinions about Davis. From 1863 to the end of the war the *New York Times* depicted Davis

> as a murderer, a cruel slaveowner whose servants all ran away, a liar, a boaster, a fanatic, a confessed failure, a hater, a political adventurer, a supporter of outcasts and outlaws, a drunkard, an atrocious misrepresenter, an assassin, an incendiary, a criminal who was gratified by the assassination of Lincoln, a henpecked husband, a man so shameless that he would try to escape capture by disguising himself as a woman, a supporter of murder plots, an insubordinate soldier, an unwholesome sleeper, and a malingerer.[18]

In Iowa City three men offered the government "$300,000 for permission to exhibit Davis around the country charging an admission to see him. They agreed to give the government half of the proceeds and to put up a bond of $100,000 as a guarantee that they would return him in good physical condition. Another petitioner recommended that Davis be hung a little higher than Haman, so that future generations could say 'hung as high as Davis,' instead of 'as high as Haman.' "[19]

Immediately after the war Davis was captured, placed aboard a Union steamer, and taken to a federal fort where he was imprisoned, chained, and humiliated for his part in the war. Jefferson Davis was to become the scapegoat for the South's rebellious sins. The myth of the scapegoat is found in almost every culture. All accounts share common characteristics including: (1) an individual is made to bear the sins of all the people; (2) the individual suffers personal punishment and supposedly removes the suffering from the people in general; (3)

---

[15]Glenn, *Between North and South,* 153.

[16]Edward A. Pollard, *The Lost Cause: A New Southern History of the War of the Confederates* (New York: E. B. Treat & Co., 1866) 685.

[17]Bell Irvin Wiley, *The Road to Appomattox* (New York: Atheneum, 1973) 42.

[18]McWhiney, "Jefferson Davis—the Unforgiven," 114.

[19]Jonathan T. Dorris, "Pardoning the Leaders of the Confederacy," *Mississippi Valley Historical Review* 15 (June 1928): 19n.

the scapegoat is expelled from the community; and (4) the scapegoat is often a god-king.[20] Davis's postwar life fulfilled each of these characteristics of the scapegoat myth. What was important for the future of the South was that Davis not only was made to suffer, but that his suffering was recognized as atonement for the sins of his fellow Southerners. Just a few months after her husband's imprisonment, Mrs. Davis told a sympathetic correspondent that her husband "is the scape goat for the putative sins of the Confederacy, but unlike the merciful law of the Jewish theocracy, he is not allowed to escape into the wilderness there to bear his load of anguish alone."[21] When an account of Davis's imprisonment, believed to be the memoir of his physician, appeared the following summer, it devoted almost an entire chapter to comparing Davis with scapegoat imagery.[22] A January 1867 article in the *Southern Review* commented that Davis had been selected "as a victim from among the whole people whom he served."[23] Mary Chesnut later remembered that when Southerners learned of the severity of Davis's treatment, most also recognized the atoning quality of his punishment, as did the Reverend Richard S. Trapier who declared, "I will pray for President Davis till I die. I will do it to my last gasp. My chief is a prisoner, but I am proud of him still. He is a spectacle to gods and men. He will bear himself as a soldier, a patriot, a statesman, a Christian gentleman. He is the martyr of our cause."[24] Davis himself recognized the symbolism of his suffering: "If I alone could bear all the suffering of the country and relieve it from further calamity," he told his wife, "I trust our Heavenly Father would give me strength to be a willing sacrifice."[25]

Unlike most myths that deal with the faraway or long-ago, Jefferson Davis's transformation was immediate and can be traced to his imprisonment and the widespread publicity it had received in the *Prison Life of Jefferson Davis*, a memoir attributed to his physician John J. Craven. This book's revelations about Davis's stringent punishment embarrassed the North, placed pressure upon the Johnson administration to ameliorate Davis's prison conditions, and ended demands for retaliatory punishment against other Southerners. In 1905 *Current Literature* declared that the *Prison Life* "was well received and it unquestionably did much to restore Davis's waning popularity in . . . [the South] and to establish him as a martyr of the Lost Cause."[26] The Lost Cause myth provided the means for Southerners to explain "the postbellum adjustment of the old chivalric concepts and the old idea of southern cultural nationalism to the traumatic experiences of devastation, defeat, poverty, and humiliation."[27] Jefferson Davis's imprisonment was a key element of this new myth.

Well into the twentieth century sympathy and partiality replaced objectivity when writers dealt with Davis and his imprisonment. The Southern agrarian poet, Allen Tate, mistakenly wrote that Davis "lay in Fortress Monroe, charged with treason, for two years, much of the

---

[20]For a fuller discussion of the scapegoat myth, see Sir James George Frazer, *The Golden Bough: A Study in Magic and Religion* (New York: The Macmillan Co., 1922) chs. 56-58.

[21]Varina Davis to Thomas F. Bayard, 2 October 1865, Bayard Family Papers, Historical Society of Delaware, Wilmington.

[22]Bvt. Lieut.-Col. John J. Craven, M.D., *Prison Life of Jefferson Davis. Embracing Details and Incidents of His Captivity, Particulars Concerning His Health and Habits, Together with Many Conversations on Topics of Great Public Interest* (New York: Carleton, Publisher, 1866) ch. 17.

[23]S. Teackle Wallis, "Imprisonment of Davis," (Bledsoe's) *Southern Review* 1 (January 1867): 243.

[24]Woodward, *Mary Chesnut's Civil War*, 819.

[25]Davis to Mrs. Davis, 26 September 1865, Jefferson Davis Collection, Transylvania University, Lexington, Kentucky.

[26]C. C. W., "The Prison Life," review of *Prison Life of Jefferson Davis*, 2d ed., *Current Literature* 38 (June 1905): 500.

[27]Rollin G. Osterweis, *The Myth of the Lost Cause, 1865-1900* (Hamden CT: Archon Books, 1973) x.

time in chains, separated from his family and friends." Tate called Davis "the sacrifice of the southern people to the passions of the northern mobs."[28] A modern, more critical biographer of Davis, Robert McElroy, became melodramatic when dealing with Davis's imprisonment. McElroy entitled chapter 27 "The Scapegoat" in his two-volume biography, *Jefferson Davis, the Unreal and the Real.* McElroy began his chapter comparing Davis with a figure of biblical lore: "In Old Testament days it was customary for the Priest at the Altar to lay his hands upon the body of a he-goat, and then send him into the wilderness bearing the sins of the people. As Davis approached Virginia, on his way to prison, he bore upon his shoulders the major part of the sin of secession."[29]

The *Prison Life* is a standard source for Davis biographers. Hudson Strode's massive three-volume hagiographic study of Davis used many of the book's stories. Strode noted, however, that "though Davis winced to read some expressions Craven had put into his mouth that were inconceivable to his nature or breeding, he recognized the work as obviously that of an admiring friend."[30] The most recent biographer of Davis, Clement Eaton, commented that Craven "did what he could do to secure better treatment for the distinguished prisoner of war. Craven and he held many conversations. The doctor came to admire him, and in 1866 published *The [sic] Prison Life of Jefferson Davis.*"[31]

The most uncritical acceptance of Craven's work came from the great Southern historian Douglas Southall Freeman, known for his biographies of George Washington and Robert E. Lee as well as his command study, *Lee's Lieutenants.* Freeman's lectures at the Alabama State College for Women were published as *The South to Posterity.* In this bibliographic study Freeman lauded the dedicated physician's work to a degree that has never been surpassed:

> It was by the sheerest chance that this physician, simple, able, understanding and with a native antagonism to cruelty, should have been summoned to advise on the treatment of President Davis. To him Mr. Davis owed the lessened rigor of treatment and to him, no less, the South owed its first dispassionate picture of the imprisonment. . . . Based on a diary Doctor Craven kept while at Fort Monroe and supplemented with reports of many conversations, it was an honest book. Had Doctor Craven been a Confederate himself, instead of an avowed Republican enemy of slavery, he could not have been more candid, nor could he have presented more clearly the courage, the character, and the high intelligence of President Davis.[32]

No one reaped more reward from the *Prison Life* than Jefferson Davis himself—symbol of an imprisoned South. He and his wife quickly realized that the book had changed Davis from the defeated leader of an unsuccessful rebellion into a martyr—far more important, heroic, and lovable than had the *Prison Life* never been published. By the end of December 1866, Clement C. Clay, who had served a brief prison term alongside Davis, already called him "the

[28]Allen Tate, *Jefferson Davis: His Rise and Fall, a Biographical Narrative* (New York: Minton Balch & Co., 1929) 299.

[29]Robert McElroy, *Jefferson Davis, the Unreal and the Real,* 2 vols. (New York: Harper & Bros., 1937) 2:524.

[30]Hudson Strode, *Jefferson Davis, Tragic Hero: The Last Twenty-Five Years, 1864-1889* (New York: Harcourt, Brace & World, Inc., 1964) 288.

[31]Clement Eaton, *Jefferson Davis* (New York: Free Press, 1977) 262.

[32]Douglas Southall Freeman, *The South to Posterity: An Introduction to the Writings of Confederate History* (New York: Charles Scribner's Sons, 1939) 55-56.

great martyr."[33] A Davis supporter, William Wilkins Glenn, saw the paroled Davis a year later and noted in his journal that "his imprisonment at Fortress Monroe and persecution by the Yankees have helped him immensely. If he had been allowed to go free, he would have had so few friends that he would have been almost forgotten in a few years. The feeling against him was so strong that he would found [sic] no sympathy from anyone. Long imprisonment has changed all this. Now he is a sort of martyr."[34] In 1879 a correspondent wrote to Davis that Theophilus H. Holmes, Davis's West Point classmate and Confederate general, had told the writer, "I look upon him [Davis] as the great sacrifice of the age, his and not [Robert E.] Lee's name should fill the hearts of the Southern people."[35]

The *Prison Life* had made Jefferson Davis's relatively short and, for the most part, lenient imprisonment transcend reality. He had become a living myth: a vanquished but unconquerable hero who had suffered for the sins of all Southerners. On 13 May 1867 Davis was released from prison by the United States Circuit Court for the District of Virginia in Richmond. Davis's wartime secretary, Burton N. Harrison, wrote to Davis's aide, William Preston Johnston, and described the scene as "the most exciting drama I ever expect to see in a court room."[36]

The rebel yell rose as Davis returned to his hotel from the courtroom. Then

all sounds creased and a deep and solemn silence fell upon the vast crowd, less demonstrative than the yell, but more tender in its sympathy.

As Mr. Davis stood up in the carriage, preparatory to alighting, a stentorian voice shouted, "Hats off, Virginians," and 5,000 bareheaded men did homage to him who had suffered for them, and with moistened eye and bated breath stood silent and still until their representative entered the hotel.

The treatment which the Federal Government had imposed upon Mr. Davis had made him a martyr, the applause was an attestation of that fact. Around the court room were thousands of men who had met danger and suffered less. Each man felt that Davis had suffered vicariously for him. If Davis was a traitor, so was he. If Davis should suffer the penalties of the law, so should he. That it was which made the feeling so intense.[37]

When Davis visited New Orleans early in 1868, one ex-rebel claimed that he went through the crowd at the Saint Charles Hotel, grasped Davis's hand and said, "I am glad the Yankees captured you—imprisoned you—put irons on you." The crowd in the lobby were startled and challenged the upstart, but they held back when he concluded, "In doing that they did for you what no other power on earth could have done—they made you the Atoning Sacrifice for our whole people. . . . Your crucifixian [sic] has sealed all the lips of criticism, and uni-

---

[33]McElroy, *Jefferson Davis*, 2:717-18.

[34]Glenn, *Between North and South*, 296.

[35]*Calendar of the Jefferson Davis Postwar Manuscripts in the Louisiana Historical Collection, Confederate Memorial Hall* (New Orleans LA, 1943) 143-44.

[36]Harrison to Johnston, 24 May 1867, William Preston Johnston Papers, Tulane University, New Orleans, Louisiana.

[37]Chesley W. Jurney, "Defense of the South by Northern Democrats, as Portrayed in the Trial of Jefferson Davis, 1865-1868," U.S. *Congressional Record*, 70th Cong., 1st sess., 1928, 10108.

versal sympathy prevails throughout the South, . . . and you will now be forever blessed by the people for whose cause you suffered."[38]

Edward A. Pollard, one of the first to use the expression "The Lost Cause," was also among the first to comment extensively on the important role the imprisonment had in creating a new image for Davis. Pollard wrote,

> The imprisonment of Mr. Davis was the best thing that could have happened for his fame. What he suffered, . . . not only disarmed much of the old resentment of his countrymen, but displayed him in an attitude so touching, and in conduct so becoming and noble, that, when released on bail in the month of May, 1867, he found himself welcomed by nearly every heart in the South, and hailed with a pride and tenderness that his countrymen had not before shown him, even in the best of his former estate.
>
> Old enmities were forgotten, old offences were forgiven, and not an injurious memory of the past war was allowed to disturb the tribute which the whole South seemed now anxious to pay to the martyr of "the lost cause."
>
> This transport of public opinion in the South concerning its ex-President, is easily explained. Mr. Davis had certainly borne imprisonment with a dignity scarcely to be expected from him. . . . From this point it was easy for his countrymen to imagine him as a vicarious sufferer, bearing punishment for the sins of the whole South; yet further, this habitual view easily passed into the romantic regard of him as an impersonation of the cause of the Southern Confederacy.[39]

Sidney Lanier, the great Southern poet and writer, mentioned Davis in his novel *Tiger-Lilies*, published in November 1867.

> If there was guilt in any, there was guilt in nigh all of us, between Maryland and Mexico; that Mr. Davis, if he be termed the ringleader of the rebellion, was so not by virtue of any intriguing act of his, but purely by the unanimous will and appointment of the Southern people; and that the hearts of the Southern people bleed to see how their own act has resulted in the chaining of Mr. Davis, who was as innocent as they, and in the pardon of those who were as guilty as he![40]

Fortunately Davis's health was strong, and he was able to see his people's immediate postwar disdain turn to respect and even affection. In 1879 Senator Richard Coke of Texas proclaimed, "We love Jefferson Davis because he represented us in a struggle in which our young men and our old men went down to their graves and by which our women were made widows and our children were made orphans. He represents us and we love him, we respect and revere him."[41]

---

[38]John M. Sandridge to ?, 15 April 1890, Samuel Richey Collection of the Southern Confederacy, The Walter Havighurst Special Collections Library, Miami University, Oxford, Ohio.

[39]Edward A. Pollard, *Life of Jefferson Davis with a Secret History of the Southern Confederacy Gathered "Behind the Scenes in Richmond"* (Philadelphia: National Publishing Co., 1869) 526-28.

[40]Sidney Lanier, *Tiger-Lilies*, vol. 5 of *The Centennial Edition of the Works of Sidney Lanier*, ed. Garland Greever, assisted by Cecil Abernethy (Baltimore: Johns Hopkins University Press, 1945) 97.

[41]"Debate on the Pensioning of Jefferson Davis," condensed from *The Proceedings of the United States Senate* (3 March 1879) 6; copy in the Jefferson Davis Collection.

Fifty years later the South still remembered fondly its only president. A Texas political aide claimed that

> the southern people had profound respect for Mr. Davis personally because of his pure character and intellectual abilities, but for him there was no deep and abiding devotion as for Lee and many of the other military chieftains. Mr. Davis impersonated their failure; the generals their brilliant success as long as success was possible.
>
> But when the victors charged him falsely with crime abhorrent to his nature, put him under ward and manacled him as a felon, and then indicted him as a traitor, he became their martyred hero, and history will so record him.[42]

In his later years Davis liked to play the role of martyr. He worked hard to perpetuate the symbolism begun by the *Prison Life.* On 10 March 1884, during his last visit to Jackson, Mississippi, Davis told his listeners, "Sectional hate concentrating itself upon my devoted head, deprives me of the privilege accorded to others in the sweeping expression of 'without distinction of race, color or previous condition,' but it cannot deprive me of that which is nearest and dearest to my heart, the right to be a Mississippian."[43] Four years later, when speaking at the Seventh Mississippi Democratic Convention, Davis greeted the gathering as "Fellow-Citizens." Then, after pausing, he continued, "Ah pardon me! The laws of the United States no longer permit me to designate you as fellow-citizens, but I am thankful that I may address you as friends. I feel no regret that I stand before you 'a man without a country,' for my ambition lies buried in the grave of the Confederacy." As the spokesman of the past, he urged the young men before him to lay aside all bitterness. "The past is dead; let it bury its dead, its hopes and its aspirations. Before you lies the future—a future full of golden promise, a future full of recompense for honorable endeavor, a future of expanding national glory, before which all the world shall stand amazed. Let me beseech you to lay aside all rancor, all bitter sectional feeling, and to take your places in the ranks of those who will bring about a consummation devoutly to be wished—a reunited country."[44] Davis had come to help bridge the gap between the Plantation South and the New South; he was the Lost Cause incarnate. And like the god-king of the scapegoat myth, he accepted his expulsion, the loss of his citizenship, without rancor, even with pride.

Mrs. Davis too recognized that Davis's imprisonment had made him a martyr for the South. As early as October 1865 she replied to Thomas F. Bayard, who had written her a note of support in which he described Davis, whom he had never met, as never "more illustrious and admirable than amid the cold stones of his military prison house and the colder hearts of those who seek to oppress his feeble body, and vainly to subdue the moral grandeur of his soul."[45] Bayard was a conservative Democrat and a United States senator from Delaware. In her response Mrs. Davis told Senator Bayard that she was mortified that no Confederate had countered the slanders about her husband or proclaimed that Davis's only crime was to "surrender all [to] the maintenance of the principle he worshipped and failing to maintain it had been overwhelmed." She admitted that few in the South "wish to battle for the silent suf-

---

[42]Jurney, "Defense of the South," 10108.

[43]Copy of the entire speech is with the Jefferson Davis Papers, Tulane University.

[44]Quoted in Clarence H. Poe, "The Tragedy of Jefferson Davis," *The Outlook* 89 (13 June 1908): 335-36.

[45]Bayard to Varina Davis, September 1865, Jefferson Davis Collection.

ferer."[46] Within a year all that had changed. The *Prison Life* had appeared, and there were many men—Northerners as well as Southerners—willing to defend "the silent sufferer."

Modern writers too have reaffirmed the symbolic value of Davis's imprisonment. Frank E. Vandiver, a renowned historian of the Civil War and the South, noted the importance of Davis's last years. "In prison, in irons, his health ravaged, his wife and family kept away, his friends fewer, Jefferson Davis performed an essential service for the South. He gathered all its wartime sins to himself and became the one great symbol of treason and waste, a symbol accepted by the North and world. His travail gave the South time for survival. He never lost hope; he did lose most of his last illusions."[47]

In the last years of his long life Davis was greeted everywhere in the South as the living legend of the Lost Cause. He was the man who had suffered for the Confederacy's sins. They knew he had, for they had read about his sacrifices in the *Prison Life*. The great Civil War historian Bruce Catton described Davis's last years in this way: "Increasingly, Southerners came to see him as one who had suffered much for the common cause; and in the course of time Davis became the most revered man in the South, a popular hero whose rare appearances were greeted by cheering crowds, with aging veterans of the war raising the Rebel yell in his honor. As leading ex-Confederates died, one by one, in the course of time, Davis came to seem the very embodiment of the adored, romantic nation that had not lived. Ranks were closed; by the end of his life Davis was the Confederate hero incarnate."[48]

Shortly after Davis's death Thomas H. Watts delivered a eulogy in Montgomery, birthplace of the Confederate government. Watts was a former colonel of the 17th Alabama Infantry and a close adviser to Davis as attorney general from March 1862 to October 1863. He focused upon the suffering Davis had endured in prison and its symbolism for the South. Colonel Watts's purple prose presented a larger-than-life Davis, worthy of veneration. According to Watts, Davis's punishment "was wanton cruelty without excuse or justification. The poor, feeble old man [Davis was fifty-six years old] resisted this indignity; not because he supposed he [could] resist successfully, the perpetration of such a foul wrong—not because he supposed the indignity was intended alone for him; but because he felt that the indignity and disgrace were for the Southern people; and hence he resisted. He was made to suffer the most brutal and inhuman indignity for the Southern people. It is no wonder, that the hearts of every true man and woman in the Southern States went out to him in love; and it is no wonder that they, now that he is dead, sorrow for him as their personal friend."[49] Through many eulogies like this one, Davis's canonization was complete.

The American public is more accustomed to marble heroes than those made of flesh and blood. Jefferson Davis would not be left to lie in peace. He had recognized that as "a man without a country" he was symbolically far more important than he would have been had his citizenship been restored. He defiantly told fellow Mississippians in 1884 that he would never apply for a pardon, for "repentance must precede the right of pardon, and I have not re-

---

[46]Varina Davis to Thomas F. Bayard, 2 October 1865, Bayard Family Papers, Historical Society of Delaware.

[47]Frank E. Vandiver, "The Shifting Roles of Jefferson Davis," in Gary W. Gallagher, ed., *Essays on Southern History, Written in Honor of Barnes K. Lathrop* (Austin: University of Texas Press, 1980) 126.

[48]Bruce Catton, intro., Haskell M. Monroe, Jr. and James T. McIntosh, eds., *The Papers of Jefferson Davis*, vol. 1: *1808-1840* (Baton Rouge: Louisiana State University Press, 1971) vi.

[49]Thomas H. Watts, "Address of Hon. Thomas H. Watts, on the Life and Character of Ex-President Jefferson Davis," 19 December 1889, 12. Thomas Hill Watts Papers, State of Alabama, Department of Archives and History, Montgomery.

pented. Remembering as I must all of which has been suffered, all of which has been lost, disappointed hopes and crushed aspirations, yet I deliberately say if it were to do over again, I would again do just as I did in 1861."[50] Despite Davis's lifelong refusal to request that his American citizenship be restored, the United States Congress returned it posthumously in 1978, thereby shredding the shroud in which he had chosen to be buried. Politicians might not have understood, but Robert Penn Warren did. "Davis died without rancor," Warren wrote, "and wishing us all well. But if he were not now defenseless in death, he would no doubt reject the citizenship we so charitably thrust upon him. In life, in his old-fashioned way, he would accept no pardon, for pardon could be construed to imply wrongdoing, and wrongdoing was what, in honor and principle, he denied."[51]

## STATE PRISONER

It was not the war that had transformed Jefferson Davis into a martyr; it was what the Union government did to him immediately after the war that made Davis into the living symbol of the Lost Cause. In April 1865 the Northern mood was dark and angry. Abraham Lincoln was dead. Secretary of State William H. Seward had been assaulted. Many believed that the murderous conspiracy emanated from the highest levels of the rebel government. Lee had surrendered to Grant, but other Confederate armies were still in the field. Most of the rebel political leaders remained at large. The new president, Andrew Johnson, unsure of his role, issued a proclamation that declared Jefferson Davis, Clement C. Clay, and other Confederates conspirators in the Lincoln assassination plot and traitors against the United States. He offered a reward of $100,000 for the arrest of Davis and $25,000 for each of the others.[52]

The Northern fears were chimeras. A conspiracy had existed, but it involved only a few insignificant plotters. Lee's surrender had forced the rest of the Confederate armies to lay down their arms. The leaders of the Confederate government failed to find a haven where they could continue the fight and preserve the cause.

Many Northerners agreed with Southern critics that the best thing that could happen to help reunite the nation was to permit Jefferson Davis to escape and be forgotten. Lincoln had told General William T. Sherman that he wished Davis would escape "unbeknown" to him.[53] Edward A. Pollard, editor of the *Daily Richmond Examiner,* wrote: "It has been said that if the Federal authorities, capturing Jefferson Davis, had turned him loose, or had wisely refrained from treating him with invidious or exceptional rigor, he would have remained today the most unpopular man in the South."[54]

Instead of escaping, Davis was captured in a wet Georgia field on 10 May 1865. The federal government now held the highest-ranking rebel, unprotected by any military conventions. No one seriously thought of releasing him or the other political leaders of the rebellion; yet no one knew what to do with them. A Baltimore editor speculated, "There has been very little excitement over the capture of Jeff Davis. That he is to be hanged appears to be a foregone conclusion—and so he will be made a martyr of as Lincoln has been. Let him alone &

---

[50]Davis speech, 10 March 1884, Jefferson Davis Papers.

[51]Warren, *Jefferson Davis,* 112.

[52]Proclamation of 2 May 1865, James D. Richardson, ed., *A Compilation of the Messages and Papers of the Presidents, 1789-1904,* 10 vols. (Washington: Bureau of National Literature and Art, 1904) 6:307-308.

[53]William T. Sherman, *Memoirs of William T. Sherman, Written by Himself,* 2 vols. (New York: D. Appleton, 1891) 2:352.

[54]Pollard, *Life of Jefferson Davis,* 525.

he will go down to his grave unmissed & unhonored though not unsung. Everything tends to show that the South fought this war against Jeff Davis who was their worst enemy."[55]

Brigadier General Joseph Holt, army judge advocate general, was among those who believed that Davis and other Confederate leaders had conspired in the assassination of Lincoln. He hired private investigators to check all leads. Davis-haters and scoundrels interested only in spending the government's money had planted most of these leads. The administration would have to charge Davis with some crime to keep him in prison. On 21 July the Cabinet unanimously agreed to indict him for treason. He was to be tried in a civilian court in the state of Virginia, where the alleged treason had occurred.[56]

On 22 May 1865 Davis, aboard the steamer *William P. Clyde,* arrived at Fort Monroe along with Clement C. Clay, former senator from Alabama and Confederate minister to Canada.[57] John Mitchel, an anglophobic Richmond editor, was the third political prisoner held at Fort Monroe. Secretary of War Edwin M. Stanton assigned his assistant, Charles A. Dana, and Major General Henry W. Halleck, army chief-of-staff, to witness Davis's incarceration. According to Dana's report to the War Department, Davis strode into the fort bearing "himself with a haughty attitude. His face was somewhat flushed, but his features were composed and his step firm. . . . His hair and beard were not so gray as has been represented, and he seems very much less worn and broken by anxiety and labor than Mr. Blair [Francis P. Blair, Sr.] reported when he returned from Richmond last winter."[58]

Major General Nelson A. Miles, newly appointed commander of Fort Monroe, had arrived at the fort the same day as Davis. Miles had not yet completed preparations to receive his important prisoners. The cells were not finished. A week before (14 May) General Miles had issued orders from Washington "Regulating Treatment of State Prisoner *Jefferson Davis.*" These directed the guards to stay awake when on duty and forbade the movement of Davis or conversations with him without the commander's express permission. The orders permitted Davis to eat hospital food instead of the ordinary soldiers' rations. The general anticipated that Mrs. Davis would accompany her husband. Miles's orders permitted her "to visit him during the day until four (4) o'clock, and during the evening from Seven (7) until half past ten (10 $^1/_2$)." Davis would be permitted an hour's walk each morning, and three hours for exercise each evening. Miles ordered a lamp to burn all night in Davis's cell. The guards were to walk their post outside his cell all night, but, Miles cautioned, "The Officer of the

---

[55]Glenn, *Between North and South,* 216.

[56]Holt's attempt to charge Davis in the Lincoln assassination conspiracy would continue for more than a year. The best discussion can be found in William Hanchett, *The Lincoln Murder Conspiracies* (Urbana: University of Illinois Press, 1983) 74ff.

[57]The federal post at Old Point Comfort, Virginia, is properly called Fort Monroe. However, it was commonly referred to as "Fortress Monroe" in the nineteenth century. In 1832 the War Department officially designated the post Fort Monroe although the Post Office did not change its postmark until 1941. A fortress refers to a large fortified place that usually includes a town within its walls. The two terms will be used interchangeably in this work, both referring to the same military installation.

[58]Blair had gone to Richmond to arrange an unofficial peace conference, which was held on 3 February 1865 at Hampton Roads, Virginia. U.S. War Department, *The War of the Rebellion: A Compilation of the Official Records of the Union and Confederate Armies,* 70 vols. (Washington: Government Printing Office, 1880-1901) ser. 2, 8:564. Cited hereafter as *OR.* All future references will be to ser. 2, vol. 8.

Guard will see that the tramping of the sentinels does not disturb the rest of the State prisoner."[59]

The War Department, however, had different plans for Davis, and Charles Dana was sent to Fort Monroe to interview Davis, to supervise Miles's preparations, and to insure that the department's more stringent instructions would be followed. They refused to allow Davis to exercise outside his cell, and refused Mrs. Davis permission to remain near her husband. Instead, she was forced to return to Georgia with the Davis children. There they were subjected to abuse and Mrs. Davis soon sent the older ones to a boarding school in Montreal. They were accompanied by Mrs. Davis's mother and Robert Brown, a black servant. Money, fortunately, would not be a problem. Former Confederate cabinet member, Judah P. Benjamin, had fled to England where he had established a trust fund for her use.[60]

Secretary Stanton feared that a despondent, defeated Davis might attempt suicide. This fear initially led to security so tight that neither Davis nor Clay was given a knife or a fork to eat his meals. Some of the guards later made oak eating utensils for the prisoners to use.[61]

The cells awaiting Davis and Clay were in the casemate, the outer wall of the fort, not the stockade that housed the common military prisoners. In this section were the apartments furnished to the officers of the post and their families. "In fact," according to Dana, "an officer with his family was moved out of the particular casemate in which Davis was placed. Any one who will take the trouble to visit Fortress Monroe can see the place still, and it certainly has not to-day [1898] a gloomy or forbidding appearance."[62] Because these casemate rooms had never been prison cells, they lacked secure doors.

Although spare, Davis's cell had all the necessities: "a hospital bed, with iron bedstead, chair and table, and a moveable stool closet. A Bible is allowed to each [Davis and Clay]. . . . The prisoners are to be supplied with soldiers' rations cooked by the guard. Their linens will be issued to them in the same way."[63]

After the initial shock of imprisonment had worn off, Clay, held in a casemate room near Davis, described his cell as "large, airy and comfortable." He also noted, "I have not suffered from the heat of the weather, but have found this casemate quite as cool as a grotto. My bedding, and indeed, all the appointments of the room are comfortable."[64]

Dana telegraphed Stanton on that first day, giving a detailed description of the arrangements that had been made to secure the two prisoners.

---

[59]Headquarters, Military District of Fort Monroe (14 May 1865), General Orders No. 7, "Regulating Treatment of State Prisoner *Jefferson Davis*," copy in William C. Braly Papers, U.S. Army Military History Institute, Carlisle Barracks, Pennsylvania.

[60]Letters from Benjamin to Varina Davis may be found in the Jefferson Davis Collection. Other offers of monetary aid to help the Davises, and to pay to educate their children in Canada may be found in the William Preston Johnston Papers.

[61]Lemuel Shipman, "Recollections of Prison Life of President Davis and Mr. C. C. Clay at Fortress Monroe, 1865-'66," handwritten copy in Henry Sale Halbert Papers, State of Alabama, Department of Archives and History.

[62]Charles A. Dana, *Recollections of the Civil War* (New York: D. Appleton and Co., 1902) 284. Dana's memoirs, like so many written well after the war, has to be used cautiously. Because memory can distort actual events, his account is used herein only when it can be confirmed elsewhere.

[63]*OR,* 564. Despite the orders, Davis and Clay were fed from the post hospital's rations.

[64]Clay to Mrs. Clay, 21 August 1865, Clay Papers, Duke University, Durham, North Carolina. Clay's letters are far more descriptive than Davis's because Davis was subjected to stricter censorship than Clay.

Each one occupies the inner room of a casemate; the window is heavily barred. A sentry stands within before each of the doors leading to the other room. These doors are to be grated, but are now secured by bars, fastened from the outside. Two other sentries stand outside of these doors. An officer is also constantly on duty in the outer room, whose duty it is to see his prisoner every fifteen minutes. The outer door of all is locked on the outside, and the key is kept exclusively by the general officer of the guard. Two sentries are also stationed without that door; a strong line of sentries cut off all access to the vicinity of the casemates. Another line is stationed on the top of the parapet overhead, and a third line is posted across the moats on the counterscarp, opposite the places of confinement. The casemate on each side and between these occupied by the prisoners are used as guard-rooms, and soldiers are always there. A lamp is constantly kept burning in each of the rooms.[65]

General Miles and the War Department realized that Jefferson Davis was the most important prisoner ever held by the United States government. The army feared either a Southern plot to free Davis or his suicide. Should either occur, the trial of the arch-rebel could never be held. Consequently, the military took actions that seem overly stringent with the hindsight of more than a century.

While he was at Fort Monroe, Dana conferred with Miles and Halleck. Dana agreed that Miles could secure Davis and Clay with manacles if necessary. Dana explained his actions to Stanton: "I have not given orders to have them placed in irons, as General Halleck seemed opposed to it, but General Miles is instructed to have fetters ready if he thinks them necessary."[66] The actual orders Dana gave Miles permitted more flexibility than the telegram indicated. The orders let Miles "place manacles and fetters upon the hands and feet of Jefferson Davis and Clement C. Clay whenever he [Miles] may think it advisable in order to render their imprisonment more secure."[67]

Dana and Halleck left the same day they arrived. On the following day (23 May), Miles, either acting on his own or with Dana's prior connivance, ordered irons to be placed upon Davis's ankles, so that the wooden door could be replaced with an iron grate. General Miles, who had not witnessed the incident, reported to Dana that when the manacles were brought to his cell, Davis "violently resisted, but became more quiet afterward. His hands are unencumbered."[68] Because the manacles had been placed on Davis immediately after Dana's brief visit, an officer assumed that "this act was done at his [Dana's] direct order and that General Miles had nothing to do with its conception, only to carry the order into execution."[69] Miles never denied that he had ordered the manacling, and Dana never claimed credit for it. Clement Clay, angry at Davis's humiliation, wrote that Davis had been manacled "*without cause &* only grew violent when they offered to iron him. I *know this* from one who was present. Facts are: Genl. M. [Miles] was authorized to iron us if necessary for safety & the ass deemed it necessary with Mr. D. [Davis] or mistook the authority as an order to do it." Clay did not

---

[65]T. K. Oglesby, *Captor and Captive: The Shackler and the Shackled; the Truth of History as to the Shackling of Jefferson Davis* (Atlanta: The Franklin Printing and Publishing Co., 1899) 9.

[66]Ibid., 10.

[67]*OR*, 565.

[68]Ibid., 571.

[69]Shipman, "Recollections," Halbert Papers. Shipman confused Assistant Secretary of War Dana with Secretary of War Stanton, and incorrectly placed the latter at Fort Monroe at the time of Davis's arrival.

hazard a guess why he was not fettered, but he did speculate to his wife why Davis might have been. Clay wrote, "Mr. D. is petulant[,] irascible & offensive in manner to officers, as they tell me, but they say he is able, learned, high toned & imposing in manner &c."[70]

The public first learned that Davis had been manacled on 26 May in an article in the Philadelphia *Evening Telegraph*. One day later the *New York Tribune* and the *Philadelphia Inquirer* repeated the story.[71] Some prominent Northerners protested to Stanton. Thurlow Weed, the influential New York Republican boss, told the secretary of war that the irons were "an error and an enormity . . . wholly unnecessary severity. If a mistake had been made I am sure it was made without authority and I pray that you will immediately correct it."[72] Secretary Stanton did disapprove of Miles's actions. On 28 May he telegraphed Miles, inquiring if the irons were still on Davis. Stanton demanded, "Please report whether irons have or have not been placed on Jefferson Davis. If they have been, when was it done, and for what reason, and remove them."[73] Miles reported back that afternoon that the fetters had been removed. The maximum time Davis could have been manacled was five days.

Two days after Davis had arrived at Fort Monroe, General Miles telegraphed General Halleck to ask if Davis and Clay could have their prayer books. Later that day Halleck approved this request. Assistant Secretary of War Dana claimed, "I believe that every care was taken during Mr. Davis's imprisonment to remove cause for complaint."[74] What were not removed were the precautions most bothersome to Davis—the constant light and the tramping of the guards. Davis had long suffered from neuralgia and insomnia, and he found these distractions torturous.

In Clay's first letter to his wife from prison, he graphically described his treatment and the prison conditions in the casemate cells:

> For I must now tell you, what I have, heretofore, tho't I would conceal till my liberation or death, that I have endured the most ingenious and refined torture ever since I came in to this living tomb—for, altho' above the natural face of the earth, it is covered with about 10 feet of earth, & is, always, more or less damp like the tomb. With a bright light in my room & the adjoining room—united to it by two door ways, closed by iron gates, wh. cover about half the space or width of the partition—& with two soldiers in this room & two & a Lieutenant in the adjoining until about 30th June; with the opening and shutting of these heavy iron doors or gates, the soldiers being relieved every 2 hours, with the tramp of these heavy armed men, walking their beats, the rattling of their arms & still more, of the guard (whose duty is to look at me every 15 minutes)—you may be sure that my sleep has been often disturbed & broken. In truth, I have experienced one of the tortures of the Spanish inquisition in this frequent, periodical & irregular disturbance of my sleep. During the 112 days of my imprisonment here I have never enjoyed one nights' [sic] unbroken sleep—yea, I have been roused every 2 hours, if asleep, by the tread of the soldiers, the clank of & the voices of officers, save not exceeding 18 times when stupefied by heavy doses

[70]Clay to Mrs. Clay, 11 August 1865, Clay Papers.
[71]*Evening Telegraph* (Philadelphia), 26 May 1865, 1; *New York Tribune*, 27 May 1865, 8; *Philadelphia Inquirer*, 27 May 1865, 4.
[72]Quoted in Burke Davis, *The Long Surrender* (New York: Random House, 1985) 181.
[73]*OR*, 577.
[74]Dana, *Recollections*, 287.

of opium. The exceptions to the rule of disturbance have been so few that I can almost enumerate them from memory. I have never known the feeling of refreshment from sleep on arising any morning of my imprisonment. Besides, I have never been allowed retirement from sight, actual or potential of my guard; having to bathe, & do all the acts of nature, in view of the guard, if they chose to look at me. I have been caged & baited, like a wild beast, by the prying eyes of (oftentimes) vulgar men both day & night. I have never been allowed an interview with anyone alone—not even with a minister of God—but have always been confronted with two or more witnesses, whenever minister, physician or any one else came to see me. —I have never been allowed my clothes, save those in present use, until the frequent disorders of my bowels made it actually necessary to keep a change of underclothing in my room. Where my other clothes are I do not know, as several of those who were represented as masters of my wardrobe denied the trust. I have found out that some things I valued have been stolen, together with all the little money I kept—I think it probable that you will never see half of the contents of my valise & dispatch bag. —The enclosed copies of letters present but a glympse [sic] of my tortures, for I know that the grand inquisitors—the Presdt. & Cabinet—knew all that I could tell & even more; & besides, my debility of body & of mind was such that I had not power to coin my thots [sic] into words to portray my sufferings. And to be frank, I was too proud to confess to them all my sufferings, &, also apprehend that they would rather rejoice & aggravate than relent & alleviate them.[75]

On 22 July, two months after Davis's arrival at the fort, Stanton ordered Miles to implement a series of changes to ameliorate Davis's condition. The secretary of war ordered the guards and the night lamp removed from Davis's cell. He permitted Davis to exercise outdoors, but still forbade the prisoner to communicate with any person other than those assigned to the fort. At least one officer accompanied Davis during these walks. Although Davis and Clay frequently saw each other on their walks, they were not permitted to talk together. Stanton also permitted Davis to have whatever newspapers or books he desired, though Davis complained that the books in the post library "are chiefly works suited to a military man, therefore not quite such as I would choose."[76] The prisoners' diet was changed. From the first Davis and Clay were given food prepared in the post hospital's kitchen. Clay described this food as "simple and spare but well prepared, and the best that could be furnished me for my health."[77] Finally, in August, two months after his arrival, Davis was granted permission to write to his wife, "under two conditions viz., that I confine myself to family matters, and that my letter shall be examined by the United states [sic] Attorney-General before it is sent to you."[78] The war secretary ordered Miles to visit Davis daily, and to report any health problems immediately. "It is not the desire of the Government," Stanton wrote, "to subject him to any hardships not essential to his secure detention."[79]

---

[75]Clay to Mrs. Clay, 11 August 1865, Clay Papers.
[76]Davis to Mrs. Davis, 13 March 1866, Jefferson Davis Collection.
[77]Clay to Mrs. Clay, 21 August 1865, Clay Papers.
[78]Davis to Mrs. Davis, 21 August 1865, in Hudson Strode, ed., "The Prison Letters of Jefferson and Varina Davis," *Comment* 4 (Spring 1966): 8.
[79]*OR*, 710-11.

These changes caused a noticeable transformation in the prisoners' mood. Clay said that his diet was better and his health stronger. "I have cause to congratulate myself on being put here, not only because of the salubriousness of the spot and the comfort of my quarters, but because of the gentle hands I have fallen into." In his letters to his wife, Clay frequently commented upon the kindness shown him by the soldiers at the fort. "All of the officers and soldiers, with scarcely any exception, have treated me with as much tenderness as their orders permitted; while they might, without incurring any charge or suspicion of cruelty, have inflicted upon me intolerable tortures." So pleased was Clay with some of the guards that he requested Mrs. Clay to send him "gallons of good old apple or peach brandy," and "some pure FRENCH brandy, for medicinal purposes. One or two bottles will do." Clay's motives were not entirely medicinal; in the same letter, he had told his wife that "the officers here have sent me juleps etc and I wish to show them some kindness in return." Davis concurred with Clay's fondness for the officers of the regiment. He told his wife, "I will be sorry to part from many of the officers—but as they are to go home, I should rejoice for such as are entitled to my gratitude." One month after the changes were ordered, Clay concluded that every effort had been made to make him comfortable. "In short," he assured his wife, "I am provided with all that is necessary for health or comfort; more than I expected to get at other people's expense, and better than any one guilty of the crimes imputed to me, ought to have."[80]

Following Stanton's orders of 22 July, a series of reports were filed on Davis's health. Dr. John J. Craven wrote the first of these on 20 August. He reported that Davis had a rash on his face, which Craven diagnosed as "erysipelas," and "a carbuncle on [his] thigh." Three weeks later Clay informed his wife that Davis "looks badly."[81]

By this time Davis was permitted to write to his wife and to contact the attorneys who had offered to represent him in his forthcoming trial for treason. In one of the first letters Davis told his wife not to be "alarmed by reports in regard to my health. Those who utter them can have no accurate information and are never to be relied on." He said that he "had fallen into a low condition the natural consequence of my situation," and complained of "carbuncles on the thigh and erysipelas in the nose." He claimed that at first he feared the latter "disease would extend to the brain," but by now it has "entirely disappeared." Davis described Dr. Craven as "both kind and skillful," and added, "I am deeply indebted to him and can assure you that while I am under his charge you need have no apprehension that any thing which is needful will be wanting."[82]

When the cool air of late summer arrived, Craven wrote Miles recommending that Davis be removed from the dank casemate to some other place on the post. "I have no other suggestions to make as to his treatment," Craven concluded. "He has the best of food and stimulants." Craven requested another physician's opinion on the conditions in the casemate cells. Davis later wrote his wife that "my kind Physician, called in the chief Medical Director who recently visited this Post, and the result of their consultation was that change to better quarters should be recommended. If their recommendations should secure to me a purer and drier atmosphere I think there will be a prompt and material improvement in my health."[83]

Miles immediately approved the physicians' recommendation, and with the approval of the War Department, he prepared cells for Davis, Clay, and Mitchel in the officers' quarters

---

[80]Clay to Mrs. Clay, 21 August 1865, Clay Papers; Davis to Mrs. Davis, 20 October 1865, Jefferson Davis Collection.

[81]*OR*, 720; Clay to Mrs. Clay, 18 September 1865, Clay Papers.

[82]Davis to Mrs. Davis, 15 September 1865, Jefferson Davis Collection.

[83]*OR*, 740; Davis to Mrs. Davis, 26 September 1865, Jefferson Davis Collection.

in Carroll Hall. Lieutenant Lemuel Shipman, who had to vacate one of the rooms Davis and Clay were to occupy, called it "most comfortable."[84] In a letter to Colonel Edward D. Town-send, the assistant adjutant general, General Miles described Davis's new room as "a very pleasant and airy one on the ground floor of Carroll Hall." He told Townsend that the quarters had been changed into a prison with "three grated doors, one opening on the piazza, one into another room to be occupied by the guard, and one into the hall. It is a room in which the prisoner can be securely confined and sentinels posted as specified in the plan."[85]

The War Department decided to check on Miles's arrangements, and sent Lieutenant Colonel Louis H. Pelouze to Fort Monroe at the end of September. While Pelouze was at Fort Monroe the decision was made to move the prisoners to the second floor of Carroll Hall. Colonel Pelouze approved these quarters and issued War Department orders to General Miles on 28 September 1865, permitting him to transfer Davis, who was moved to his new cell four days later.

Writing before the move was complete, Clay feared that the new cells would be less com-fortable than his present one, "altho' of fairer appearance." He also had heard rumors that Davis was "to be put in a cage there." But Davis was satisfied with the new arrangements. Shortly before the move he wrote Mrs. Davis: "There is now no reason to suppose that my imprisonment will so impair my health as soon to terminate my life." Davis rejoiced that the "dry air, good water and a fire when requisite have already improved my physical condition and with increasing strength all the disturbances due to a low vitality it is to be expected will disappear as rapidly as has been usual with me after becoming convalescent." Finally, Davis remembered Craven, his "attending Physician[,] who has been to me much more than that term usually conveys."[86]

John Mitchel was the first of the three political prisoners held at Fort Monroe to be re-leased. He wrote to Mrs. Davis on 1 November 1865 that he had been permitted to say good-bye to her husband. Mitchel described Davis "as comfortably settled as any prisoner can well expect to be. . . . When he [Davis] dresses to go out he looks as well, steps as firmly & holds his head as high as ever he did on Capitol Square [Richmond]." Mitchel also told her that Dr. Craven said that Davis's "health is at present pretty good."[87]

All correspondence to and from Davis was censored. General Miles, and perhaps others, read Davis's letters before they left Fort Monroe. All incoming mail for him had to be sent to Attorney General James Speed. In response to a protest from Mrs. Davis that one of her letters had been released to the press, Speed told her that "all of your letters that come to my care are read by no one but myself, and these few have been promptly forwarded. Mr. D's letters come to me open; who may have read them before they reach me, I do not know; after they reach me no one else reads them." Finally, the attorney general assured Mrs. Davis that "I have never spoken of the contents of the letters either way—I would not speak of their contents & feel like a gentleman."[88]

General Miles, ever cautious and obedient, sent the War Department a copy of a letter that Davis had written to Mrs. Davis on 23 October. The commandant objected to Davis's complaint that he had slept poorly while in the casemate. Miles wrote, "The statement is false

[84]Shipman, "Recollections," Halbert Papers.
[85]OR, 746.
[86]Clay to Mrs. Clay, 11 August 1865, Clay Papers; Davis to Mrs. Davis, 15 September 1865, Jef-ferson Davis Collection.
[87]Mitchel to Varina Davis, 1 November 1865, Samuel Richey Collection, Miami University, Ohio.
[88]Speed to Varina Davis, 2 December 1865, Jefferson Davis Collection.

in every particular as I know he rested and slept more than he says. His usual answer on being asked how he slept was invariably 'very well.' " By this time General Miles had become irritated at the sympathy Davis's imprisonment had evoked in some newspapers. Miles recognized that, as Davis's jailer, he would be the chief villain in all future accounts. The general complained, "As the newspaper reports were so favorable he [Davis] assumed more the airs of a prince than a prisoner."[89]

Both Jefferson Davis and Clement Clay constantly warned their wives that all the newspaper accounts of their imprisonment were highly exaggerated and not based on firsthand observation. "Let me assure you," Clay wrote, "that letter writers for the newspapers have no access to this fort, and that they either fabricate their reports or get them from soldiers, or, perhaps, officers, who furnish them for their own amusement, as I throw crumbs into the moat beneath my window, to the hungry minnows and enjoy the avidity with which they seize them." Davis wrote his wife, "You should have known how little you could trust the statements in regard to occurrences in my prison. It is true that nothing happened which does not somehow pass to newspaper correspondents, but as is usually the case with monopolies they abuse their privilege by perverting their knowledge and building a superstructure with but little regard for the foundation. You say the papers tell you every thing, but I warn you that the things they tell are not realities." Davis illustrated his caution with the story of an overcoat that some newspapers incorrectly reported he had received. "The matter being of such public importance as to have been followed in its progress through the tailor's shop, and down the Bay, the journals may give you the future history before it is known to me." Despite such inaccuracies, the War Department refused correspondents access to interview Davis or to report on his condition.[90]

Mrs. Davis asked her husband for a fuller description of his new quarters in Carroll Hall. On 23 October Davis extensively described them only to have almost four pages of text deleted from his letter. Mrs. Davis, unaware of the censoring of Davis's description of his cell, complained that he had ignored her request. On 3 November 1865 Davis emphatically told her, using a heavier hand and darker ink, "Your renewed request for a description of my room & accounts of my clothes is noted."[91]

Despite this graphic hint, Mrs. Davis pleaded for more information since she had been frightened by pessimistic newspaper reports on Davis's health. Davis replied, "I am sorry that the newspapers have distressed you by accounts of my condition and treatment, . . . I yielded to your renewed request and wrote a minute description of my room, its furniture, the beats of the sentinels &c. &c. &c. That part of my letter was objected to and was rewritten accordingly."[92]

---

[89]OR, 769-70, 840.

[90]Clay to Mrs. Clay, 21 August 1865, Clay Papers; Davis to Mrs. Davis, 2 December 1865, Jefferson Davis Collection.

[91]A copy of Davis's description may be found in the Jefferson Davis Collection at Transylvania University. The copy is not in Jefferson or Varina Davis's hand. A note at the top, written by their grandson, Jefferson Hayes-Davis, who had donated the collection to Transylvania University, said, "I think this letter was censored and never sent." In other handwriting is a second note, "Nov. 5th this and the next returned by Genl. because he objected to the passage marked by a cross." Much of the document is in Mrs. Davis's memoir; see Varina [Howell] Jefferson Davis, *Jefferson Davis, Ex-President of the Confederate States of America, a Memoir by His Wife*, 2 vols. (New York: Belford Co., 1890) 2:726-28; Davis to Mrs. Davis, 3 November 1865, Jefferson Davis Collection.

[92]Davis to Mrs. Davis, 21 November 1865, ibid.

In another letter Mrs. Davis complained of "heavy erasures," and Davis once again explained what had happened.

> The "heavy erasures" concerning which you inquire, assuming that they were made by me, as the Atty. Genl. had politely informed you that he did not do it, were not by my choice. To your repeated request to be informed as to my room, my clothes, and the change of the garrison as effecting me, I replied in the letter to which you refer. Two leaves containing the answers to the first two questions were returned to me as matter which would not be forwarded, and they were rewritten omitting the answers described. Subsequently my attention was called to a sentence on another page responding to your inquiry about the new garrison and stating a consequent alteration in the matters of sentinels, which I was required to obliterate. I drew the pen through it and sent it back.[93]

In fact, the Davises had anticipated some censorship of their correspondence. Before they parted on the *Clyde,* they had formulated a simple code. A few key words could convey more than a casual reader would discern. Once Davis had to remind his wife of this code: "You say you have lost the clue to the meaning of 'The:' add Holmes and I suppose it will give it."[94]

Although Davis could not describe his quarters, he was permitted to tell his wife about a typical day in prison.

> In the morning as soon as dressed I read the morning prayer (family) sometimes adding a chapter of the new Testament and a Psalm. After breakfast read, at this time Bancroft's History of the United States. Soon after 11—read the morning service, on Sundays, Wednesdays & Fridays, add the communion service, the Collect, Epistle and Gospel and the Litany. In the afternoon read whatever book occupied me and when Genl. Miles comes, go out to walk say, for an hour on the parapet. In the evening read the service as appointed. Family prayer at night . . . of food I am quite satisfactorily supplied by the Doctor's family, and my appetite is to blame for any want of appreciation. My cot is now comfortable and I have plenty of water and fire—Do not imagine horrible things and suffer vicariously for me.[95]

But mostly Davis wrote about his concern for his wife and children, fraternal and parental advice, corrections of some news reports, his general health, and philosophical reflections. As in almost all personal letters from a loving husband to his wife, Davis devoted much of the space to talk about family matters. He wrote of "Maggie," then in a convent school in Montreal, where her "loving temper will suit the . . . Nuns." He told his wife, "I am hungry for the children's little faces and have habitually to resist the power of that and other tender feelings which may not be gratified." In another letter he pleaded for more information about his family: "Tell me as much as you can of the sayings doings and looks of the children." Davis frequently professed his love to his wife. "My heart longs for your presence," he wrote on 3 February 1866. "How gladly would I shield you from every pain," he assured her. Davis occasionally sent her locks of his hair for the children to cherish, and he requested photo-

---

[93]Davis to Mrs. Davis, 7 December 1865, ibid.
[94]Davis to Mrs. Davis, 17 February 1866, ibid.
[95]Davis to Mrs. Davis, 20 October 1865, ibid.

graphs of the children, which Mrs. Davis did send him. At times Davis had to comfort his wife. He wrote of his own faith and assured her "that He who rules only permits injustice for some counterbalancing good of which the sufferer cannot judge." In the same letter he prayed, "Daily and nightly I beseech the Father [to] conduct you and the little ones to a place where you should be, trusting that He will protect and guide you all, and if it be his will reunite me with you whenever it is best that you & I be."[96]

Anxiety for his family and himself caused emotional illness and occasional depression. "My days drag heavily on to what I have no means to direct or to foresee." Combined with this uncertainty were the constant noise from the pacing guards and the light in the hall outside his cell. In September 1865 Davis complained that "the loss of sleep has created a morbid excitability [sic]." His most poignant complaints came a month later when he suffered a loss of memory, which he described as "the saddest effect" of his imprisonment, and then lamented,

> For say three months after I was imprisoned here two hours of consecutive sleep were never allowed to me, more recently it has not been so bad, but it is still only broken sleep which I get at night, and by day my attention is distracted by the passing of the Sentinels who are kept around me as well by day as by night. I have not sunk under my trials, am better than a fortnight ago and trust shall be sustained under any affliction which it may [be] required of me to bear. My sight is affected, but less than I would have supposed if it had been foretold that a light was to be kept where I was to sleep, and that at short intervals to be aroused and the expanded pupils that frequently subjected to the glare of a lamp.[97]

A month later things had improved and Davis assured his wife, "My sleep is less disturbed than formerly."[98] Mrs. Davis sent him goggles to shield his eyes, but the attacks of erysipelas prevented him from wearing them, and in January 1866 he requested her to send him an eyeshade.

Davis's letters frequently mentioned ill health, but never hinted at any disease worse than neuralgia, rashes, or boils. In November 1865 he told his wife: "My health is better than it was three months ago, my food is suited to my health and is abundant as I desire." In January 1866 Davis complained of neuralgia that made even writing difficult. He assured Mrs. Davis that, "I use caution in all things so that my strength may be preserved for whatever ails me." Less than three weeks later Davis told her that the neuralgia had subsided and an earlier case of dyspepsia "has been diminished by more proper diet." Shortly thereafter he assured her, "My health is now as good as usual." In that same letter, however, Davis complained that his attacks of neuralgia "sometimes render me almost blind." To relieve the pain he took "chloroform mixed with aconite, and also a preparation of spirits of camphor which served in the milder attacks." By March Davis was feeling better. "My health is about the same as heretofore," he told Mrs. Davis, "and the effects of close confinement has [sic] been less deleterious than might have been anticipated." Davis's last mention of his health came nine days later. "Do not permit yourself to be unhappy through fears for my health," he wrote his wife, "the injury sustained has been less than was reasonably to be anticipated under treatment so unusual. In the matter of diet there is nothing now to complain of; and the officers of the

---

[96]Davis to Mrs. Davis, 20 October 1865; 3 February 1866; 21 April 1866; 3 February 1866; 28 January 1866; 21 November 1865, ibid.

[97]Davis to Mrs. Davis, 2 December; 26 September; 20 October 1865, ibid.

[98]Davis to Mrs. Davis, 21 November 1865, ibid.

guard treat me with all the consideration compatible with their position. The daily walk of an hour is continued and the exercise in the open air usually revived me."[99]

Davis tried to make his letters appear as optimistic as possible. His handwriting was clear, bold, and neat. He rarely dwelt on his own problems, but usually tried to comfort his wife by answering her questions and reassuring her about his condition. There was a noticeable change, however, in the temper and tone of his letters in December 1865 and January 1866. A combination of foul weather, the holidays, and neuralgia made him despondent. "My own Winnie fear not what man can do," Davis counseled, "it is God disposed—Now I am shut up and slander runs riot to destroy my fair repute, but any investigation must redeem my character and leave it for an inheritance to my children of which in after times they will not be the worse for possessing. The treatment I have received will be compared with my treatment of others and it will be the reversal of the picture my enemies have drawn."[100]

Davis's complaints about his health are not surprising; they fit the pattern of behavior throughout his life. Both he and Varina leaned toward hypochondria, and they complained most of their lives about actual and imagined illnesses. Poor health was an escape and formed an important part of their relationship with each other. Illness offered them a haven from the world's demands and an excuse to demonstrate affection.[101] The confined prisoner Davis was no less healthy than President Davis had been outside. Naturally, the psychological pressures from the imprisonment—the guards and the light, along with the pending trial for treason— must have excited his nerves and disrupted accustomed habits. Yet even with these pressures, Davis's health did not significantly deteriorate at Fort Monroe.

Davis worried that his imprisonment might trigger a reaction in his wife. He cautioned her not to let "imaginary ills distress you." A few weeks later he wrote, "I fear that you have confined yourself too much to the house. Your mental anxiety and physical ills will act and react on each other. If you can master one it will help you overcome the other."[102]

Davis's health had always worried Miles. Frequent, sometimes weekly, medical reports described Davis's problems with boils, insomnia, neuralgia, dyspepsia, and a host of other ailments from poor appetite to muscle weakness. The doctors' description of Davis's general condition ranged from "deteriorating" to "improving." A team of army surgeons checked Davis's health several times during his confinement. Their reports agreed that Davis's health would improve if the light in the hallway outside his cell were extinguished, if the guards would stop their pacing, and if he would be permitted more exercise. Dr. George E. Cooper, who replaced Dr. Craven in December 1865, described Davis's ailments as "more the result of confinement than anything else."[103]

Initially Dr. Cooper appeared less sympathetic to the prisoners' plight than his predecessor, but Cooper had a hidden side. Before her first trip to Fort Monroe, Mrs. Clay wrote to Dr. Craven and asked him to meet her. Although Craven had been replaced by the time Mrs. Clay arrived, he met her secretly and warned, " 'My successor is the blackest of black Republicans, and I fear rigorous in his treatment of the prisoners,'—adding, 'the less you are

---

[99]Davis to Mrs. Davis, 21 November 1865; 17 January; 3, 17, 19 February; 13, 22 March 1866, ibid. The last letter was mistakenly dated 22 March 1865 by Davis.

[100]Davis to Mrs. Davis, 28 January 1866, ibid.

[101]Psychosomatic illness was an important refuge for nineteenth-century Americans. See Howard M. Feinstein, *Becoming William James* (Ithaca NY: Cornell University Press, 1984) for information on how another prominent family coped with it.

[102]Davis to Mrs. Davis, 26 November; 7 December 1865, Jefferson Davis Collection.

[103]*OR*, 896, 31 January 1866.

seen with me, the better for your cause.' " When Mrs. Clay met Dr. Cooper she found him to be "barely civil. I dare not ask one favor so stern and implacably did he impress me as hostile to my husb.[,] myself, my section & the cause for wh. we were struggling."[104]

Despite this cool reception, Dr. Cooper personally sympathized with the Davises and the Clays, and despite Craven's misgivings, Cooper was not the "blackest of black Republicans." In fact, Mrs. Clay soon found a new friend. Dr. Cooper confessed to her, "'My wife's the darnedest rebel out there except yourself.'" He brought Mrs. Clay to his quarters where she found herself "in the arms of a beautiful woman, the good fairy of childhood, for from her sweet lips dropped gems and jewels of comfort, while enfolding me in her arms & mingling her tears with mine she said 'be of good cheer my sister there is nothing under Heaven that you wd. do for J. D. or C. C. C. that I will not do. I am an old P. C. [Point Comfort] girl, nursed the milk of a Virginia mother & am ready to die for the Cause.' " Mrs. Clay later wrote that although Dr. Cooper "has lain in his grave for years, . . . his memory is green in my heart & my devotion to his wife & daughter unimpaired."[105]

Davis liked Dr. Cooper every bit as much as Dr. Craven. Cooper changed Davis's diet and "relieved me from the effects of indigestion." Cooper quickly befriended Davis. He taught the prisoner how to make coffee in a pot provided by Mrs. Clay, and at times took his daughter to visit Davis. "If more were needed," Davis told his wife, "Dr. Cooper would readily do it so far as the healing art extends. So that you may rest assured that whatever is practicable in my present imprisonment for the preservation of my health is as freely done now as when Dr. Craven was here."[106]

As early as 3 October 1865, Mrs. Davis told a close friend, "I have offered again and again to live in prison with him, to take a parole not to tell him anything about the public."[107] Finally on 25 April 1866, after almost a year in prison, Jefferson Davis received permission from the War Department for his wife to visit him. She was forced to sign a "Parole of Honor" in which she promised "to engage in or assent to no measures which shall lead to any attempts to escape from confinement, on the part of my husband, or to his being rescued, or released from imprisonment, without the sanction and order of the President of the United States nor will I be the means of conveying to my husband any deadly weapons of any kind."[108]

Mrs. Davis was housed in quarters in the casemate. The Davises' two-year-old baby, Varina Anne (Winnie) Davis, accompanied her. A Maryland sympathizer described the apartment as "sufficiently comfortable quarters," and Burton N. Harrison called them "tolerably comfortable."[109] At first Mrs. Davis had limited hours to visit her husband. Soon these visits included almost the entire day. At the end of May 1866, upon his word of honor that he would not attempt to escape from the fort, Davis was given the freedom to leave Carroll Hall and, with Mrs. Davis, walk the grounds of the fort unguarded from sunrise to sunset.[110] "But at sun down he is regularly locked up in a vile jail room, with bars, sentinels, light in the room &c."[111]

---

[104]Virginia Clay-Clopton, "Prisons & Prisoners," Clay Papers.

[105]Ibid.

[106]Davis to Mrs. Davis, 17 February 1866, Jefferson Davis Collection.

[107]Varina Davis to Johnston, 30 October 1865, William Preston Johnston Papers.

[108]Dated 1866, Jefferson Davis Collection.

[109]George William Brown to Franklin Pierce, 14 July 1866, Franklin Pierce Papers, Library of Congress; Harrison to Johnston, 4 August 1866, William Preston Johnston Papers.

[110]Davis's parole, 25 May 1866, is in the Richey Collection.

[111]Harrison to Johnston, 4 August 1866, William Preston Johnston Papers.

According to her memoirs, written a quarter-century later, Mrs. Davis was shocked by her husband's emaciated condition. "Through the bars of the inner room I saw Mr. Davis's shrunken form and glassy eyes; his cheek bones stood out like those of a skeleton. Merely crossing the room made his breath come in short gasps, and his voice was scarcely audible."[112] Davis's close friend, Burton N. Harrison, confirmed Mrs. Davis's observations. Harrison wrote to William Preston Johnston, another Davis intimate, in August 1866 that Davis's "health is very, very bad. He is emaciated & feeble—his voice weak—his step uncertain—his gait shaky & his feet carried along draggingly [sic]. We have great hopes of a speedy release—otherwise it seems certain he cannot live long."[113] Mrs. Davis soon let the friendly press and solicitous politicians know what she thought of her husband's condition.

A year of imprisonment had taken its toll. Yet Davis was never as sick as his wife or his close friends made him appear. In November 1867 he met Robert E. Lee for the first time since the end of the war. The Confederate general wrote his wife that "Davis looked 'astonishingly well, and is quite cheerful.'"[114] Later in his life Davis would complain that "exposure in both high and low latitudes and two years of close imprisonment together with mental suffering of no ordinary severity, have made me feel older than such a a [sic] hardy constitution should have made me feel [at] even a more advanced age."[115] Despite this complaint, written on his seventieth birthday, there is no evidence that his imprisonment permanently damaged his health. Charles Dana wryly commented, "That Davis's health was not ruined by his imprisonment at Fortress Monroe is proved by the fact that he came out of the prison in better condition than when he went in, and that he lived for twenty years afterward, and died of old age."[116]

Regardless of Davis's true condition, his wife used her pessimistic assessment to mount a successful effort to ameliorate Davis's still-stringent prison conditions. Less than three weeks after Mrs. Davis had arrived at the post, General Miles complained to the War Department that she was circulating false reports about Davis's condition to her friends and sympathetic reporters. Miles requested permission "to admit reliable representatives of the press inside the fort that they may give to the country the true facts in the case as they are, and I feel confident that there will be no reason for complaint either regarding his condition or treatment."[117] Stanton, surprisingly, turned down Miles's request. Miles continued, unsuccessfully, to pressure the War Department to permit reporters to interview Davis and to inspect his quarters.

Mrs. Davis's efforts to press the case for her husband's release were more successful in gaining favorable public attention. Dr. Cooper's contributions to her efforts were invaluable. In May 1866 she traveled to Washington, taking with her a copy of Dr. Cooper's report of 9 May 1866 on Davis's health. Cooper's prognosis was very pessimistic.

> He [Davis] is considerable [sic] emaciated, the fatty tissue having almost disappeared[,] leaving his skin much shriveled. His muscles are small, flaccid and very soft, and he has but little muscular strength. He

---

[112]Varina Davis, *Jefferson Davis,* 2:759.

[113]Harrison to Johnston, 4 August 1866, William Preston Johnston Papers.

[114]Lee to Mary Custis Lee, 25 November 1867, quoted in Charles Bracelen Flood, *Lee, the Last Years* (Boston: Houghton Mifflin Co., 1981) 170.

[115]Davis to ?, 3 June 1878, Jefferson Davis Collection.

[116]Dana, *Recollections,* 287.

[117]*OR,* 909.

is quite weak and debilitated, consequently his gait is becoming uneven and irregular. His digestive organs at present are in comparatively good condition but become quickly deranged under anything but the most carefully prepared food. With a diet disagreeing with him dyspeptic symptoms promptly make their appearance, soon followed by vertigo, severe facial and cranial neuralgia, an erysipelatous inflammation of the posterior scalp and right side of nose, which quickly affects the right eye (the only sound one he now has) and extends through the nasal duct into the interior nose. His nervous system is greatly deranged, being much prostrated and excessively irritable. Slight noises, which are scarcely perceptible to a man in robust health[,] cause him much pain, the description of the sensation being as of one flayed and having every sentient nerve exposed to the waves of sound. Want of sleep has been a great and almost the principal cause of his nervous excitability. This has been produced by the tramp of the creaking boots of the sentinels on post round the prison room and the relieval [sic] of the guard at the expiration of every two hours which almost invariably wakens him.

Prisoner Davis states that he has scarcely enjoyed over two hours of sleep unbroken at one time since his confinement. Means have been taken by placing matting on the floors for the sentinels to walk on to alleviate this source of disturbance, but with only partial success. His vital condition is low and he has but little recuperative force. Should he be attacked by any of the severe forms of disease to which the tidewater region of Virginia is subject, I, with reason, fear for the result.[118]

Mrs. Davis also carried a personal letter from Dr. Cooper regarding her husband's condition. Cooper wrote his letter in response to a letter from Mrs. Davis, who had told the doctor that she needed his personal observations on Davis's condition because she soon planned to leave the fort. Dr. Cooper responded on the same day, telling Mrs. Davis, "I have done all in my power to keep his health up but I must own I see him becoming more weak day by day. He has been well cared for in the matter of food, the tramp of the sentinels he no longer hears. He has exercised one hour in the morning and as much as he wishes for after four in the afternoon." Cooper prescribed "mental & bodily rest and exercise at will. This can be only by having the parole of the Fort with permission to remain with his family now residing there." Following such a change, Dr. Cooper concluded, Davis "will then probably recuperate."[119]

Dr. Cooper's report soon reached several newspapers, creating a hysterical outburst. Later Mrs. Davis claimed that "a wave of indignation swirled throughout the land" and prompted editorials denouncing the government's stringent measures.[120] The New York *World,* for example, castigated "the persons who have prostituted their official position to inflict upon the American name an ineffaceable brand of disgrace by the wanton and wicked torture of an invalid lying a helpless prisoner in the strongest fortress of the Union." The *World* claimed that Cooper's report revealed that Davis's health "has been systematically broken down by a cruel and deliberate perseverance in applying to him one of the worst tortures known to humanity." The *World* waxed eloquent in its vituperative account:

In a very minute and horrible treatise on the tortures practiced by the Inquisition an Italian writer tells us that a certain grand inquisitor at

---

[118]Ibid., 908.
[119]Cooper to Varina Davis, 23 May 1866, Jefferson Davis Collection.
[120]Campbell MacCulloch, "The Last Days of the Confederacy," *Spare Moments* 2 (March 1907): 7.

Rome, famous for his skill at jangling God's work in the human body, pronounced this special form of torment—the torment by insomnia—to be "the most exquisite and victorious of all he had ever essayed." No picture in all that dread gallery of imperial madness and misery which Suetonius has bequeathed to us is so fearful as his portraiture of Caligula roaming through the vast halls of the palace of the Caesars night after night with bloodshot eyes, sleeplessness, and driven on by sleeplessness to insanity. And in what a light are we, this triumphant American people of the nineteenth century, to appear before posterity weighted with the damning image of our most conspicuous enemy thus tied by us to the stake and tortured by us with worse than Indian tortures unto death? We make and seek to make no party issues with any man or men on this matter. It is the honor, the humanity, the Christianity, the civilization of the American Republic which are here involved.[121]

General Miles was no fool; he realized what was afoot. He sent the *World* editorial, along with similar clippings from the *New York News* and the *Richmond Times,* to the War Department. In a confidential letter he claimed that "Surgeon Cooper is entirely under the influence of Mr. and Mrs. Davis, the former of whom has the happy faculty that a strong mind has over a weaker to mold it to agree with its views and opinions." Mrs. Cooper, Miles continued, "is a secessionist and one of the F. F. V.'s [First Families of Virginia] of this state." Miles warned, "In my opinion there are other reasons than the 'waves of sound' to make Mr. Davis nervous and excitable; for instance, his age and the diseases to which he has been subject in previous years. The disappointment of his hopes and ambitions must necessarily affect the nervous system of a man of his pride while a prisoner. Since Mrs. Davis' appearance at this place there has been a determined effort made that as he could not be a hero to make a martyr of him."[122]

Miles requested that another doctor examine Davis. In response to his request, and in answer to the shrill public accounts, the War Department dispatched Surgeon General Joseph K. Barnes to examine Davis. On 6 June 1866 Dr. Barnes reported his findings to Secretary of War Stanton.

> Considering the age of the prisoner, his temperament, and all attending circumstances, his present condition is remarkably good, and, although thin and gray, his carriage is erect, his voice strong, and his general appearance not more altered since I saw him several years ago than was to be reasonably expected from natural causes. Having the freedom of the fort from sunrise to sunset, he walks at will either upon the ramparts or the parade ground, and to and from his meals, which are furnished by the surgeon of the post through Mrs. Davis, with whom he now takes them. The bill of fare furnished me by General Miles . . . constitute[s] a most wholesome and nutritious diet. Since a change in posting sentinels the inconvenience and irritation produced by disturbed rest has been relieved and is less complained of.
> Surgeon Cooper states that "Mr. Davis has improved in all respects at least 50 per cent. since his report of May 9, 1866," while General Miles considers his condition about the same; and that he takes less exercise

---

[121]*OR*, 915-16.
[122]Ibid., 919.

since all restrictions upon it have been removed. The prisoner's own statement was distinctly to the effect that his health is and has been much better than has been represented, and he expressed great annoyance at the reports of his condition which had reached the public, acknowledging that if the sentinel could be removed from such close proximity to his sleeping room and the light at night dispensed with he would be quite as comfortable as it was possible for any one under duress to be.

At this season there is no malarious disease at Fort Monroe. . . . the healthful climate of Old Point [Comfort] has made it for years a favorite resort. I do not consider him more liable to an attack of any of the severe forms of disease of the tide-water region than any other inmate of the fort, nor have I reason to suppose that such disease would be less amenable to treatment in his case than in others.

By extending the prisoner's parole from guard mounting to guard mounting instead of from sunrise to sunset, the objectionable sentinel and night lamp, the only present grounds of complaint[,] would be removed.[123]

Dr. Barnes's prescription would not be implemented immediately. But from the time of his visit until Davis's release almost a year later, weekly written medical reports were kept on Davis's condition. Mrs. Davis believed that her husband's life had been saved by Dr. Cooper's report. The furor it caused "cleared the air, and the official investigation, which was then set on foot, resulted in a decided improvement in the health of Mr. Davis."[124]

In August Dr. Cooper set off yet another scare when he reported that Davis might have contracted malaria, and prescribed quinine for his patient. The War Department quickly dispatched two army surgeons, Charles H. Crane, the assistant surgeon general, and Josiah Simpson, to examine Davis. These physicians contested Dr. Cooper's latest diagnosis. They concluded that Davis's

health has improved in every respect during the last few weeks. . . . The prisoner stated that his appetite was fair and digestion good; that his dyspepsia had been much relieved since the arrival of his wife at Fortress Monroe, as she was able to have food prepared that he had a preference for and could readily digest (all his meals being now taken with her and under her supervision); that he had been free from neuralgia for some time past and slept quite well at night. . . . From our examination of the prisoner and from the evidence presented we are of the opinion that prisoner Davis' health is now better than at any time since his arrival at Fortress Monroe. The measures adopted and now in use to preserve his health appear to be ample.[125]

The feud between General Miles and Mrs. Davis continued to fester. The antagonists had more in common than either would admit. Both were supercilious and haughty, overly impressed with their own self-importance and contemptuous of all who opposed their strong wills. Miles found Mrs. Davis overbearing and all too demanding. From the start he feared her cleverness and had suspected her of seeking to embarrass him. His worst fears were confirmed when President Johnson reassigned him, effective 1 September 1866. Miles wrote a letter marked "private" to Stanton in an unsuccessful effort to stall his transfer. Miles re-

---

[123]Ibid., 924.
[124]MacCulloch, "Last Days of the Confederacy" (March 1907): 7.
[125]OR, 953.

minded Stanton that he had "been here fifteen months during the imprisonment of Jefferson Davis and [I have] been the subject of every kind of abuse, which I consider has been unjust and an injury to my reputation. His [Davis's] friends have demanded my removal and are still doing so through their papers."[126] Miles went to see Stanton in person and asked the secretary of war if he might remain on duty until 1 October. In a letter to his mentor, Major General Oliver Otis Howard, Miles explained that he desired to stay at Fort Monroe until October to prevent the "Copperhead [Democratic] Party" from claiming that "I was removed at their request."[127] Despite his protest, Miles's wartime brevet rank of major general was removed and he was commissioned a regular army colonel on 6 September. He was given command of a black infantry regiment and assigned to North Carolina as assistant commissioner of the Freedmen's Bureau.

One biographer of Miles called his frustrating assignment as Davis's jailer an impossible task: "Despite his tactful handling of a difficult situation, and the fact that he was acting on the orders of superiors, he was censured by Southern sympathizers for the alleged ill-treatment of the former president of the Confederacy."[128] General Miles was never able to outlive the charges that he had abused Jefferson Davis. He finally permitted his version of the events at Fort Monroe to be told in an anonymous pamphlet published in 1902, a year before his retirement.[129]

The fort's new commander, Brigadier General Henry S. Burton, did not have his predecessor's troubles with the Davises. Soon after he had assumed command, General Burton visited Davis in his cell. The general asked Davis if he could do anything for him. Davis requested that his bed be moved from the middle of the room to a wall where it would be away from the window in the door, which permitted a draft and the night-light to disturb his sleep. According to a letter in the *San Francisco Examiner* in 1885, "General Burton ordered a heavy and dark blanket to be hung at the door, to darken the room and stop the draught, and in addition ordered the officer of the day to put the bed in the most sheltered corner of the room." The correspondent concluded that from that day on, Davis was able to sleep well every night.[130] Mrs. Davis immediately liked General Burton. She told a friend, "Since Genl Burton came into position here, he has been very civil and kind to me and kind to him [Davis]—his [General Burton's] wife is a sympathetic[,] warm hearted[,] talented Mexican woman who is very angry with the Yankees about Mexican affairs, and we get together quietly and abuse them—though to say [the] truth since Miles departed all here are kind to us, and considerate."[131] Years later Mrs. Davis described General Burton as having a "kindly, generous nature."[132]

General Burton soon permitted Mrs. Davis to join her husband in Carroll Hall, where a four-room suite with a kitchen was set aside for their use. Friends sent furniture and other items to decorate the prison apartment. Now the family was together—father, mother,

---

[126]Ibid., 975.

[127]Peter R. DeMontravel, "The Career of Lieutenant General Nelson A. Miles" (Ph.D. diss., St. John's University, 1983) 126.

[128]C[harles] D[udley] R[hodes], "Nelson Appleton Miles," *Dictionary of American Biography*, 1933.

[129]This pamphlet, *A Statement of the Facts Concerning the Imprisonment and Treatment of Jefferson Davis while a Military Prisoner at Fort Monroe, Va. in 1865 and 1866*, is printed in its entirety as an appendix to this book.

[130]Clipping from the *San Francisco Examiner*, 3 August 1885, Richey Collection.

[131]Varina Davis to Johnston, 27 September 1866, William Preston Johnston Papers.

[132]Varina Davis, *Jefferson Davis*, 2:773.

daughter, sister-in-law, and two servants. Davis was permitted to receive gifts, including bottles of green chartreuse from the bishop of Montreal. This liqueur, Mrs. Davis claimed, was "a powerful digestive stimulant" that helped Davis following meals.[133]

Even with the new accommodations and the easing of most restrictions on her husband, Mrs. Davis tumbled to the nadir of her hopes shortly after General Miles left. In a remarkably candid letter, Mrs. Davis confessed her worst fears to Mrs. Montgomery Blair, wife of Lincoln's postmaster general, who was drifting back into the Democratic party. Mrs. Davis greeted Mrs. Blair as "My Dear Old Girl" and confessed, "I see so little for the future but anguish and poverty for him that I try to be willing that God if he thinks it good should 'give his beloved sleep.' . . . I seem perfectly apathetic. It has taken me a long time to come to this but this 'peine fort et dur' [strong and hard punishment] to which I have been subjected has crushed hope out of me. Justice I did not expect, but hoped for humanity, these I now know exist no more."[134]

Yet Jefferson Davis not only survived, he grew healthier and stronger during the last six months at Fort Monroe. Not only had his physical condition improved, but his attitude had changed. He was free to walk the post and receive visitors. The public no longer chastised him for prolonging the war. Now his people rallied to demand his release. "He suffered," Mrs. Davis wrote, "as only men of his temperament can, but held aloft the standard of Confederate fealty and Christian virtue."[135]

Jefferson Davis lived with his family in the post officers' quarters much longer than he had been alone in the casemate cell. His was an imprisonment fit for an ex-president. Mary Day Burchenal, sister of Selden Allen Day, an officer at the fort, fondly recalled her memories of the Davises' last six months at Fort Monroe. Mrs. Burchenal's memoirs, "A Yankee Girl Meets Jefferson Davis," described how her brother and his fellow officers often sneaked favors to Davis. They even brought an easy chair so that he could read more comfortably. Mrs. Burchenal claimed that she had frequently visited Mr. and Mrs. Davis in their prison apartment. Indeed, so close did they become that Davis often called her "daughter." She fondly remembered the Davises' confinement and their private life. Her account leaves the reader with the impression that the Davises' prison life was one of quiet and dignified poverty.[136]

From the autumn of 1866 until Davis's release the following May, there was little official comment. His health seemed to rise and fall along with the weather. In these last months he spent increased time with his attorneys preparing for his pending trial. When not at the fort Mrs. Davis spent much of her time in Washington trying to get the president to order her husband's release. Perhaps she saw what some historians have called the "soft side" of Johnson "where the helpless, the uprooted, the distressed, were concerned—and he was particularly vulnerable to the feminine-sex regardless of whether they wore blue or gray."[137] Johnson was willing to release Davis, but the president insisted on upholding " 'his inviolate rule never to grant a pardon unless the application was made by a personal appeal from the prisoner,' and Mr. Davis could not bring himself to make the appeal, for as he said: 'an appeal for clemency or pardon was in itself a confession of previous guilt,' which he emphatically denied."[138]

---

[133]Ibid., 775.

[134]Varina Davis to Mrs. Montgomery Blair, 27 September 1866, Francis P. Blair Family Papers, Library of Congress.

[135]Varina Davis, *Jefferson Davis*, 2:775.

[136]Mary Day Burchenal, "A Yankee Girl Meets Jefferson Davis," *Holland's, The Magazine of the South* 50 (October 1931): 17-18, 43, 45.

[137]Leroy P. Graf, Ralph W. Haskins, et al., eds., *The Papers of Andrew Johnson*, 6 vols. (Knoxville: University of Tennessee Press, 1967-1983) 6:lxxvii.

[138]MacCulloch, "Last Days of the Confederacy" (March 1907): 7.

But the trial would never be held. The federal government knew that it could not try Davis for treason without raising the constitutional issue of secession. Edward A. Pollard described this impending confrontation as "the trial of the North. It was to determine whether a man could be punished as a traitor for acting on an opinion which had divided three generations of Americans."[139] Since any trial would have to take place in Virginia, where the "crime" had been committed, the federal government wisely recognized that it would never be able to convict Jefferson Davis for treason in a Southern court. Two years had passed since the war had ended. Congress was more interested in impeaching Andrew Johnson than in trying Jefferson Davis. Rather than permitting the war itself to be tried, the government released Davis on bail on 13 May 1867; on 15 February 1869 the case against Davis was dismissed.

## RECONSTRUCTION POLITICS

No small factor in obtaining the release of Davis was a remarkable book attributed to his Union surgeon at Fort Monroe who cared for him from May to December 1865. It appeared on 16 June 1866, less than a month after Mrs. Davis reached Washington and Dr. Cooper's report on Davis's condition reached many newspapers, prompting a number of shrill editorials. This memoir, based on the alleged diary of Dr. John J. Craven, was published under the title, *Prison Life of Jefferson Davis. Embracing Details and Incidents in His Captivity, Particularly Concerning His Health and Habits, Together with Many Conversations on Topics of Great Public Interest.*

Initially the North had gloated over the incarceration of the chief rebel. The day after Davis arrived at Fort Monroe a *New York Herald* editorial stated, "At about three o'clock yesterday, all that is mortal of Jefferson Davis, late so-called 'President of the alleged Confederate States' was duly, but quietly and effectively committed to that living tomb prepared with the impregnable walls of Fortress Monroe. . . . No more will Jeff'n Davis be known among the masses of man. . . . He is buried alive."[140] Yet instead of the indignity of oblivion, Davis's quiet, dignified suffering in prison helped to transform him into a martyr and a hero. By the end of 1866 several Northern leaders, including Horace Greeley, the influential editor of the *New York Tribune,* had launched a successful campaign that eventually would free the Confederate president. That the *Prison Life* could succeed in winning such sympathy for Davis is not difficult to understand when one examines the facts of the case.

Much had happened since that fateful June day in 1864 in Baltimore when the National Union party convention had placed Andrew Johnson as the vice-presidential candidate alongside Abraham Lincoln. A poor son of the Appalachian South, Johnson was an illiterate tailor. After his wife taught him to read, he tried a second career in politics. A Jacksonian, Johnson had fought against the vested, planter interests in Tennessee that he claimed were responsible for secession. When the war came Johnson remained in the United States Senate until he was appointed military governor of his state, promising "just penalties" for "the leaders of the rebellion. . . . Treason must be made odious and traitors must be punished and impoverished. . . . The tall poppies must be struck down."[141]

Concerned about his own reelection, Lincoln had sought a coalition ticket with Democrat Johnson as his running mate. Later many Republicans would be delighted to have Johnson as president. Remembering his threats against the planters, Republicans expected him to bar

---

[139]Pollard, *Life of Jefferson Davis,* 535.

[140]Quoted in Hudson Strode, ed., *Jefferson Davis, Private Letters, 1823-1889* (New York: Harcourt, Brace & World, Inc., 1966) 167.

[141]Graf and Haskins, *Papers of Andrew Johnson,* 6:336.

Southern Democrats from important positions in the restored nation. Initially President Johnson pursued just such a policy: prosecuting the assassins, punishing rebel leaders, and encouraging emancipation. But the president never forgot his Democratic roots. His vision of the restored South was a South of middle-class democracy: "For this end, a reorganized and strengthened Democratic party, cleansed of its disloyal prewar leadership, would be a reliable instrument; and with an agrarian-oriented Democracy in control, the country would return to first principles and paradise would be regained."[142]

Although Johnson had placed planters in a special class requiring presidential action, he handed out pardons like candy. Some authors have claimed that Johnson's postwar control over the planters fulfilled a psychological need. "Like the southern common people for whom he spoke, Johnson's resentment of the planter class was, after all, combined with a certain grudging admiration. If his vanity demanded that he gain recognition and respect, then nothing could satisfy him more than forcing this class to seek mercy from his hands. . . . Those who had scorned him were now flattering him, appealing to his generosity, begging for the franchise and the protection of their property."[143] It soon became obvious to Johnson that the obstacle standing in the way of his dream of a restored democracy was no longer the defeated rebels, but the victorious Republicans. The Republicans opposed his postwar goals in the same way that the planters had opposed his vision of an antebellum yeoman democracy. The Republicans had misread the president. The editors of Johnson's papers have called him "a controversial figure . . . a man generally uncompromising and sometimes intractable, a maverick never comfortable in any party harness, a sworn enemy of 'the interests' irrespective of time and place, a provincial *southern* in almost everything but secession."[144]

Johnson had hoped for a smooth and rapid restoration of the Union so that, with the Southern Democrats, he would have a working majority in Congress. He always had believed that secession was illegal and unconstitutional. Johnson held that the president, via his executive power of pardon, could restore civil rights to the rebel leaders and return the states to their ordinary relationship. He had told Congress in his first annual message (4 December 1865) that "the true theory is that all pretended acts of secession were from the beginning null and void. The States cannot commit treason nor screen the individual citizens who may have committed treason any more than they can make valid treaties or engage in lawful commerce with any foreign power. The States attempting to secede placed themselves in a condition where their vitality was impaired but not extinguished; their functions suspended, but not destroyed."[145]

By 1866 Johnson faced serious opposition from congressional Republicans. They feared that if Johnson quickly restored the Southern states and pardoned the former rebel leaders, the Democratic party would regain its prewar power and thereby frustrate the Republican plans for economic and social reform of the South. Thwarting the Republican vision was precisely what Johnson wanted. "He did not welcome the vast acceleration of social and economic changes for which the Civil War was responsible. In an age of railroads, manufacturing corporations, and commercialized agriculture, Johnson still romanticized the self-sufficient yeoman farmer, still regarded cities as centers of moral decay."[146] Johnson's only recourse was

---

[142]Kenneth M. Stampp, *The Era of Reconstruction, 1865-1877* (New York: Alfred A. Knopf, 1966) 59.

[143]Ibid., 70-71.

[144]Graf and Haskins, *Papers of Andrew Johnson,* 6:lx.

[145]Richardson, *Messages and Papers of the Presidents,* 6:357.

[146]Stampp, *Era of Reconstruction,* 54.

promptly to restore the Southern states to the Union, and to return the pardoned—and, one hoped, repentant—rebel leaders to Congress.

A political watershed had arrived. Few elections in American history were as important as the congressional race of 1866. The future of constitutional government seemed to rest on its outcome. Since Congress had refused to seat the senators and representatives from the Southern states, congressional elections in the fall would determine whether the president or the Congress would control the course of Reconstruction. The National Union Movement had been formed in the spring of 1866 to oppose the proposed Fourteenth Amendment, to "affirm the right of each state to regulate its local institutions, subject only to the Constitution of the United States" and "to prescribe its own term of suffrage."[147] The only Americans in full agreement with President Johnson's program were the members of the old Democratic party, but Johnson saw no harm in trying to gain support from moderate Republicans. The president went directly to the national electorate, where he tried to convince the voters that his lenient Reconstruction policy would preserve liberty, promote national unity, and foster prosperity. The president would need all the help he could get.

In March 1866 President Johnson received a letter from the editor of the staunchly Democratic newspaper, the *New York Citizen*. Its editor, Charles G. Halpine, told Johnson that disclosure of information about Davis's imprisonment "could not but modify the rampant passions and hatreds on which such men as [Charles] Sumner and [Thaddeus] Stevens make their trade." Halpine offered to prepare a book, and he assured the president that revelations about Davis's prison life would be "the most powerful campaign document ever issued in this country—a document that could not but abate the fanaticism of the radicals . . . & strengthen & rally the conservative opinions of the country to your increased support."[148]

As a matter of fact, Johnson had anticipated Halpine's proposal, for he already had recognized the political significance of Davis's imprisonment in securing sympathy for the South as well as for his own Reconstruction plans. In July 1865 he had told a prominent Southern lady, "Madam . . . the interests of the South require the blood of Mr. Davis."[149] Halpine's book interested Johnson. It would be neither a memoir nor a biography; it would be a political tract for the Democratic party. A sympathetic portrayal of Davis and the Southern viewpoint would demonstrate the wisdom of Johnson's treatment of the rebel leaders and restore confidence in their desire to live peaceably in the reconstituted Union. As Halpine himself put it, such a work would "strengthen the sound, constitutional and conservative opinion of the country in support of your policy and views."[150] Andrew Johnson "was decidedly interested and Halpine went promptly to work."[151]

The real author of the *Prison Life of Jefferson Davis* was not Dr. John J. Craven, but Charles Graham Halpine, a largely unknown but most interesting character of the Civil War era. Christened Charles Boynton Halpin, he was born in County Meath, Ireland, on 20 November 1829, the son of a priest of the Irish (Protestant) Church. A Protestant minister's duties in Catholic Ireland were not onerous, and the elder Halpin devoted most of his time to literature. Charles, inheriting his father's love for words, quit his study of medicine at Trinity Col-

---

[147]Eric L. McKitrick, *Andrew Johnson and Reconstruction* (Chicago: University of Chicago Press, 1960) 399.

[148]Halpine to Johnson, 20 March 1866, Andrew Johnson Papers, Library of Congress.

[149]Glenn, *Between North and South*, 238.

[150]Halpine to Johnson, 20 March 1866, Johnson Papers.

[151]William Hanchett, "Reconstruction and the Rehabilitation of Jefferson Davis: Charles G. Halpine's *Prison Life*," *Journal of American History* 56 (September 1969): 282.

lege to pursue a career in journalism. When only nineteen, Charles married Margaret G. Milligan. Although above him in station, Margaret would prove to be a loyal and loving wife.[152]

Halpine sailed to America in 1850 to make his fortune. He arrived in Boston and earned his living writing advertisements, amusing essays, and poetry for the short-lived magazine *Carpet-Bag*. Halpine's early writings demonstrated the style and characteristics he used throughout his career. He liked pseudonyms and disguised his fictitious characters as first-hand observers who commented upon important personalities or events. Their observations were embellished with an Irish wit that endeared them to Halpine's readers. His wife did not join him in the United States for three years. To pass his lonely hours, Halpine sought solace in the bottle—a habit that plagued him the rest of his life. Alcoholism, a fine wit, a gift for story telling, and a penchant for politics made Halpine a real-life caricature of the Irish immigrant in the antebellum United States.

By the time Margaret had arrived in America, Halpine had moved to Brooklyn and was writing stories and poetry for several New York newspapers. He enjoyed considerable renown from the appearance of a collection of his poems, *Lyrics by the Letter H*. A lover of literary mystery, he had attributed this collection to others, but contemporary critics quickly penetrated the ruse, identified him, and acclaimed the work a success. During this same period he became a member of the reform wing within the New York Democratic party.

Halpine was among the first to volunteer when the Civil War began. He became a lieutenant and adjutant of the famous "Fighting Sixty-Ninth" Regiment, largely composed of fellow Irishmen from New York City. Halpine spent much of his time during the war as an aide to the controversial Union general David Hunter. A member of an important Virginia family, Hunter won more than his share of Southern enmity for his attempt to use fugitive slaves in the federal army, and for his success in ravaging the Shenandoah Valley, which included burning the buildings at the Virginia Military Institute in 1864. Initially Halpine was Major General Hunter's aide on the Sea Islands off the South Carolina and Georgia coast. The seashore was not congenial to Halpine. He had constant headaches and feared losing his sight from the brilliant sun reflected off the white sand. When, for reasons that are still unclear, Hunter was removed from his command in June 1863, Halpine obtained a medical discharge.

When Halpine returned to New York City, he served on the staff of Horatio Seymour, New York's Democratic governor. There, in July 1863, he helped subdue the passions of the draft rioters, many of whom were Irish. But when General Hunter received a new command, Halpine rejoined him as his aide and participated in Hunter's famous Shenandoah Valley raid. A year after his first resignation, Halpine resigned a second, and final, time.

Halpine's wartime duties allowed him the time to write a series of essays under the pseudonym Miles O'Reilly. Largely forgotten today, Private O'Reilly's witty, satiric comments on the war were a favorite in their day. Halpine told his tales so convincingly that many believed his character to be a real soldier. The Miles O'Reilly stories and some of Halpine's earlier poems were collected and published in two different and highly successful books, *The Life and Adventures, Songs, Services and Speeches of Private Miles O'Reilly* (1864) and *Baked Meats of the Funeral* (1866).

---

[152]The best study of Halpine's life is William Hanchett, *Irish, Charles G. Halpine in Civil War America* (Syracuse NY: Syracuse University Press, 1970). Hanchett's biography is written with an objectivity, decisiveness, and wit that does well by his subject. Other accounts are John D. Hayes and Doris Maguire, "Charles Graham Halpine: Life and Adventures of Miles O'Reilly," *New York Historical Society Quarterly* 51 (October 1967): 326-44, and F[rank] M[onaghan], "Charles Graham Halpine," *Dictionary of American Biography*, 1932. Readers are advised to use the last with caution since it contains factual errors.

After his second resignation from the army, Halpine resumed his journalistic career, writing as many fictitious news stories as factual reports. At first he wrote for the anti-Lincoln organ, the *New York Herald,* but soon after the war Halpine took over the *New York Citizen,* the paper of the reform wing of the New York Democrats. There he met Robert B. Roosevelt of the influential East New York family, who became a lifelong friend. Halpine first met Andrew Johnson in the summer of 1865 and soon became a frequent visitor to the White House. Under Halpine's editorship, the *New York Citizen* consistently backed President Johnson's lenient plan for reconstructing the South. Johnson returned the favor when he promoted Halpine to brevet brigadier general in February 1866. "Nothing but the privilege of using the military title was involved, but General Halpine was the last man to consider the honor an empty one!"[153]

While serving on the Sea Islands, Halpine had met Dr. John J. Craven and the two soon became close friends. Craven was a self-educated physician. In 1851 he began "to read medicine" under the tutelage of Dr. Gabriel Grant of Newark. Later Craven himself would admit, "My reading of medicine in Dr. Grant's office was interrupted to a great extent from the fact that during the time I was studying medicine my time was occupied in earning a livelihood for myself and family so that I did not occupy the time as did an ordinary student of medicine in the office of my preceptor."[154] At that time American medicine was moving beyond the unscientific age, and with it came the end of the practice of prescribing massive doses of purgatives, and the free-market, no-regulation practices of the Jacksonian era.[155]

When the Civil War began Craven enlisted in the First New Jersey Regiment as a surgeon. His appointment caused much controversy among the degree-holding physicians of New Jersey. The Essex District Medical Society of Newark protested Craven's appointment, calling him "an irregular practitioner, who is without any claim whatever to a medical position, and that the credit and dignity of the profession demand a respectful representation of the facts to the Department [of War]." The New Jersey State Medical Society endorsed the district organization's protest. Most medical schools in the United States were proprietary ones, more interested in making money than educating competent physicians. Professional medical societies, primarily composed of graduates from the proprietary schools, were formed to protect their own interests and to prevent self-taught physicians from practicing medicine. There is no evidence that Civil War patients benefited from one group more than the other. In response to these charges Craven obtained a letter of recommendation from Dr. Willard Parker, a New York City surgeon, who wrote: "I beg leave to state that the bearer, J. J. Craven, is very well posted in the practical parts of his profession; that he has a zeal and a determination also in his profession which must make him efficient and reliable in every emergency." Craven took this letter to President Lincoln, who ordered that Craven be examined by an

---

[153]Hanchett, *Irish,* 143.

[154]Chester D. Bradley, "Dr. Craven and the *Prison Life of Jefferson Davis,*" *Virginia Magazine of History and Biography* 62 (January 1954): 83.

[155]For additional information on medical education in the antebellum United States, see John Duffy, *The Healers: A History of American Medicine,* 2d ed. (Urbana: University of Illinois Press, 1979); Donald Fleming, *William H. Welch and the Rise of Modern Medicine* (Boston: Little, Brown, 1954); and Richard Harrison Shyrock, *Medicine and Society in America, 1660-1860* (New York: New York University Press, 1960).

army board. Craven passed his examination, and the War Department permitted him to continue as an army surgeon.[156]

Craven was a scientific gadfly of the first order. Only a year before the *Prison Life* appeared, his friend Halpine wrote a witty and fictitious sketch in the *New York Citizen* about Craven's scientific thirst. Halpine's humorous portrait of Craven is a good example of the journalist's facile pen. As Halpine recalled, Craven "is a devotee of science in all its branches, and more fully fills my ideal of a savant than any other medical man it has been my luck to meet in the army. . . . When a scoundrelly deserter, convicted of going over to the enemy and other crimes too abominable to mention was 'shot to death with musketry' in pursuance of his sentence, Dr. Craven obtained the privilege of skinning him and tanning his hide—the skin itself tattooed all over while the fellow was a sailor with pictures too blasphemously and obscenely horrible for contemplation, being a dreadful commentary on the subsequent claims of which the soul therein dwelling had been greedily guilty."[157] Craven held a variety of wartime assignments before his final appointment as medical purveyor and chief medical officer for the Department of Virginia and North Carolina. In this position Craven was stationed at Fort Monroe where he attended Jefferson Davis.

When Halpine learned that his old friend had been Jefferson Davis's attending physician for several months at Fort Monroe, he hit upon an ingenious idea: support the Democratic cause by providing a sympathetic account of Davis's imprisonment. For additional insights into Davis's personality, Halpine contacted Richard Taylor, Jefferson Davis's brother-in-law. As the only son of President Zachary Taylor, Richard admitted that "I had a larger acquaintance with influential politicians than other Southern commanders."[158] For that reason, Taylor was spending time in New York City and Washington seeking pardons and financial support for prominent Southerners.

But why would a devoted Union man fabricate an account designed to make a martyr out of the Confederate leader? In truth, Halpine did not care a whit about Jefferson Davis's fate; when the prisoner was released on bail in May 1867 Halpine wrote Johnson to congratulate him "on the partial riddance of your white elephant, Jefferson Davis."[159] But Halpine did have clear political motives along with the obvious pecuniary considerations he would receive from a successful book. He confessed to a friend that he hoped "to put the whole present plea of the South in the mouth of Mr. Davis, interpolating political matters from Southern sources in his real conversations with Dr. Craven which were chiefly on scientific & social subjects, though not altogether so."[160]

In addition, the *Prison Life* itself disclosed that the primary purpose for its publication was the author's "deep conviction that the Union can best be reconstructed, and its harmony of relationship restored by pursuing a moderate policy."[161] Chapter 16 especially developed the

---

[156]*Arthur M. Eastman* v. *Western Union Telegraph Company,* Circuit Court, Southern District of New York (November 1874) 518, 520, 956. Copy of the testimony is with the John J. Craven Papers, Library of Congress.

[157]*New York Citizen,* 1 July 1865, 1. This story was a favorite of Halpine, who reprinted it a year later in the *Citizen,* 7 July 1866, 4. Some authors have accepted this fanciful sketch as accurate; see Burke Davis, *The Long Surrender,* 180.

[158]Richard Taylor, *Destruction and Reconstruction: Personal Experiences of the Late War* (New York: D. Appleton, 1879) 239.

[159]Halpine to Johnson, 14 May 1867, Johnson Papers.

[160]Halpine to Samuel L. M. Barlow, 23 April 1866, quoted in Hanchett, "Reconstruction . . . of Jefferson Davis," 282.

[161]*Prison Life,* 19-20.

writer's arguments for a lenient policy by expressing the political issues in Davis's words. Because this motive was the central reason behind the book, Halpine had sent Craven back to Fort Monroe to gather notes concerning Davis's ideas on Reconstruction. Unable to meet personally with Davis, Craven engaged a sympathetic friend, most likely Dr. Cooper, to smuggle out written statements from Davis. Interestingly, despite this primary material, Davis later would complain that the opinions about Reconstruction attributed to him in the *Prison Life* were inaccurate.[162]

Halpine was a consistent supporter of President Johnson's Reconstruction policy. Halpine's convictions were expressed as editor of the *Citizen,* in independent essays, and even in verse. In "Mr. Johnson's Policy of Reconstruction," Halpine took the part of "the boys in blue," asserting that many Union soldiers had fought to restore the Union and nothing more.

> "His policy," do you say?
> By Heaven, who says so lies in his throat!
> 'Twas our policy, boys, from our muster-day,
> Through skirmish and bivouac, march and fray—
> "His policy," do you say?
> . . . . . . . . . . . . . . .
> We are with him none the less—
> He works for the same great end we sought;
> We feel for the South in its deep distress,
> And to get the old Union restored we press—
> 'Twas for this end we enlisted and fought.
>
> Be it his or whose it may,
> 'Tis the policy, boys, that we avow;
> There were noble hearts in the ranks of gray,
> As they proved on many a bloody day,
> And we would not oppress them now.[163]

Halpine especially feared the Republican demand for black political and economic rights in the South because he saw parallels between the Republicans' position regarding the South and England's oppressive rule in his homeland. Bitterly he wrote,

> Either we must treat the South as Cromwell treated Ireland—uprooting all the ancient laws and proprietors of the soil, and replanting it with the families of his own soldiers, holding by military tenure and with sufficient garrisons to repress and keep in subjection an enslaved and utterly ruined people; or we must pass liberal acts of oblivion and amnesty in favor of all who took part in the secession movement, only excluding those . . . who have been guilty of individual crimes placing them outside the laws of civilized warfare.[164]

---

[162]Jefferson Davis's marginal comments in his personal copy of: John J. Craven, *Prison Life of Jefferson Davis* (New York: Carleton, Publisher, 1866) 253. This book is in the Rare Books Section of the Special Collections Division, Tulane University Library, New Orleans, Louisiana. Cited hereafter as *Prison Life,* Davis Copy.

[163]Robert B. Roosevelt, ed., *The Political Works of Charles G. Halpine (Miles O'Reilly)* (New York: Harper & Brothers, 1869) 257-58.

[164]Quoted in Hanchett, *Irish,* 143.

Seizing the opportunity, Halpine placed similar statements, comparing the South with Ireland, into the mouth of Davis in the *Prison Life*.[165]

Halpine's acquaintance with Dr. Craven, already introduced to many of his readers as "the physician attending another distinguished prisoner—Miles O'Reilly," offered Halpine's fertile mind the unique opportunity to aid the cause of the Democratic party by writing a sympathetic account of Jefferson Davis's imprisonment. Halpine was an ardent Democrat who feared postwar Republican rule in the North as well as in the South. Apparently, Dr. Craven shared Halpine's political outlook. Although some authors, including Halpine, had described Craven as a Republican, not only was Craven willing to help the Democratic cause by providing information for the *Prison Life,* he was nominated by President Johnson for a postmastership, only to be rejected by the Republican Senate. Later in life Craven unsuccessfully ran as a Democratic candidate for the New York State Assembly.[166]

Although it was already too late to rescue President Johnson's personal fortunes, Halpine recognized the potential political impact of the *Prison Life*. He hoped that a compassionate account of Davis's suffering in prison might turn Northerners away from Republican excesses. "If the great Union party was not beyond the reach of accident," Halpine wrote in the columns of the *Citizen,* "Dr. Craven's book might be turned into a campaign document, furnishing, as it does, from Davis' own lips, first-rate Copperhead replies to Republican arguments."[167] He hoped that the book would strengthen the Democratic party by forcing a quick readmission of the Southern states with Democratic senators and representatives. Generosity and magnanimity to Davis could lead to generosity and magnanimity to the South as well. The end result would be a rejuvenated national Democratic party.

Even if the measurable political impact of the *Prison Life* was negligible, its political motivation cannot be doubted. It is not surprising that one of the earliest and most extensive reviews of the *Prison Life* devoted more than twenty-two pages to the political implications of the work while largely ignoring the narrative of Davis's imprisonment. The essay concluded, "We have said nothing of Dr. Craven's book, for the simple reason that there is nothing to say. It belongs to what is called the 'sensational' class, and although apparently written with good feeling and in good faith, was still prepared for its market and seasoned accordingly."[168] Halpine himself gloated that the *Prison Life* "has proved a perfect bombshell in the radical [Republican] camp. They squirm under its revelations like dead frogs under a galvanic battery."[169] Finally, despite its obvious political purpose, it also significantly contributed to the efforts to arouse public sympathy for Davis, and eventually made it possible for the federal government to avoid a difficult constitutional predicament by releasing Davis.

## FICTION DISTORTING FACT

Obviously the person in the best position to judge the authenticity and reliability of the *Prison Life* was Jefferson Davis himself. In fact, he is the source of perhaps the most damning testimony against the book. Yet that testimony was unknown in his lifetime and has been little known and less often cited to this day. Throughout their lives, neither Davis nor his wife commented unfavorably on the book. Both knew that the book had made Davis into the man he had wished to be. Having lost all else in the war, enhanced public stature was the

---

[165]*Prison Life*, 243-45.
[166]*Portrait and Biographical Record of Suffolk County (Long Island)* (New York: Chapman, 1896) 1025-26.
[167]*New York Citizen*, 30 June 1866, 2.
[168]Wallis, "Imprisonment of Davis," 255.
[169]*New York Citizen*, 7 July 1866, 4.

thing most cherished by Davis in the last decades of his life. The war had destroyed his farm, freed his slaves, and revealed his personal shortcomings. The *Prison Life* salvaged his reputation. In it he appeared abused, kindly, intelligent, noble, and forgiving. Davis the man had become Davis the symbol. Any criticism of the work could ruin this image and subject him again to the scorn of his people.

Richard Taylor, a Confederate general and Davis's brother-in-law by his first marriage, wrote in his memoirs that he and Davis had discussed Davis's new prominence as a result of his imprisonment. Taylor "remarked that the curse of unexpected defeat and suffering" had alienated many of the Southern people toward Davis. However, Taylor continued, "now his calamities had served to endear him to all. I think he derived consolation from this view."[170]

Both of the Davises found the memories of his imprisonment painful. It brought back the shame Davis had suffered when manacled, his bodily aches, the initial symptoms of Mrs. Davis's subsequent nervous illnesses, and the general disdain people had felt for him. Much later in his life, when Davis mentioned the *Prison Life,* he recalled those sad memories, "the renewal of which is always painful."[171] Whatever kindness or mercy that could be extracted from his prison experiences was preserved and nurtured, not attacked or denied.

But when Davis acquired his own copy of the *Prison Life* in August 1866, it was not the memory of the experience that troubled him. Privately he fumed about the inaccuracies in the book. George William Brown, a Maryland attorney and Southern sympathizer who had spent fifteen months in a federal prison during the war, visited Davis in July 1866. After Brown returned to Baltimore, he wrote a letter describing Davis's condition to ex-president Franklin Pierce. Brown noted, "Dr. Craven's book is doing a great deal of good, but it contains a great deal that annoys Mr. Davis very much. It is, he says, sensational in parts and that is particularly disagreeable to him, and in some things is incorrect."[172]

At the time of Brown's visit, the *Prison Life* was still fresh in Davis's mind, and the public had not had time to react to it. Two months after Brown's visit James A. Bayard, Jr. of Delaware saw Davis in prison. He told friends that Davis was critical of the work. William Wilkins Glenn wrote in his journal that Bayard had told him that Davis "says that there is not one word of truth of what Craven says in his book about [General] Hunter. He never uttered such words." Furthermore, Davis had guessed the real author of the work. "The Book he says was prepared by Miles O'Reilly who had been on Hunter's staff. O'Reilly put all this in himself." Finally, Davis claimed that the book had received the approval of the Johnson administration. "The book was reviewed in the war office & expurgated before going to press."[173] This claim cannot be substantiated today.

Halpine knew that Davis was infuriated with the *Prison Life.* Word already had begun to leak out that Davis disliked the book. To contradict these reports and to create additional interest in the work, Halpine created a fictional exchange with Davis and printed it in the *Citizen.* Halpine assured the public that "we have authority to contradict the report that Jeff. Davis repudiates any portion of Col. Craven's book. On the contrary, Mr. Davis bore testimony no later than last Tuesday (July 17) to the marvelous accuracy with which his conversations are reported in the 'Prison Life'—adding that he wished Craven had not been so

---

[170]Taylor, *Destruction and Reconstruction,* 247.

[171]Davis to Col. C. W. Frazer, 21 July 1887, in Dunbar Rowland, ed., *Jefferson Davis, Constitutionalist: His Letters, Papers, and Speeches,* 10 vols. (Jackson MS: Department of Archives and History, 1923) 9:583.

[172]Brown to Pierce, 14 July 1866, Pierce Papers.

[173]Glenn, *Between North and South,* 273.

accurate, 'as some of the reported remarks about Southern politicians and generals were extremely embarrassing.' "[174]

The *Prison Life* was a conversational narrative that claimed to present the stories Davis shared with his physician. Persons familiar with Davis's personality recognized him in the book. Davis was garrulous and freely offered his opinions on a wide range of subjects from literature to political philosophy. Glenn remembered that Davis "will talk to you about everything from science down to the shape of a dog's tail, and have something to say about everything, showing that he has read or talked about it before."[175] The portrait of the ex-president in the *Prison Life* was a complimentary one. He was shown to be a man less worried about his own condition than that of his wife, children, and the entire South. Davis was portrayed as a religious man, a student of natural history and literature, and a kindly soul who fed crumbs from his prison plate to a mouse he had befriended. Readers could only be impressed with Davis's forgiveness toward those who had punished or maligned him, his stoical acceptance of his own fate, and his hope of redeeming himself in his anticipated trial. Davis spoke of Lincoln and many Union generals with sincere admiration and demonstrated paternal concern for the recently freed slaves. "Mr. Davis is remarkable for the kindliness of his nature and fidelity to friends. Of none of God's creatures does he seem to wish or speak unkindly; and the same fault found with Mr. Lincoln—unwillingness to sanction the military severities essential to maintain discipline—is the fault I have heard most strongly urged against Mr. Davis."[176]

Despite the book's favorable portrayal of Davis based upon Dr. Craven's observations, in truth, Craven's involvement in its publication left Davis disappointed and bitter. Prior to that time he had been impressed with the kindness Craven had shown him. In their private letters during the first year of his imprisonment, Davis and Varina frequently mentioned Dr. Craven. Most of these references are laudatory; none is negative. In Davis's first letter from prison to his wife, he wrote, "To the surgeon and regimental chaplain I am under many obligations." Two months later Davis thankfully acknowledged, "I am deeply indebted to my attending physician who has been to me much more than that term usually conveys." As late as April 1866, more than three months after Craven's removal and three months before the *Prison Life* appeared, Davis still recalled the kindness shown by his physician and Craven's family. "I can never be less grateful for their attentions," Davis wrote, "than when like the good Samaritan they gave me relief and proved that I had not passed the limits of humanity. Benefits are to be measured by the motive with which they are conferred and by the effect which they produce. I therefore feel deeply indebted to the Dr. and the Ladies of his family; for a benevolence which had much to suppress and nothing selfish to excite it and but for which my captivity would soon have ended in death."[177] In October 1865 Mrs. Davis had noted her own gratitude, assuring Davis, "I will teach my children to pray for dear Dr. Craven all his life."[178] She even dismissed Craven's refusal to answer her first letters as a virtue, saying, "I suppose that is a rigid adherence to his duty."[179] Craven became such a favorite of Mrs. Davis that she kept his *carte de visite* along with those of forty other men whom she called her "particular favorites." Of these, Craven was one of only five who were neither political nor military of-

[174]*New York Citizen,* 21 July 1866.
[175]Glenn, *Between North and South,* 297.
[176]*Prison Life,* 373.
[177]Davis to Mrs. Davis, 21 August, 14 October 1865; 8 April 1866, Jefferson Davis Collection.
[178]Strode, *Davis, Private Letters,* 182.
[179]Mrs. Davis to Davis, 23 October 1865, ibid., 193.

ficers of the Confederacy.[180] Davis's relationship with Craven was so close that Halpine melodramatically described it as "the tenderest & even most pathetic attachment."[181]

Publication of the *Prison Life* ended Davis's friendship with Craven. The kind care Davis had received from Craven, whose motives Davis earlier had described as "nothing selfish," now appeared to have emanated from pecuniary and political considerations. Despite Craven's vow that he would say nothing in the book to violate "the relations of physician and patient [which] have a sacredness of confidence," he indeed had betrayed his professional oath.[182] Twenty years later Mrs. John T. Brodnax, a third and neutral party, contacted Davis at Craven's request. Now old and visiting New Orleans, Craven hoped to make up with Davis before he died. The doctor sent his ex-patient a message that was a marvel of understatement, admitting that he feared "he may have done something which might have given you offence, and to find out . . . *what it was* so he might offer some explanation." Craven, of course, knew what he had done to provoke Davis's wrath. Mrs. Brodnax, the would-be peacemaker, assured Davis, "Could you hear him [Craven] relate the many little incidents and warm up under a vivid recollection, you might recall some tender touch or look which he could not give expression to in those dark days."[183] Along with her letter was an unidentified newspaper clipping of an interview with Craven. Therein a journalist related Craven's motives, as recounted to him by the physician. Craven had this account sent to Davis as an apology for the inaccuracies in the book. In the newspaper story Craven denied that he had ministered to Davis for personal profit. Instead, he claimed,

> There were three great reasons why I should faithfully care for Mr. Davis. First, from a military standpoint, he was a vanquished enemy; second, he was a prisoner of war, and third, and above all, he was my patient. Standing as I did as the representative of the nation and my profession at his bedside my duty was plain. All his interests had in a moment become as dear to me as the apple of my eye, and I watched him with as jealous care as though he had been my brother, knowing that such treatment would be recognized by my people and the world at large.[184]

Craven's explanation did not mollify Davis. The two men were never friends again.

Almost half of the pages in Davis's copy of the *Prison Life* have some sort of comment by him. The ex-president remarked on more than 180 passages. Seventy of his comments deal with minor errors of fact; many of these were brief, often no more than underlining, placing a message in parentheses, or adding an "X" or a question mark. Only once does Davis emphasize his agreement with a story in the book. At the end of chapter 7, the *Prison Life* recalled Davis's fond thanks for Craven's daughter, who "had undertaken to be his [Davis's] housekeeper, and sent over his meals. . . . He begged me to carry the assurance of his grati-

---

[180]Ishbel Ross, *First Lady of the South: the Life of Mrs. Jefferson Davis* (New York: Harper & Bros., 1958) 186, incorrectly claimed that Craven was the only non-Southerner among thirty men. I am grateful to Dr. Edward D. C. Campbell, former director of the Museum of the Confederacy, Richmond, Virginia, who arranged for copies of all of Varina Davis's *cartes de visite* to be sent to me.

[181]Halpine to Johnson, 20 March 1866, Johnson Papers.

[182]*Prison Life*, 18.

[183]Mrs. John T. Brodnax to Davis, 13 March 1887, in Rowland, *Jefferson Davis, Constitutionalist*, 9:535.

[184]Ibid., 9:536.

tude, and hoped—if he might never see her himself—that his children would some day have an opportunity to thank the young lady who had been so kind to their father." Davis had not forgotten. He wrote, "Sweet girl your kindness is gratefully remembered."[185] While misrepresentations of stories about Davis's curiosity, erudition, or kindness may be excused as tall tales, statements about his political philosophy, the management of the war, and his previous career elicited vigorous response from Davis. Some of Davis's most strenuous dissent came in regard to the book's account of Confederate physicians and prisons—issues that would not only embarrass Davis, but might even implicate him in worse crimes.

While many of the accounts offered in the book were labeled false by Davis, one in particular revealed Craven's personal participation in some of the humiliation heaped upon the prisoner. To prove the inhumanity of General Miles and some other officers, the *Prison Life* mentioned that they had gathered snippets of Davis's hair as mementoes. The custom of collecting hair was common in the nineteenth century, and young ladies learned to make parlor decorations of elaborate hair wreaths that contained clippings from the locks of loved ones. Davis protested the indignity of having his hair taken, and General Miles ordered the clippings returned. Davis remembered that Craven himself had taken some of the purloined hair and had hidden it away because he feared punishment for stealing the relics. Davis recalled that "Dr. C. became alarmed when he heard of the event and ask[ed] me to keep the hair for the present[,] promising to send it at a future time."[186]

Davis also thought the *Prison Life* minimized some of his experiences. The book claimed, "Upon the whole, he had been most kindly and considerately treated by officers and men." Davis retorted, "The Dr. should not in remembrance of the brutality with which he knew I was treated during the earlier part of my imprisonment have made his statement so broad."[187]

But Davis particularly objected to the doctor's failure to safeguard Mrs. Davis's private correspondence from the public eye. He knew his distraught wife had written things in her letters to Craven that she would not have expressed had she known they were to be published. Davis revealed his ire in his marginal note regarding one such instance: "To publish it was base enough, even had it been accurately done."[188]

Near the end of his long life Davis wrote his own memoirs, *Rise and Fall of the Confederate Government*. He referred to his imprisonment in brief but bitter terms, never mentioning either Craven or the *Prison Life*.

> Bitter tears have been shed by the gentle, and stern reproaches have been made by the magnanimous, on account of the needless torture to which I was subjected, and the heavy fetters riveted upon me, while in a stone casemate and surrounded by a strong guard; but all these were less excruciating than the mental agony my captors were able to inflict. It was long before I was permitted to hear from my wife and children, and this, and things like this, was the power which education added to savage cruelty; but I do not propose now and here to enter upon the story of my imprisonment, or more than merely to refer to other matters which concern me personally, as from my connection with the Confederacy.[189]

---

[185]*Prison Life,* Davis Copy, 103.
[186]Ibid., 355.
[187]Ibid., 327-28.
[188]Ibid., 333.
[189]Jefferson Davis, *The Rise and Fall of the Confederate Government,* 2 vols. (New York: D. Appleton and Co., 1881) 2:705.

Shortly before his death Davis wrote a brief autobiography for *Belford's Magazine*. Therein he advised readers, in a footnote, that for additional information on "my life at Fortress Monroe, [see] 'The Prison Life of Jefferson Davis,' by Dr. L. J. J. Craven [sic]; New York: Carleton, 1866."[190]

Mrs. Davis, on the other hand, did not seem to feel as personally violated by the book as had her husband; furthermore, she believed that Craven's ministrations had saved her husband's life. She liberally quoted the *Prison Life* in her memoirs. With few intrusions she lifted thirty-seven pages from the *Prison Life*. She was careful, however, to use only the sections she knew were accurate from consulting Davis's annotated copy, comparing it to the letters from prison that he had written to her.

One dramatic incident recounted in the book did trouble her. The *Prison Life*'s account of the manacling of Davis was too melodramatic and maudlin. Mrs. Davis not only had Davis's annotated copy of the *Prison Life* and his letters to consult, but she also had an unpublished, and since lost, account of this indignity written by Davis and kept with his personal papers.[191] She knew that Craven had not been present when Davis had been placed in irons, and she excused his tale by noting, "The good doctor probably received the account from some unreliable person. . . . There are certainly many persons in the North now who have not accepted it as a fact."[192]

For additional information Mrs. Davis contacted Captain Jerome Titlow, who had witnessed the manacling of Davis, but Titlow's memory had faded during the quarter-century since the event. His account repeated the *Prison Life*'s, which she already knew was inaccurate.[193]

Mrs. Davis prepared her own account while cautioning readers not to believe the "dramatic account published in Dr. Craven's book." She said that Davis had told her, "It could not have been written by anyone who either knew the facts, or had such personal knowledge of him as to form a just idea of what his conduct would be under such circumstances." She assured her readers, "Very little was said by Captain Titlow or by himself [Davis], and that whatever was said was uttered in a very quiet, practical manner. For himself, he would say he was too resolved and too proudly conscious of his relation to a sacred, though unsuccessful cause, for such exclamation and manifestation as were imputed to him by Dr. Craven's informant, and given to the public in his book."[194] Mrs. Davis's account of the manacling scene reaffirmed

---

[190]From Jefferson Davis, "Autobiography of Jefferson Davis," *Belford's Magazine* 4 (1889-1890): 255-66, quoted in Monroe and McIntosh, *Papers of Jefferson Davis*, 1:lxiv.

[191]"Jefferson Davis' written account of the fettering of his person at Fortress Monroe" was included among the many papers, books, pamphlets, and relics given by Mrs. Davis to the Louisiana Historical Association in 1899, as recorded in the minutes of the association's meeting of 5 July 1899 (Louisiana Historical Association Collection, Administrative Records, Tulane University). The account, however, had been lost by the time the Works Progress Administration catalogued the collection (*Calendar of the Jefferson Davis Postwar Manuscripts in the Louisiana Historical Association Collection*, New Orleans, 1943).

[192]Varina Davis, *Jefferson Davis*, 2:658n.

[193]For an account of the correspondence between Varina Davis and Captain Titlow, see Bradley, "Dr. Craven and the *Prison Life*," 71-78. Titlow and Mrs. Davis corresponded at other times. After her memoirs had appeared, she sent him a copy, for which he thanked her and noted, "I can find nothing in the Prison Life of Jefferson Davis, that is not truthful as far as my knowledge goes." Titlow to V. Jefferson Davis, 4 May 1891, Jefferson Davis Collection.

[194]Varina Davis, *Jefferson Davis*, 2:658.

Davis's own comments in his copy of the *Prison Life,* where he had written in the margins, "My resistance resulted from a sense of right and duty; though desperately, it was calmly quietly made."[195]

In many ways Varina Davis's memoirs offer the best biography of Davis. Never meant to be objective, her personal account provided the most human and penetrating study of her husband's personality. Shortly after her husband's death, Mrs. Davis described her project to Davis's longtime friend, William Preston Johnston, whom she told, "My husband relied upon me to show him forth to the world as far as my poor power would avail to do this. . . . Like you I know I cannot bear a Shaft to his memory but I can paint him as he should stand before the world."[196] Although most historians would consider her work a success, it failed to reap the financial rewards she had hoped to obtain, and it caused further alienation between Varina Davis and the kin of Jefferson Davis. Lucy Bradford Mitchell, Davis's niece, told her daughter Lise that Varina Davis "is suing the Belfords [her publishers] for $4000. It is not worth 25 cts it is a history of the Howells and they were beneath notice when alive and their memory only remains to disgrace them."[197]

Recalling in her memoirs those painful months of Davis's imprisonment, Mrs. Davis stated her belief that the suffering he had experienced at Fort Monroe was worse than that borne by Napoleon on St. Helena. Mrs. Davis was more sentimental about Davis's imprisonment than any other aspect of his life. To contrast Davis's noble character with the lack of restraint and the bad manners shown to him by his captors, she recounted all the melodramatic tales. "Never during this extreme torture and harrowing anxiety did his dignity give way, or his high bearing quail before the torment. He was too refined and dignified to be abusive, and too proud[,] in general Miles' delicate phrase, 'to beg.' He suffered as only men of his temperament can, but held aloft the standard of Confederate fealty and Christian virtue."[198]

Shortly before her death in 1906, Mrs. Davis wrote an extensive article on "The Last Days of the Confederacy" that Campbell MacCulloch edited and published in *Spare Moments* magazine. Mrs. Davis spoke freely about her husband's imprisonment, hoping to correct the many false stories she believed had been circulated by her old nemesis, General Miles, who had recently published his own account of Davis's imprisonment. She criticized unnamed persons who maintained that the stories of Davis's suffering in prison "were merely gross fabrications created for the purpose of inducing sympathy." Never mentioning the *Prison Life* at all, and only referring to Craven once, Mrs. Davis warned that "many of the facts are at variance with the accounts of them." She told readers that the most accurate account of Davis's incarceration could be found in "the official records," and she refrained from giving "any comment other than the bare facts as to be found in the Department of War in Washington."[199]

Despite their bitterness and irritation with the inaccuracy of the *Prison Life,* the Davises soon realized that it would be best to let the book run its course. The public had reacted favorably. People began to sympathize with the ex-Confederate president and to demand his release. Davis perceived that his suffering did have a purpose. The book he had so despised had begun his transformation from defeated rebel into martyred hero. It would serve no pur-

---

[195]*Prison Life,* Davis Copy, 39.
[196]Varina Davis to Johnston, 18 March 1890, William Preston Johnston Papers.
[197]Lucy Bradford Mitchell to Lise Mitchell, 13 March 1892, Lise Mitchell Papers, Tulane University.
[198]Varina Davis, *Jefferson Davis,* 2:775.
[199]MacCulloch, "The Last Days of the Confederacy" (October 1906): 1; (February 1907): 7.

pose for him to deny the authenticity of the work. He and Mrs. Davis would have to ignore the errors and accept the acclaim.

So Jefferson and Varina Davis let the *Prison Life* stand unchallenged. The book was misleading, but who was willing to write a more accurate account? It was too painful for the Davises to retrace the sad days of defeat, the suffering, and the humiliation. Davis knew, at best, that the work was a colorful and sympathetic rendering of a highly emotional, personal experience; at its worst, the *Prison Life* was a self-serving, fictionalized account of a proud man's suffering, written to gain financial profit and political reward for the author and his cronies. Though Davis never publicly repudiated the book, his personal copy is so full of corrections and comments that only the most careless scholars will rely on an unannotated copy. With his accustomed gentlemanly grace, Davis made the quintessential comment about the book, "It is most charitable to suppose that in this as in many other instances he has attributed to me the opinion of some one else, not knowing what I thought, and only careful to fill his book according to programme."[200]

## PROVENANCE

Davis did not allow the *Prison Life* to go totally unchallenged. In the margins of the copy he acquired in August 1866 he made extensive annotations. The flyleaf of the copy is inscribed "Jefferson Davis," followed by "Fortress Monroe, Va." and the date, "7th August 1866." The autograph, like the marginalia, was done in pencil.

In 1891, after disposing of Beauvoir, the Davises' home on the Gulf Coast in Mississippi, Mrs. Davis donated her husband's annotated copy of the *Prison Life* along with many other books, pamphlets, letters, and personal relics to the Louisiana Historical Association.[201] In 1899 she completed the bequest, thereby creating a collection that the association called "immeasurably superior to any collection of [Davis] relics now existing or that will ever exist." The minutes of the 5 July 1899 meeting of the association estimated that the combined Jefferson Davis collection it had received from Mrs. Davis "comprised over 3000 of his books, 1200 pamphlets and magazines, 200 photographs and engravings, 400 relics and articles that were his, Miss. Winnie's [Varina Anne Davis's] and his family's; with more than a thousand letters addressed to him; hundreds of his manuscript writings; his message books; his letter books; his Official papers, that alone contain over 2000 different documents, his swords and other [items] too numerous for enumeration. When fully catalogued the collection will certainly exceed 6000 articles in number."[202]

Under the terms of the donation, the papers in the collection were to be sealed until five years after Mrs. Davis's death. She died in 1906 and early the following year, Walter L. Fleming, soon to become a noted Southern historian, contacted members of the Davis family for permission to examine private papers. Professor Fleming explained, "It is my desire to write a full and complete life of Mr. Davis, something to correspond with Nicolay's and Hay's life of Lincoln."[203] Fleming's inquiries prompted the Davis's only surviving child, now calling herself Mrs. Margaret Howell Jefferson Davis Hayes, to request the Louisiana Historical Association to return one box of papers marked "private." These papers, mostly letters written

---

[200]*Prison Life,* Davis Copy, 182.

[201]The 1891 *First Circular and Catalogue of the Louisiana Historical Association* lists Craven's *Prison Life* as one of Davis's books donated by Mrs. Davis to the association.

[202]Report of the meeting of 5 July 1899, Louisiana Historical Association Collection, Administrative Records, Tulane University.

[203]Fleming to Mrs. M. E. Harner [Hamer], 12 April 1907, Lise Mitchell Papers, Tulane University.

by her father and mother to each other during her father's imprisonment, would later be donated by her son, Jefferson Davis-Hayes, to Transylvania University.

Mrs. Hayes told the head of the Louisiana Historical Association that her "mother only intended them [the private papers] to be used if *necessary,* in my father's defense[,] not to injure any one living or dead." As for Professor Fleming's projected biography of her father, Mrs. Hayes admitted that it would "no doubt be of historical value, but we feel my father's book & my mother's memoir[s,] if more generally read by Southern people, would satisfactorily cover *all* that could or should be told concerning my father's life."[204]

Unfortunately, the minimal care provided by the Louisiana Historical Association for this priceless collection was inadequate to prevent widespread losses. In the 1930s the Works Progress Administration catalogued the items that remained in the association's Jefferson Davis collection. The persons working on the project noted, "In 1917 it was discovered [that] 362 items were lost, *not magazines.* We must presume they were *books* and *pamphlets,* since anything like a 'relic' was carefully eliminated in the count."[205] Even this inventory did not prevent further losses from the collection. In 1957 Miss Dora L. Pool, custodian of the collection that was housed at the Confederate Memorial Hall in New Orleans, explained that "years ago, a sword and other relics belonging to President Davis were stolen from Memorial Hall."[206]

Finally, at about the same time that Miss Pool wrote her letter, the Louisiana Historical Association decided to turn the collection over to Tulane University for safekeeping. By then, only 403 of Jefferson Davis's books were left from the original donation and innumerable documents also were missing. In all likelihood, most of the missing items probably had not been stolen for monetary reasons, but rather "borrowed" as souvenirs or remembrances of times past from the unguarded collection.

One of the missing items was Davis's copy of the *Prison Life,* which had somehow come into the possession of Mrs. Tobias G. Richardson (nee Ida Ann Slocum), a well-known New Orleans book collector and a wealthy patroness of Tulane University. She willed it along with thousands of other, miscellaneous books to the university in 1911.

Mrs. Richardson's husband was dean of the University of Louisiana Medical School (subsequently Tulane) from 1865 to 1885. Although Tulane's acquisition records do not indicate how Mrs. Richardson acquired the volume, according to Mrs. Connie Griffith, former director of manuscripts, the "Richardsons were friends of Davis and of William Preston Johnston, Davis's aide-de-camp during the Civil war and the first president of Tulane."[207] Throughout her life Mrs. Richardson gave generous gifts of money and important books to Tulane.

As is clear from his marginal comments in his copy of the *Prison Life,* Davis's opposition to the book focused upon Craven, who had lent his name, his position, and—most important of all—his confidential relationship with Davis to this fictional memoir designed to serve Democratic party purposes. The *Prison Life* was supposedly based on a diary that Craven kept while caring for Davis. In a letter to President Johnson, Halpine wrote of Dr. Craven's "minute diary of his attendance on Mr. Davis, noting down in it his physical condition[,] the effects

---

[204]M. H. J. D. Hayes to Joseph A. Chalaron, 26 January 1908, Jefferson Davis Papers.

[205]*Calendar of the Jefferson Davis Postwar Manuscripts,* intro.

[206]D. L. Pool to Ray M. Thompson, 30 December 1957, Louisiana Historical Association, Administrative Records.

[207]Letter of Mrs. Connie G. Griffith, director, Manuscripts Division and Rare Book Room, Howard-Tilton Memorial Library, Tulane University, to Professor William Hanchett, 29 August 1967. Professor Hanchett kindly sent a copy to the author.

of different therapeutic agents, & also the conversations of the prisoner on all subjects of public interest."[208] Yet, despite determined efforts to document Craven's contribution to the *Prison Life,* no one has ever produced that diary. All that remain are three partial pages—287 words. A diary probably would have been kept in a bound volume, but these three pages with cross-outs and corrections are of differing sizes. They are haphazardly dated—one says "June 9th," another "24th," and the third "24." Since these sheets do not show diary entries, it is more likely that they are only some of the notes Craven wrote for Halpine to use when writing the *Prison Life.*[209] Yet even these notes were incomplete. Craven had to return to Fort Monroe in April 1866 to obtain more information about Davis, especially his views on reconstructing the South. Halpine requested Johnson to grant Craven permission to visit Davis, "a not unnatural wish to the former medical attendant of so eminent a person."[210] Although Craven was not permitted to visit Davis, he did travel to Fort Monroe and obtained a written reply from Davis about his views of Reconstruction.[211]

Dr. Craven's credentials as Jefferson Davis's physician during a portion of his imprisonment had lent the *Prison Life* the credibility it needed if it were to serve its political purpose. Still, word of Halpine's role leaked out soon after the book appeared. In an unrelated court case in 1874, an interrogator tried to discredit Craven's testimony by asking him about the authorship of the *Prison Life.* The testimony included the following exchange:

> Q. "Did you write a book entitled 'The Prison Life of Jefferson Davis?' "
> A. "I did."
> Q. "Did you write that book yourself?"
> A. "I did, sir."
> Q. "Did you publish it under your own name?"
> A. "I did."
> Q. "Did not Charles G. Halpin [*sic;* Halpine's name was consistently misspelled in the testimony] write that book?"
> A. "No, sir, Charles G. Halpin assisted me in the arrangement of the book, and in the compilation of the book,—put it in a book shape,—but the book or the subject matter of the book was prepared by me from minutes or data, that I had accumulated while at Fortress Monroe."
> Q. "Did you give any credit to Mr. Halpin for his share of the composition and compilation of that book, or of publication thereof?"
> A. "I did, sir, give him credit, and give him pecuniary compensation."
> Q. "Do you mean you gave him any credit in the book itself?"
> A. "I don't know that I did, in the book itself."
> Q. "Did you not publish it wholly as your own?"
> A. "I did. I think I was entirely justified in so doing, the book was my own."
> Q. "Charles G. Halpin was the person popularly known as Miles O'Reilly?"

---

[208]Halpine to Johnson, 20 March 1866, Johnson Papers.
[209]John J. Craven Papers.
[210]Halpine to Johnson, 20 March 1866, Johnson Papers.
[211]*Prison Life,* Davis Copy, 243-53.

A. "Yes, sir. Charles G. Halpin and myself were a long time together during the war, both upon the staff of Maj.-Gen. David Hunter. Gen. Halpin as Adjutant General, and myself as Chief Medical officer, on the staff of Gen. Hunter."

The interrogation moved to other subjects, but later returned to the question of the authorship of the *Prison Life*.

Q. "You have spoken of the book titled, 'Prison Life of Jefferson Davis.' Was the composition of it arranged in this way:—You furnished the notes and materials, and Mr. Halpin wrote them up, and put them in form?"

A. "As I said before, the subject matter of the book was mine. I had no knowledge or experience in book making, and work was revised and corrected by General Halpin, and he lent me, in accordance with the contract, such assistance in the arrangement and construction of the book as was deemed necessary to make it complete."

Q. "Was not the text of the book written by him from your notes?"

A. "No sir; cannot say that that was the case; don't mean to say, but what many words, perhaps sentences, in the book were written by, and composed by, Gen'l Halpin; but again I repeat, the subject matter of the book was mine."[212]

Clearly Craven's testimony cannot be used as evidence of his authorship; it was actually a crafty admission on Craven's part that while Halpine had written, composed, corrected, arranged, and revised the work, the book was based on Craven's observations.

Halpine, for his part, never denied writing the *Prison Life*. The book was frequently advertised for sale in the *Citizen* along with the two Miles O'Reilly anthologies. All three volumes had been published by the firm of George W. Carleton, and all three were available for sale at the *New York Citizen*'s editorial offices. The advertisements for the *Prison Life* left out Craven's name and listed the three volumes together so no one would have any trouble realizing that all had been written by the same man. One of the most popular features in the *Citizen* was the book-review column, but Halpine never included his own review of the *Prison Life*. Instead, he included reviews from other newspapers. One, from the *Washington Chronicle*, claimed that the book "reads like 'a Democratic speech in Congress.'" And Halpine himself was the ultimate source of many of the charges that he was the author of the *Prison Life*. As early as 7 July 1866 he was reporting that a "radical *canard*" was circulating that the book was "written for him [Craven] by George Bancroft, Private Miles O'Reilly, George W. Curtis," or "Bayard Taylor."[213] The real canard, of course, was this item. Except for the fictional O'Reilly, the other individuals mentioned were prominent, popular writers who, according to one author, "hated Mr. Davis with a satanic hatred and never at any time showed him the slightest sympathy—in prison or out of it."[214] Two months later Halpine printed another humorous denial requesting "the wiseacres who insist that *Miles O'Reilly* helped Dr. Craven to

---

[212]*Eastman* v. *Western Union*, 525-26, 676, Craven Papers. The pages cited are not in proper order and take some effort to locate in the bound transcript.

[213]*New York Citizen*, 7 July 1866, 4.

[214]Quoted in David R. Barbee, "Dr. Craven's 'Prison Life of Jefferson Davis'—an Exposé," *Tyler's Quarterly Magazine* 32 (April 1951): 285.

write this book would also be kind enough to inform us how said *O'Reilly* may extort like payments from Carleton and the English publishers."[215]

In March 1869 an essay in *The Historical Magazine* attributed the work to Halpine, citing a friend of Halpine who claimed he had heard Halpine admit "that HE had written the book within three weeks; and that with the exception that it was founded on a few notes furnished, and on an intimate acquaintance with the tastes and habits of Davis, it was nothing more than a fancy sketch."[216] The origins of the *Prison Life* were described in greater detail in an article published the previous autumn in the *Charleston Mercury*, a paper owned by Robert Barnwell Rhett, Jr., a friend of Halpine and a longtime political enemy of Davis—a man not likely to help Davis become a hero. Rhett dismissed the work as "a novel woven upon slender threads of fact" and charged that Halpine had written the book in nine days. He based his claim on information from an interview with Halpine in March 1868, "when he communicated to us the above facts from his own graphic and eloquent lips." The *Mercury* continued with this account of how the *Prison Life* came to be written.

> Soon after the admission of Mr. Davis to jail, Craven the surgeon of the post, went to New York, where he met his quondam messmate of the same staff, Gen. Halpine. This literary friend congratulated him forthwith on this opportunity he had to immortalize himself in print, and, at the same time, make money by a book on Jeff. Davis. The idea seemed new to Mr. Craven, and he said it was impracticable. Halpine asked him where were his notes. He replied that he had none and could not do it. Then said Halpine, "give me whatever material you have, and I will write in your name, and we will share the profits." This was agreed to.
>
> Craven furnished three letters of Mrs. Davis to him and some notes written on the margin of a *Herald* by Mr. Davis, touching the points he desired Reverdy Johnson to make in defending him for treason. This was all the authentic matter supplied.
>
> At the request of Gen. Halpine, Craven also made out a list of the officers of the post and their days for going on duty, and other little details of the post and garrison and of Mr. Davis.
>
> Halpine then called to see several Confederates in New York, and among others General Dick Taylor. He pumped them as to Mr. Davis, his views and opinions on public matters; also in regard to leading Southern men and Mr. Davis' reflections and feelings towards them, etc.
>
> A Philadelphia publishing house now advertised that it was soon to put out a life of Davis, and Halpine saw the importance of anticipating this publication by his book. It was arranged in New York to get it out immediately. He agreed to furnish his publisher forty pages of foolscap material daily. And he set [*sic*] down to write and wrote forty pages daily for nine days, when the book was completed—the web of his fervent brain and accomplished mind.[217]

Other reviews were content to question the reliability of the *Prison Life.* An essay by Baltimore attorney S. Teackle Wallis, in the January 1867 issue of Bledsoe's *Southern Review,*

---

[215]*New York Citizen,* 8 September 1866.

[216]ANCHOR, "Disputed Authorship," *The Historical Magazine* 5, 2d ser. (March 1869): 210-11.

[217]Typescript copy of article, "A Curiosity of Literature," from *Louisville Daily Democrat,* 29 October 1868, taken from *Charleston Mercury,* 22 October 1868, with David R. Barbee Papers, Library of Congress.

claimed that the book should be relegated to "the 'sensational' class" and that some of the accounts were "melodramatic" or even "fanciful."[218] An editorial in the *New York Times* pointed out some of the book's inaccuracies. "To picture a prisoner as so without dignity, and full of querulous complainings, to say nothing of describing his frantic struggles and outcries during the 'ironing' scene, was to lower one's conception of what a great 'martyr' chieftain should be." The article also noted that the author had used "a high sensation style," and portrayed Davis in an "utterly undignified attitude." The editorial labeled the entire work "very *maladroit*" and incorrectly predicted, "We question whether Mr. Davis will occupy so prominent a place in history as he might have done had this idea of his being a martyr not been insisted on by certain writers."[219]

In 1905 a letter printed in the *Boston Globe* disclosed that Halpine had bragged of his ruse to at least one other person. George Alfred Townsend was a popular nineteenth-century journalist whose satiric columns on society and politics frequently appeared in the *New York Herald* and the *New York World* under the pseudonym "Gath." Townsend's letter revealed that "my editorial associate, Gen. Charles G. Halpine, wrote the book of Dr. Craven, the fortress doctor, on the ironing, etc., of Davis, the whole grossly exaggerated."[220]

Contemporary criticism and court testimony are not the only evidence demonstrating the fraudulent nature of the memoir. Davis's own negative comments in the margins serve as additional, damning proof. The *Prison Life* was not the only book Davis annotated during his imprisonment. Professor Walter L. Fleming wrote in an article about Davis's religious life, "A small worn copy of the 'Imitation of Christ' used by Davis while in prison is still preserved. The marginal notes and marks made by the prisoner indicate his appreciation of certain passages."[221] Davis frequently made marginal notations in his books. Most of his prewar personal library has suffered an unknown fate.[222] But the extant copies of his later books and magazines often displayed comments on the flyleaves or along the margins. Davis often marked books or articles that dealt with controversial wartime subjects, and usually only marked the passages with which he disagreed. Most of his comments are not as extensive as those he made in the *Prison Life,* but, of course, none of the other books caused him as much personal anguish.

In the marked books from Davis's personal library, now in the Tulane University collection, the most frequent word Davis used to begin his marginal comments was "not" written with a lowercase "n," often followed by the word "true." It is significant that in his personal copy of the *Prison Life* Davis marked forty-eight passages beginning with "not," eight of which are followed by "true." It was a habit of Davis to note his disagreement with authors by marking the margins. While the *Prison Life* may have caused him more anguish than most other books, Davis's marginal comments were not unusual.

Not only are the marginal markings in other volumes from Davis's library similar to those used in the *Prison Life,* but the handwriting in these other volumes is identical to that in the margins of his copy of the *Prison Life* as well as to the handwriting in his letters. Davis had

---

[218]Wallis, "Imprisonment of Davis," 255.

[219]*New York Times,* 26 June 1866, 4.

[220]Quoted in C. C. W., "The Prison Life," 502.

[221]Walter L. Fleming, "The Religious Life of Jefferson Davis," *The Methodist Quarterly Review* 49 (April 1910): 337. This volume is not included in the Louisiana Historical Association inventory, and is missing today.

[222]See Lynda Lasswell Crist, "A Bibliographical Note: Jefferson Davis's Personal Library: All Lost, Some Found," *Journal of Mississippi History* 45 (August 1983): 186-93.

a clear, careful, yet bold hand. The capital D's and C's are uniquely his own. When he combined them to form "Dr. C.," as he did frequently in the margins of the *Prison Life* and in early letters from prison, they stand out as his personal hallmark. No one who has carefully worked with his papers can doubt that the marginal notes were made by Jefferson Davis. It is true that Mrs. Davis imitated his signature and in later years assumed his name, calling herself V. Jefferson Davis. Mrs. Davis, however, never tried to imitate his handwriting in an entire document, let alone marginal comments written in a personal copy of a book not meant to be shared with anyone else.[223]

Despite common knowledge that the *Prison Life* was not a genuine memoir, but the fictional product of the pen of Charles G. Halpine, the book was an enormous success. The *Prison Life* quickly became the standard source on Davis's imprisonment. New editions appeared in 1905, 1960, and 1979. The only changes in the 1905 edition were a new sketch of Davis in prison and a brief preface added by Dr. Craven's son, William Darcy Craven, who "graciously offered [this edition] to a new generation of readers" and defended his father's book from the recent criticism that had been leveled by General Miles and his supporters. The last two editions were souvenirs published for the "Davis Shrine," Beauvoir, near Biloxi, Mississippi. The introduction to the 1979 edition, written by James W. Thompson, historian-in-chief of the Sons of Confederate Veterans, inaccurately claimed that "historians in general have paid little attention to the account of his [Davis's] experiences written by Dr. Craven and published in 1866, and history is the poorer for this neglect."[224] In truth, the book was a best-seller netting the authors substantial royalties, at least $14,000, and it still remains widely known among professional and amateur historians who have used it when writing about Davis's imprisonment. The preface to this same edition, written by Newton W. Carr, Jr., superintendent of "Beauvoir, the Jefferson Davis Shrine," offered it "to the seekers of justice and truth." Carr "hoped that the prison episode in the life of Jefferson Finis Davis will fill the gap in the 'Davis Shelf' of the libraries across the nation."[225] In addition to these American editions, a British edition and a French translation of the work were published in 1866.

When Charles G. Halpine's biographer, William Hanchett, published an article in 1969 calling attention to Davis's comments in the Tulane University copy of the *Prison Life,* Chester D. Bradley, a self-described "practicing physician in Newport News, Virginia," who has spent a lifetime

---

[223]Cy Courtney, a New Orleans attorney and handwriting specialist, examined the Tulane University copy and concluded,

> Examination of the original noted copy of *Prison Life of Jefferson Davis* has been completed. From the known writings I am prepared to defend the opinion that the notations are written by the same hand as the exemplars.
>
> This is based on the over 150 separate notations on various pages of the book, and the 3 letters of 6 Nov 1870, 17 Feb 1882 and the 25 of February 1882.
>
> Firstly, the original was studied for the purpose of analyzing the nature and scope of the task. Secondly, Xerox copies which satisfactorily represented the originals were examined for the final processing of the task. Thirdly, individual letters were taken and mounted in an alphabetical array from the first page of the 6 Nov 1870 letter, giving a range array of Mr. Davis' individual letter characters.
>
> Lastly, these were critically compared with the set of Xerox pictures of twenty pages most prolifically marked. Only after being satisfied that all of the letters were within the writer's range and style was I prepared to send this opinion to you. Further, in the 150 notations, there was no different or unlike style seen.

[224]*Prison Life of Jefferson Davis,* 4th ed. (Beauvoir MS: The Jefferson Davis Shrine, 1979) intro., first page.

[225]Ibid., preface.

defending Craven's authorship, rose again to dispute the authenticity of the annotated copy. He rested his case on the question of Davis's presence at Fort Monroe before his imprisonment. The *Prison Life* clearly placed Davis at Fort Monroe between 1853 and 1857. The marginal comments in the Tulane University copy just as clearly challenge this assertion. Since both versions could not be correct, a choice had to be made. Dr. Bradley convincingly argued that if he could disprove a specific, substantial annotation, he would discredit Tulane's "Davis Copy" and cast doubt on all the remaining marginalia. If the book's account was correct, the marginal comments must have been made by someone other than Davis.

The *Prison Life* placed Davis at Fort Monroe in the 1850s by asking, "Was he [Davis] thinking of those days under President Pierce in which on his approach the cannon of the fortress thundered their hoarse salute to the all-powerful Secretary of War, the fort's gates leaping open, its soldiers presenting arms, and the whole place under his command?" The marginal notes in the Tulane University copy scuttled this conjecture by commenting, "never was at Ft. Monroe until brought to it as a captive."[226] A later annotation reemphasized this point when the book stated that Davis's "transfer to Carroll Hall had brought back many curious reminiscences of his past life. In the very building he now occupied, he had once, as Secretary of War[,] extended the prerogative of clemency to an officer, since eminently distinguished on the Federal side, who was before (or sentenced by) a court-martial under grave charges as an officer, though not affecting his honor as a man." The marginalia commented, "not true[,] I was never in the building until removed to it as a prisoner."[227]

Which was correct: the *Prison Life* or the author of the marginal comments? Bradley asserted that the book was correct, but all internal evidence suggests a different conclusion. Other than the *Prison Life* itself, the only other credible account of a previous Davis visit to the fort is a passage from the memoirs of Virginia Clay-Clopton, wife of Clement Clay, fellow prisoner of Davis at Fort Monroe. This work, like so many Civil War era "memoirs," must be used carefully. Too often such works first appeared years after the events they described. Facts and fantasies were often blurred, and as C. Vann Woodward has shown, the famous "diary" of Mary Chesnut was actually a novel. Two other historians working with such materials have warned that Mrs. Clay's book "must be used with caution as it contains many exaggerations and numerous errors."[228]

According to Mrs. Clay,

> Secretary [of the Navy, James C.] Dobbin was my escort on my first (a most memorable) visit to Fort Monroe. The occasion was a brilliant one, for the President and his Cabinet had come in a body to review the troops. Jefferson Davis, then Secretary of War, and but recently the hero of the battle of Buena Vista, directed the manoeuvers, his spirited figure, superb horsemanship, and warlike bearing attracting general attention. An entire day was given up to this holiday-making, and the scene was one of splendid excitement. At night the fort and the waters beyond were lit up by a pyrotechnic display of great gorgeousness, and enthusiasm rose to its highest when, amid the booming of cannon and

---

[226]*Prison Life,* Davis Copy, 31.
[227]Ibid., 325-26.
[228]Carol K. Bleser and Frederick M. Heath, "The Impact of the Civil War on a Southern Marriage: Clement and Virginia Tunstall Clay of Alabama," *Civil War History* 30 (September 1984): 198n.

the plaudits of happy people, an especially ingenious device blazed across the night sky the names of Franklin Pierce and Jefferson Davis![229]

In an unpublished manuscript written in 1908, Mrs. Clay reaffirmed her memories of former Davis visits to Fort Monroe when he was secretary of war. Despite Mrs. Clay's reminiscences, no primary evidence places Davis at the fort before 1865. Unfortunately, Mrs. Clay gave no specific dates in either source for the alleged visits. All she remembered was that Davis had accompanied President Pierce, who had come with his Cabinet "in a body" to the fort.[230] During the four years when Davis was secretary of war neither his personal papers, nor his official ones, mention a visit to Fort Monroe. Pierce's only presidential trip to Fort Monroe or to Old Point Comfort occurred in June 1854. There is no notation of any other presidential visit or of any visit by the secretary of war during the Pierce administration (March 1853-March 1857). Extant official letters sent from Fort Monroe for the same period also do not show any visit there by Jefferson Davis.[231]

Jefferson Davis had remained in Washington while Pierce and some members of his official family enjoyed a brief holiday. Davis had not been able to keep up with his work for several weeks prior to the presidential trip. During those days he had spent most of his waking hours at the side of his son, Samuel Emory, whose life slipped away from his grieving parents' hands. Varina Davis's biography of her husband recalled those trying days of June 1854 when their world collapsed:

> Our only child sickened, and after several weeks of pain and steady decline, died at twenty-three months old; and his lovely personality had even at that early age impressed itself on many people. He was Mr. Davis's first thought when the door opened, and the little fellow would wait as patiently as possible, sometimes a quarter of an hour, at the door to kiss his father first.
>
> For many months afterward, Mr. Davis walked half the night, and worked fiercely all day.[232]

War Department letters signed by Jefferson Davis and dated in Washington for 23, 24, and 26 June 1854 can be seen at the National Archives.[233]

---

[229]Virginia Clay-Clopton, *A Belle of the Fifties; Memories of Mrs. Clay of Alabama Covering Social and Political Life in Washington and the South, 1853-1866,* Ada Sterling, ed. (New York: Doubleday, Page & Co., 1905) 68.

[230]Clay Papers, Duke University.

[231]See Fort Monroe letters sent from the Post and Artillery School, 1855-1863, National Archives, Old Army Records, Record Group 393.

[232]Varina Davis, *Jefferson Davis,* 1:534-35.

[233]See "Letters Sent by the Secretary of War Relating to Military Affairs, 1800-1889," National Archives microfilm group M-6, reel 35. There are many other sources confirming that Davis had not accompanied the presidential party to Fort Monroe in June 1854. A front-page obituary in the *Daily National Intelligencer* (Washington), 15 June 1854, reported, "Death, on Tuesday evening, the 13th instant, at 5 o'clock, Samuel Emory, only child of Hon. Jefferson Davis, aged 22 months and 14 days. The funeral will take place at the residence of his parents, on Thursday, the 15th instant, at 4 P.M." In addition, John Hill Wheeler, a North Carolina attorney soon to become the American minister to Nicaragua, kept a daily diary in which, on 15 June 1854, he noted: "Afternoon went to funeral of the only child of Genl Davis (Secy of War) rode to cemetery in Georgetown in carriage . . . President & Cabinet were present—very affecting scene." Eight days later Wheeler recorded in his diary, "President with Mr. Dobbin went to Old Point today." Wheeler's diary is in the John Hill Wheeler Papers, Manuscripts Division, Library of Congress.

The only other evidence that Jefferson Davis might have visited Fort Monroe before his imprisonment stemmed from a front-page article in the *Philadelphia Inquirer* on 20 June 1865. The unsigned story, citing no sources, was really an article about the building of the Rip Raps, the curious pile of rocks a mile offshore from the fort. Prisoner Davis had been brought to the fort only a month before this article had appeared; at that time he was still held incommunicado. The first paragraph of the article was an obvious attempt to build reader interest in a mundane subject. It sensationalized the reporter's evidence.

> Although no conversation is permitted with the imprisoned arch-rebel, he . . . is being garrulous in his old days. A few days ago he talked of the times when he was Secretary of War. And he told the walls and his mute mechanical guards, and the immobile commissioned officer who bear [*sic*] him company, that during his administration of the War bureau, he was struck by the large number of bills pouring in for stone deposited on the Rip Raps shoals. . . . Secretary Jeff's suspicions were aroused, he procured him a boat, and he had himself conveyed to the Rip Raps, to see for himself what became of all the stones for which Uncle Sam had paid.[234]

The reader was asked to believe that the proud and defiant Confederate ex-president, threatened with a capital offense, ranted to the walls and his silent jailers about an insignificant boat trip supposed to have occurred more than a decade before.

In sum, four questionable sources attributed a pre-1865 visit by Jefferson Davis to Fort Monroe. The first, the *Prison Life of Jefferson Davis,* a creative fantasy by a New York City journalist, Davis himself labeled as false. The next two were Mrs. Clay's memoirs, one published and one not, written fifty years after the event supposedly took place. Mrs. Clay, confused by the years, her close friendship with the Davises, the appearance of the *Prison Life,* and her memories of a presidential visit to Fort Monroe five decades before, believed that Davis had accompanied the president on his visit. She had forgotten that Davis had remained in the capital to catch up on the work he had ignored during his young son's final illness. The fourth account of a Davis visit was a journalist's creation of a senile, imprisoned Davis, chattering away to the walls of his cell about a trivial event that supposedly had happened more than a decade earlier. The "evidence" does not merit further consideration.

Dr. Bradley's spirited defense of Craven did, however, convince the historical popularizer Burke Davis. His recent book, *The Long Surrender,* claimed that the *Prison's Life*'s account was correct. Bradley had sent Burke Davis copies of his correspondence with Professor Hanchett, and Mr. Davis sided with Bradley. In *The Long Surrender* Burke Davis described Bradley's arguments as "valuable contributions to the understanding of the capture and imprisonment of Davis, and of Craven's book and its influence."[235]

There is mention of one other copy of the *Prison Life* that might have been annotated by Jefferson Davis. In 1887 Colonel C. W. Frazer of Memphis, Tennessee, reminded Davis that a mutual friend, Mrs. Virginia Boyle, had sent Davis a copy of the *Prison Life,* more than a year before, "for some corrections, which you kindly promised to make." Frazer also noted that Davis had not yet returned the book to Mrs. Boyle nor had he sent her an acknowledgment that he had received it.[236] A few days later Davis replied to Frazer's inquiry. "Please say

---

[234]*Philadelphia Inquirer,* 20 June 1865, 1.

[235]Davis, *The Long Surrender,* 301.

[236]Frazer to Davis, 18 July 1887, in Rowland, *Jefferson Davis, Constitutionalist,* 9:580. The Frazer letters are missing from the Louisiana Historical Association Collection.

to my friend Virginia that her request being made to me as a command, I expected to make marginal notes on Dr. Craven's book, but a little work now goes a great way with me and as the subject is one, the renewal of which is always painful[,] I have postponed the reading of the book and frankly would say I would like to be let off from the task of annotating it."[237] Whether Davis was "let off" or not remains a mystery, but obviously Davis must have expressed some reservations about the veracity of the *Prison Life,* or he would never have mentioned the need for "some corrections" in the first place.

If another annotated copy of the *Prison Life* exists, it would not change the purpose or the importance of the work; in fact, it would only serve to emphasize further Davis's long-standing anger concerning the book. The *Prison Life of Jefferson Davis* was not written to be a literal account of Davis's imprisonment. The book was written to show the extremes that could be expected from uncontrolled Republican rule. If a man of Davis's character and reputation could be made to suffer such severe reprisals, what could the South as a whole expect? Although serious contemporary critics were not fooled by Halpine's work, his symbolic narrative soon became part of the "Lost Cause" myth. Unlike most other parts of this complex myth, Davis's role as the Southern scapegoat was "documented" by a primary source, and what was conceived as fancy soon became accepted as fact.

This new edition of the *Prison Life of Jefferson Davis* will correct the errors that have grown up around Davis's imprisonment. Along with this brief narrative chronology is the fictitious memoir amplified with Davis's own comments, and General Miles's defense is included as an appendix. Readers will be able to see for themselves not only what the *Prison Life* said about Davis but, even more important, what Davis really thought about the persons and events mentioned in the fraudulent memoir. What no edition can do is to diminish either the reality of Davis's suffering or the importance of the *Prison Life* in helping to provide a meaning for the Southern loss in the Civil War.

---

[237]Davis to Frazer, 21 July 1887, ibid., 9:580.

## NOTE

For purposes of clarity as well as composition exigencies, this edition of the *Prison Life of Jefferson Davis* is not an exact reproduction, but a reasonable approximation of Jefferson Davis's personal copy of the 1866 Carleton edition, which contains Davis's own manuscript annotations and emendations. In that volume Davis's editorial—and censorial—hand can be seen in three ways. Most commonly, Davis wrote notes in the margins; these marginal notes are shown as italic sidenotes in this edition. In addition, Davis underlined some words and drew vertical lines in the margins alongside text he questioned or wished to emphasize; all underlining and marginal vertical lines in this edition of the text closely approximates that of the original. Finally, Davis changed words or added signs in the text itself. These emendations are shown enclosed in bold braces (**{ }**). Thus, "**{** ( **}**" indicates that Davis added an open parenthesis in his own copy, and "penned **{***pinned***}**" means that Davis changed the word "penned" to read "pinned" (see page 57).

My notes to the text and to Davis's handwritten marginalia appear as footnotes, keyed to the text or to the marginalia by one of several pi characters (*, †, ‡, §). In addition, occasional editorial notes to the original text or to Davis's sidenotes are enclosed in brackets ([ ]). (But note that the author of the original text enclosed one complete paragraph of the text in brackets—in chapter 14, page 83.)

*Edward K. Eckert*

WILLIAM NOTMAN  MONTREAL, OTTAWA, TORONTO,
PHOTOGRAPHER                              TO THE QUEEN
COPYRIGHT

*Jefferson and Varina Davis had this portrait taken in Montreal soon after his release from prison in May 1867. Courtesy The Museum of the Confederacy, Richmond, Virginia.*

*Many Americans agreed with Thomas Nast's cartoon (in the 30 June 1866 issue of* Harper's Weekly) *that Jefferson Davis's treatment at Fort Monroe was too lenient, especially when compared with the suffering borne by Union prisoners at Andersonville. Courtesy Richard Gates, St. Bonaventure University.*

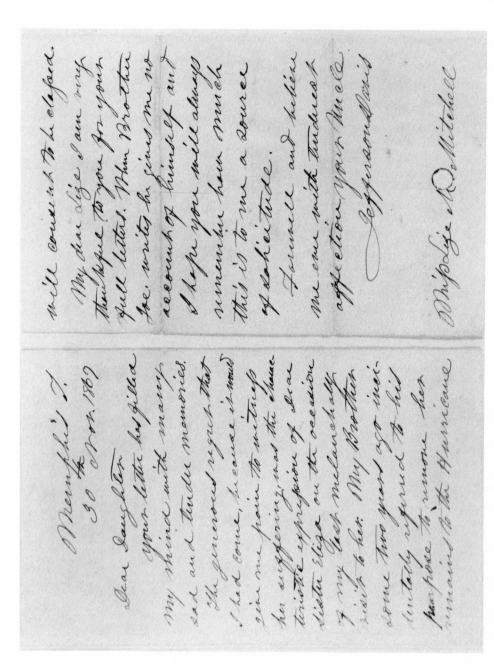

*A sample of Davis's handwriting, from a personal letter, which may be compared with the annotations in Davis's copy of the Prison Life (see facing page). Courtesy Rare Book Room, Special Collections Division, Tulane University Library.*

officer who superintended the search. They then told my servants that they could go ashore, if they did not desire to go to Savannah. The husband of my negro nurse forced her to go, and the white girl left from an unwillingness to be exposed to a Southern climate. I entreated to be permitted to debark at Charleston, as my sister, Miss Howell, still continued to be ill, and I feared to return on the ship with a drunken purser, who had pre-

*This example of a Davis annotation is taken from page 333 of the original edition of the Prison Life. Courtesy Rare Book Room, Special Collections Division, Tulane University Library.*

THE NEW YORK PRINTING COMPANY
81, 83, *and* 85 *Centre Street*,
NEW YORK.

# Prison Life

of

# Jefferson Davis.

EMBRACING DETAILS AND INCIDENTS IN HIS CAPTIVITY, PARTI-
CULARS CONCERNING HIS HEALTH AND HABITS, TO-
GETHER WITH MANY CONVERSATIONS ON
TOPICS OF GREAT PUBLIC INTEREST.

BY

BVT. LIEUT.-COL. JOHN J. CRAVEN, M.D.,

Late Surgeon U. S. Vols., and Physician of the Prisoner during his Confinement
in Fortress Monroe, from May 25, 1865, up to December 25, 1865.

*" Had I died on the throne, enveloped in the dense
atmosphere of power, I should to many have remained a problem. Now, misfortune will enable
all to judge me without disguise."*—NAPOLEON
BONAPARTE TO D. BARRY O'MEARA.

NEW YORK:

*Carleton, Publisher, 413 Broadway.*

LONDON: S. LOW SON & CO.

M DCCC LXVI.

To

## The Hon. Hugh McCullough,

*Secretary of the Treasury,*

WHO FIRST

Of all our Northern Public Men
Has had the WISDOM, MAGNANIMITY, and COURAGE
To express Sympathy for the Misfortunes

of

### The Subject of our Memoir,

by

A Visit to Mr. Davis in his cell at Fort Monroe,

*This Volume Is Inscribed.*

# •CHAPTER 1•

*An Introduction by Anecdote.—The Old-Fashioned Preface in a New Dress.*

Late one summer evening, hot, hungry, dusty, thirsty, tired, exasperated, and full of vengeful thoughts, I was riding down the road from the bloody and resultless encounter near Bermuda Hundreds, to where my field hospitals had been established.* Saul journeying to Damascus, breathing out threatenings against his enemies, was in no fiercer spirit. The day had been oppressively warm, our losses enormous, our gains nothing; and worn out with the labor and wretchedness of superintending the removal of the wounded, I was cantering wearily but rapidly back to where many hundred sufferers, in all stages of manglement, lay awaiting the painful remedy of the surgeon's art. Never before had the rebellion, with its attendant horrors, appeared so inhuman to my mind; and if the hot hatreds of my soul could have taken shape in words, I would have exclaimed, addressing the Confederates under Beauregard:

*Oh, that each slave had forty thousand lives,*
*One is too poor, too weak for my revenge!*

Half way between the battle-field and my hospitals, I overtook four of our boys in blue, under a corporal, tenderly carrying to the rear a stretcher on which lay a wounded rebel.

Something tempted me to halt and dismount. God forgive me if it was a desire to assure myself that all the suffering had not been on our side. If so, the unworthy feeling was of brief duration; for no sooner, throwing the reins to my orderly, did I stand beside the litter and gaze upon the pale, pinched features of the wounded man, than all promptings of patriotic hatred vanished; and there was nothing left in my ex-

---

*On 5 May 1864 the Army of the James, commanded by Benjamin Butler, had landed at Bermuda Hundred on the south bank of the James River about 25 miles southeast of Richmond. Butler's forces were in support of the Union drive in Virginia. Confederate forces under Pierre G. T. Beauregard stopped Butler's army at Drewry's Bluff (16 May), halfway to Richmond, and forced the Union troops to withdraw back to Bermuda Hundred. On 15-16 June Butler's forces were unable to break through a much-weakened Confederate defense to support General Ulysses S. Grant's attack on Confederate forces near Petersburg. Federal forces continued to hold Bermuda Hundred until the end of the war.

istence but the deep, overwhelming sympathy of the medical man for a patient needing aid to call him back from death.

He needed aid, indeed. His left arm was shot through; his right leg shattered and badly mangled above the ankle; his hip was torn by the fall of his horse, and life appeared fast ebbing. In his horse, by the way, as it fell under him, there were sixteen bullets. He had ridden right in on top of the 6th Conn. regiment, and our boys had given him what we called "a blizzard."

"My poor man," I said, "you are wounded nearly unto death."

*was not a staff officer but a commander of a Brigade.*

"I feel it," he faintly replied. "I am General Walker,* of Beauregard's staff. Let me rest somewhere, and dictate some last words to my Wife and Commander."

Where was my hatred now? Where the fierce thirst of retribution that should have looked on this unfortunate's agony as a just judgment?

Giving him some brandy from a pocket-flask, I told the corporal in charge to carry him to my own tent, next General Gillmore's† headquarters at Hatcher's House; and hastily scribbling a line to my hospital steward, "Take charge—will be with you soon," I remounted, and galloped off to the sickening scenes always presented in a field hospital after a severe engagement.

It was midnight, or some little later, before my duties to the hundreds of our boys would allow me to visit the sufferer in my tent. His case needed immediate amputation of the lower leg, and there was no sufficient light for performing the operation.

"Tear down that smoke-house and kindle a big bonfire," was my order. "We must get light somehow, and quickly, or this man will die. He is seven-eighths on his way to death already."

Never before had I been so painfully anxious. The feeling arose, no doubt, from an instinct of conscience punishing my unprofessional thoughts—or half thoughts—when first halting beside his litter. The man had to be saved, or an unhappy recollection would haunt my life. No appliance that care or skill could furnish must be wanting. It had been against Beauregard all day that my anger had been specially kindled. I recalled our first defeat at Bull Run. His memorable "beauty and booty" proclamation. Was I always to witness defeat when opposed to this enemy? And it was against Beauregard and all belonging to him, that day, while the contest lasted, that the imprecations of my soul, if not uttered, had been most vehemently felt.

But here now was a military part of Beauregard—one of his eyes or arms—over whom I yearned as if with a brother's sympathy. My business was to heal the wounded, not to wound. By what right had I indulged the vengeful thoughts which filled my breast when first meeting on the road this shattered human wreck?

---

*William S. Walker.
†Quincy A. Gillmore.

The bonfire was soon blazing, and before the operation commenced—as a happy result could scarce be hoped—I procured an
amanuensis for General Walker, to whom he hurriedly dictated two
letters. They were farewells to his Wife and General Beauregard. Will
the loyal world think worse of me, if I confess, that while hearing the
few feeble whispers in which this wounded rebel communicated to a
strange soldier of the hostile force what he expected to be his last words
on earth—his last messages to the Commander he reverenced, and
the Wife he was to see no more—I found an unusual moisture making
my sight uncertain?

General Walker, however, was not destined to die. By the flicker-
ing light of the bonfire, and with the aid of Surgeons Janeway and
Buzelle,* the amputation was successfully performed, and his other
wounds properly treated. He remained at once my guest and patient
until sufficiently restored for safe transfer to the General Hospital at
Fortress Monroe, and is now hopping around the earth somewhere,
blythe and hearty on the leg that is left him; perfectly willing to be
"reconstructed," I should imagine, in more senses than one; nor any
the less likely in future to make a loyal citizen, from such recollections
as he may yet preserve of the bonfire and the tent, the amanuensis and
the attending doctors of that midnight scene.

This is the material part of my preface, and contains the only apology I shall offer in case any over-sensitively loyal readers may feel, or
affect to feel, shocked on finding in the following pages some record
of the imprisonment of Jefferson Davis, not written to gloat over the
misfortunes of a fallen enemy—certainly not aiming to palliate his political or other errors; but to depict so much of him as was revealed to
the Writer during a medical attendance of many months while Mr.
Davis lay a prisoner in Fortress Monroe. Should any such objectors be
found, the Writer believes himself safe in predicting that they will be
drawn pretty exclusively from that loyal class who were non-bellig-
erent, except in the contracting line, and strictly non-combatant, save
for higher percentages of profit, during the recent contest for the
Union.

---

For the rest, the following pages have been prepared from a conscientious conviction of duty, under the advice of eminent and respected friends, and with the sanction of many gentlemen in our public
life, who are not more exalted by station than by loyalty, intelligence,
and moral worth.

The book aims to introduce no discussion of any political questions
connected with the late rebellion; nor to be a plea influencing public
judgment, either for or against, the gentleman who was for so many
months the Author's patient. It will report him as he was seen during
a protracted and confidential medical attendance, extenuating nothing of public interest, and setting down naught in malice.

---

*John H. Janeway and Andrew J. H. Buzzell.

Of course, the relations of physician and patient have a sacredness of confidence which the Writer would be the last to violate; and all such restrictions, in this volume, will be found rigidly observed. No knowledge gained during such relationship that might injure Mr. Davis if published, could properly or without flagrant infidelity, be given to the world by his medical attendant; and it is from a sincere conviction that the reverse must prove the fact, and from a sincere personal sympathy and respect for the subject of this memoir, that the present volume has been undertaken.

It may here be proper to remark—lest partisan malice should attempt from interested motives to distort the Writer's position—that he has been through all the years of his thinking life an earnest and active opponent of slavery, and of all the other cardinal doctrines on which the leaders of the late Rebellion claimed to base their action. He was a member of the Republican party from its birth down to the present day—an uncompromising supporter of the Union; and it is from his deep conviction that the Union can best be reconstructed, and its harmony of relationship restored, by pursuing a moderate policy and seeking to understand, in their present frame of mind, what are the views of the men who were recently our leading enemies, that he would now beg the earnest attention of all classes in the Country to such portions of this volume as shadow forth the opinions of Mr. Davis in regard to the future of the South.

# •CHAPTER 2•

*Fortress Monroe.—The Ceremonial of delivering Mr. Davis into Custody.—His first Day in the Casemate.*

Fortress Monroe is too well known to need any description in these pages. It is the most powerful regular fortification on the Continent; and, with its subordinate works, is the grim Cerberus guarding the approach by water to our National Capital. It has witnessed the initial movements of many most interesting chapters in the recent war, though itself never within reach of hostile guns, save when the *Merrimac* made its brief raid upon our fleet in Hampton Roads—the raid so notably checked by Captain Worden* in his little Monitor.

Either from it, or past it from Annapolis, had sailed the chief expeditions, marine and military, of the Southern coast. Beneath its ramparts the transports of McClellan's army had made brief rendezvous when hastening to the campaign of the Peninsula; and here again they had to pass, when returning with diminished ranks and soiled plumage to save the National Capital after General Pope's disaster.†
It witnessed the sailing of Sherman's Port Royal expedition, to which the writer had the honor to belong; the expeditions of Burnside, Butler, Banks, and all the other joint military and naval movements which thundered for three years along the coast, from Cape Hatteras to Sabine Pass.‡ Farragut, Du Pont and Porter stepped ashore on its hospitable beach when returning from their most famous exploits.§

---

*John L. Worden.

†George B. McClellan was commander of the unsuccessful Peninsula campaign (February-June 1862), in which federal troops tried to take Richmond, and John Pope led a federal army to defeat at Second Manassas (August 1862).

‡General Thomas W. Sherman left Hampton Roads (29 October 1861) for Port Royal with a naval expedition under Flag Officer Samuel F. DuPont. Ambrose E. Burnside, as commander of the Department of North Carolina, led an unsuccessful expedition against the North Carolina coast (January-March 1862). Butler and Nathaniel P. Banks led numerous federal expeditions (1863-1865) in Louisiana, where the latter afterward commanded the Department of the Gulf.

§David Glasgow Farragut, the first American admiral, achieved victories at New Orleans (April 1862) and Mobile (August 1864). DuPont led an unsuccessful campaign to reduce Charleston (April 1864). His failure here caused his removal, an action that Charles G. Halpine, an admirer of DuPont, bit-

Of a truth, Fortress Monroe, though not properly in the war, was of the war—a rendezvous for our greatest naval, military and civil chiefs in some of their greatest moments; nor will its least interesting reminiscence to the future tourist be this which records, that in one of its granite casemates, and looking out through the bars of a grated embrasure on the Empire he had lost, lay for many months in solitary confinement, and awaiting trial, the defeated Chief of the mightiest rebellion which this earth has yet witnessed; or, at least, the vastest in extent and the most formidable in its resources, of which history gives any clear and credible record.

And never before, indeed, did the old fort witness such excitement, though partially suppressed and held in check by military discipline and the respect due to a fallen enemy, as on the 19th day of May, 1865, when the propeller *William P. Clyde* dropped anchor in Hampton Roads, and the news spread on shore—first in eager, questioning whispers, then in the full assurance of conviction—that she had on board as prisoners Jefferson Davis, late President of the late Confederacy and his family; Alexander H. Stephens, Vice-President; John H. Reagan, late Postmaster-General; Clement C. Clay,* and several more State prisoners belonging to his now scattered and ruined house.

"What will they do with him?" "When will they bring him ashore?" "Guess they'll take him right on to Washington and hang him by Military Commission?" "Guess you're a jackass; they can't hang him, unless they hang all." "Jackass yourself; the papers say he was partner with the assassins in killing Lincoln." "Who are the other chaps with him?" "Will they keep him in the woman's toggery he had on when caught?" "Guess there's no truth in that." "It's just as true as preaching—all the papers say so." "They'll hang Clem. Clay sure." This was something of the conversational buzz I had to pass through, while hastening down from my quarters inside the fort, to get an early view of the little steamer, which, with her imprisoned freight, was the centre of attention.

For the next three days these speculations continued, colloquially and in the papers; but meantime, and for some days previously, preparations had been going on within the fort, under the direction of Colonel Brewerton† of the Engineers, which gave evidence to the initiated that the State prisoners on board the propeller in the offing would

---

terly resented. Halpine originally had created Miles O'Reilly to defend DuPont against the Lincoln administration. David Dixon Porter was the commander of the flotilla that successfully passed the Confederate defenses at Vicksburg (16 April 1863) and later led the naval expedition that took Fort Fisher NC (October 1864-January 1865).

*Clay was a United States and Confederate senator from Alabama; he also served the Davis administration as a special envoy to Canada, where he hoped to be able to negotiate a peace treaty with special envoys from the Lincoln administration. Clay was Davis's fellow political prisoner at Fort Monroe.

†Henry Brewerton.

soon be transferred—at least some of them, and for the present—to securer quarters. Blacksmiths and carpenters were busily at work fitting up casemates number two and four in first front, and near the postern, for the reception of prisoners. They were being partitioned off into regular cells by busy bricklayers; heavy iron bars were placed across the external embrasures, and windows opening on the interior; and the cells intended for the prisoners were partitioned off into two apartments, that next the embrasure being intended for the captives, while the room or cell opening on the interior of the fort was for his guard.

"And it has come to this," was my reflection, as I stood with folded hands first contemplating these arrangements. "But a few months ago, the man for whose reception these preparations are being made, was the acknowledged ruler of many millions of American citizens. He had armies at his command; cabinet officers; a staff of devoted adherents; and ambassadors, though not officially recognised, at all the courts of Europe. Nearly a million of lives—by battle, disease, and starvation— have been sacrificed for, and against, the cause of which he was the chosen representative. And it has come to this with him!" Aye, and was soon to come to worse. But this is anticipating.

On the morning of the 21st of May some of the minor State prisoners on board the *Clyde*—the rebel General Wheeler* and his staff— were placed on board the gunboat *Maumee,* which then steamed for Fort Warren in Boston harbor; while Alexander H. Stephens, ex-Postmaster Reagan, and some others, were soon after transferred on board the gunboat *Tuscarora,* which immediately started off to Fort Delaware, as was presumed. Intense excitement, on shore and in the neighboring vessels, accompanied all these changes; but Major-General Halleck,† who had come down some days before to superintend the arrangements, would make no sign, and speculation consequently ran higher and higher every moment as to whether the chief prisoner of all was destined to remain at the fort, or be transferred elsewhere in custody without halting.

At last, on the afternoon of the 22d, all doubts were set at rest by the arrival of Major-General Miles‡ in a special steamer from Baltimore, this officer being now assigned to the command of the fort, relieving Colonel Roberts;§ and simultaneously therewith, from the posting of chains of sentinels and guards to keep back the crowd along the Engineer's Landing, and from thence along the route to the Water

---

*Joseph Wheeler was one of the few Confederate military commanders imprisoned after the war. Wheeler had opposed Joseph E. Johnston's surrender to William T. Sherman (26 April 1865), and had followed the Davis government into Georgia where he was captured.

†Henry Wager Halleck.

‡Nelson A. Miles.

§Joseph Roberts had been promoted to brevet brigadier general on 9 April 1865.

Battery Postern, it became clear that the important prisoner was about being landed, and that his route would lie in this direction.

The parting between Mr. Davis, his wife, four children,* and the other members of his family and household who were on board the *Clyde,* was extremely affecting, as I have been told, by officers who were present—the ladies sobbing passionately as the chief prisoners—Messrs. Clay and Davis—were handed over the ship's side and into the boat, which was to convey them, under guard, to their unknown fate.

The procession into the fort was simple though momentous, and was under the immediate inspection of Major-General Halleck, and the Hon. Charles A. Dana, then Assistant Secretary of War; Colonel Prichard,† of the Michigan cavalry, who immediately effected the capture, being the officer in command of the guard from the vessel to the fort. First came Major-General Miles holding the arm of Mr. Davis, who was dressed in a suit of plain Confederate grey, with a grey slouched hat—always thin, and now looking much wasted and very haggard. Immediately after these came Colonel Prichard accompanying Mr. Clay, with a guard of soldiers in their rear. Thus they passed through files of men in blue from the Engineer's Landing to the Water Battery Postern; and on arriving at the casemate which had been fitted up into cells for their incarceration, Mr. Davis was shown into casemate No. 2 and Clay into No. 4, guards of soldiers being stationed in the cells numbered 1, 3, and 5, upon each side of them. They entered; the heavy doors clanged behind them, and in that clang was rung the final knell of the terrible, but now extinct, rebellion. Here, indeed, is a fall, my countrymen. Another and most striking illustration of the mutability of human greatness. Let me here give a picture of the earliest scene in the cell of Mr. Davis, as related immediately after its occurrence by one who was a passive actor therein, my own connection with Mr. Davis not commencing until two days after (May the 24th), when I was first detailed by Major-General Miles as his attending physician.

Being ushered into his inner cell by General Miles, and the two doors leading thereinto from the guard-room being fastened, Mr. Davis, after surveying the premises for some moments, and looking out through the embrasure with such thoughts passing over his lined and expressive face as may be imagined, suddenly seated himself in a chair, placing both hands on his knees, and asked one of the soldiers pacing up and down within his cell this significant question: "Which way does *fabrication* the embrasure face?"

The soldier was silent.

Mr. Davis, raising his voice a little, repeated the inquiry.

---

*The remaining Davis children were Jefferson, Jr., Margaret Howell (Maggie or Pollie), Varina Anne (Winnie), and William (Billie).

†Benjamin D. Pritchard.

But again dead silence, or only the measured footfalls of the two pacing sentries within, and the fainter echoes of the four without.

Addressing the other soldier, as if the first had been deaf and had not heard him, the prisoner again repeated his inquiry.

But the second soldier remained silent as the first, a slight twitching of his eyes only intimating that he had heard the question, but was forbidden to speak.

"Well," said Mr. Davis, throwing his hands up and breaking into a bitter laugh, "I wish my men could have been taught your discipline!" and then, rising from his chair, he commenced pacing back and forth before the embrasure, now looking at the silent sentry across the moat, and anon at the two silently pacing soldiers who were his companions in the casemate.

*Fiction should be probable this is absurd.*

What caused his bitter laugh—for even in his best days his temper was of the saturnine and atrabilious type, seldom capable of being moved beyond a smile? Was he thinking of those days under President Pierce,* in which on his approach the cannon of the fortress thundered their hoarse salute to the all-powerful Secretary of War, the fort's gates leaping open, its soldiers presenting arms, and the whole place under his command? Or those later days under Mr. Buchanan† when, as the most powerful member of the Military Committee of the Senate, similar honors were paid on his arrival at every national work— even during those final moments when he was plotting "to secure peace" by placing in command of all our forts and armories, such officers as he thought might be relied upon to "go with the South if the worst came?"‡ And was not his question significant:—"Which way does this embrasure face?" Was it north, south, east, or west? In the hurry and agitation of being conducted in, he had lost his reckoning of the compass, though well acquainted with the localities; and his first question was in effect: "Does my vision in its reach go southward to the empire I have lost, or North to the loyal enemies who have subdued my people?"—for it is always as "his people" that Mr. Davis refers to the Southern States.

*never was at Ft. Monroe until brought to it a captive*

*As original as it is infamously false.*

His sole reading-matter a <u>Bible and prayer-book</u>, his only companions those two silent guards, and his only food the ordinary rations of bread and beef served out to the soldiers of the garrison—thus passed the first day and night of the ex-President's confinement.

*Not given immediately though they were in my trunk. The prayer book was for some time witheld [sic] after the Bible was given.*

---

*Franklin Pierce, president of the United States (1853-1857), and a close friend of the Davis family.

†James Buchanan, president of the United States (1857-1861).

‡The Johnson administration had charged Davis with treason. Such groundless accusations as Halpine placed here were grist for these charges.

# •CHAPTER 3•

*Placing Mr. Davis in Irons.—His Protest and his Struggles.—My First Visit to the Prisoner.*

On the morning of the 23d of May, a yet bitterer trial was in store for the proud spirit—a trial severer, probably, than has ever in modern times been inflicted upon any one who had enjoyed such eminence. This morning Jefferson Davis was shackled.

It was while all the swarming camps of the armies of the Potomac, the Tennessee and Georgia—over two hundred thousand bronzed and laurelled veterans—were preparing for the Grand Review of the next morning, in which, passing in endless succession before the mansion of the President, the conquering military power of the nation was to lay down its arms at the feet of the Civil Authority, that the following scene was enacted at Fort Monroe:*

Captain Jerome E. Titlow, of the 3d Pennsylvania Artillery, entered the prisoner's cell, followed by the blacksmith of the fort and his assistant, the latter carrying in his hands some heavy and harshly-rattling shackles. As they entered, Mr. Davis was reclining on his bed, feverish and weary after a sleepless night, the food placed near to him the preceding day still lying untouched on its tin plate near his bedside.

"Well?" said Mr. Davis as they entered, slightly raising his head.

"I have an unpleasant duty to perform, Sir," said Captain Titlow; and as he spoke, the senior blacksmith took the shackles from his assistant.

*fiction distorting fact.* Davis leaped instantly from his recumbent attitude, a flush passing over his face for a moment, and then his countenance growing livid and rigid as death.

He gasped for breath, clutching his throat with the thin fingers of his right hand, and then recovering himself slowly, while his wasted figure towered up to its full height—now appearing to swell with indignation and then to shrink with terror, as he glanced from the captain's face to the shackles—he said slowly and with a laboring chest:

"My God! You cannot have been sent to iron me?" **{not true}**

"Such are my orders, Sir," replied the officer, beckoning the blacksmith·to approach, who stepped forward, unlocking the padlock and

---

*The Army of the Potomac passed in a Grand Review in Washington on 23 May 1865 and Sherman's army did the same on the following day.

preparing the fetters to do their office. These fetters were of heavy iron, probably five-eighths of an inch in thickness, and connected together by a chain of like weight. I believe they are now in the possession of Major-General Miles, and will form an interesting relic.

"This is too monstrous," groaned the prisoner, glaring hurriedly round the room, as if for some weapon, or means of self-destruction. "I demand, Captain, that you let me see the commanding officer. Can he pretend that such shackles are required to secure the safe custody of a weak old man, so guarded and in such a fort as this?" *fiction perverting fact.*

"It could serve no purpose," replied Captain Titlow; "his orders are from Washington as mine are from him."

"But he can telegraph," interposed Mr. Davis, eagerly; "there must be some mistake. No such outrage as you threaten me with, is on record in the history of nations. Beg him to telegraph and delay until he answers."

"My orders are peremptory," said the officer, "and admit of no delay. For your own sake, let me advise you to submit with patience. As a soldier, Mr. Davis, you know I must execute orders."

"These are not orders for a soldier," shouted the prisoner, losing all control of himself. "They are orders for a jailor—for a hangman, which no soldier wearing a sword should accept! I tell you the world will ring with this disgrace. The war is over; the South is conquered; I have no longer any country but America, and it is for the honor of America, as for my own honor and life, that I plead against this degradation, *coloring laid on.* Kill me! kill me!" he cried, passionately, throwing his arms wide open and exposing his breast, "rather than inflict on me, and on my People through me, this insult worse than death."

"Do your duty, blacksmith," said the officer, walking towards the embrasure as if not caring to witness the performance. "It only gives increased pain on all sides to protract this interview."

At these words the blacksmith advanced with the shackles, and seeing that the prisoner had one foot upon the chair near his bedside, his right hand resting on the back of it, the brawny mechanic made an attempt to slip one of the shackles over the ankle so raised; but, as if with the vehemence and strength which frenzy can impart, even to the weakest invalid, Mr. Davis suddenly seized his assailant and hurled him half-way across the room.

On this Captain Titlow turned, and seeing that Davis had backed against the wall for further resistance, began to remonstrate, pointing out in brief, clear language, that this course was madness, and that orders must be enforced at any cost. "Why compel me," he said, "to add the further indignity of personal violence to the necessity of your being ironed?"

"I am a prisoner of war," fiercely retorted Davis; "I have been a soldier in the armies of America, and know how to die. Only kill me, and my last breath shall be a blessing on your head. But while I have life and strength to resist, for myself and for my people, this thing shall not be done."

*The sergeant had no musket*

*Gross misrepresentation no part of the affair truthfully reported: my resistance resulted from a sense of right & duty; though desperately, it was calmly quietly made.*

Hereupon Captain Titlow called in a sergeant and file of soldiers from the next room, and the sergeant advanced to seize the prisoner. Immediately Mr. Davis flew on him, seized his musket and attempted to wrench it from his grasp.

Of course such a scene could have but one issue. There was a short, passionate scuffle. In a moment Davis was flung upon his bed, and before his four powerful assailants removed their hands from him, the blacksmith and his assistant had done their work—one securing the rivet on the right ankle, while the other turned the key in the padlock on the left.

This done, Mr. Davis lay for a moment as if in stupor. Then slowly raising himself and turning round, he dropped his shackled feet to the floor. The harsh clank of the striking chain seems first to have recalled him to his situation, and dropping his face into his hands, he burst into a passionate flood of sobbing, rocking to and fro, and muttering at brief intervals: "Oh, the shame, the shame!"

It may here be stated, though out of its due order—that we may get rid in haste of an unpleasant subject—that Mr. Davis some two months later when frequent visits had made him more free of converse, gave me a curious explanation of the last feature in this incident.

He had been speaking of suicide, and denouncing it as the worst form of cowardice and folly. "Life is not like a commission that we can resign when disgusted with the service. Taking it by your own hand is a confession of judgment to all that your worst enemies can allege. It has often flashed across me as a tempting remedy for neuralgic torture; but thank God! I never sought my own death but once, and then when completely frenzied and not master of my actions. When they *false* came to iron me that day, as a last resource of desperation, I seized a soldier's musket and attempted to wrench it from his grasp, hoping that in the scuffle and surprise, some one of his comrades would shoot or bayonet me."

What has preceded this, with the exception of the preceding paragraph and of things I saw—such as the cell, procession, etc.—has been based on the evidence of others who came fresh from the scenes they pictured.* I now reach the commencement of my personal relations with the prisoner, and for all that follows am willing to be held responsible.

On the morning of May 24th, I was sent for about half-past 8 A.M. by Major-General Miles; was told that State-prisoner Davis complained of being ill, and that I had been assigned as his medical attendant.

Calling upon the prisoner—the first time I had ever seen him closely—he presented a very miserable and afflicting aspect. Stretched upon his pallet and very much emaciated, Mr. Davis appeared a mere fascine of raw and tremulous nerves—his eyes restless and fevered, his head continually shifting from side to side for a cool spot on the

---

*Craven had not witnessed Davis's first days at the fort; he had arrived two days after Davis had been placed in his cell.

pillow; and his case clearly one in which intense cerebral excitement was the first thing needing attention. He was extremely despondent, his pulse full and at ninety, tongue thickly coated, extremities cold, and his head troubled with a long-established neuralgic disorder. Complained of his thin camp mattress and pillow stuffed with hair, adding, that he was so emaciated that his skin chafed easily against the slats; and, as these complaints were well founded, I ordered an additional hospital mattress and softer pillow, for which he thanked me courteously.

"But I fear," he said, as, having prescribed, I was about taking my leave, accompanied by Captain Evans,* 3d Pennsylvania Artillery, who was officer of the day; "I fear, Doctor, you will have a troublesome and unsatisfactory patient. One whose case can reflect on you little credit. There are circumstances at work outside your art to counteract your art; and I suppose there must be a conflict between your feelings as a | *not so* soldier of the Union and your duties as a healer of the sick."

This was said with a faint smile, and I tried to cheer him, assuring him, if he would only keep quiet and endeavor to get some rest and sleep, which my prescription was mainly addressed to obtain, that he would be well in a few days. For the rest, of course a physician could | *compliment* [sic] have no feelings nor recognise any duties but towards his patient. | *of the above*

Mr. Davis turned to the officer of the day, and demanded whether he had been shackled by special order of the Secretary of War, or whether General Miles had considered this violent course essential to his safe-keeping? The Captain replied that he knew nothing of the matter; and so our first interview ended.

On quitting Mr. Davis, at once wrote to Major Church,† Assistant Adjutant-General, advising that the prisoner be allowed tobacco—to the want of which, after a lifetime of use, he had referred as one of the probable partial causes of his illness—though not complainingly, nor with any request that it be given. This recommendation was approved in the course of the day; and on calling in the evening brought tobacco with me, and Mr. Davis filled his pipe, which was the sole article he had carried with him from the *Clyde*‡ except the clothes he then wore.

"This is a noble medicine," he said, with something as near a smile as was possible for his haggard and shrunken features. "I hardly expected it; did not ask for it, though the deprivation has been severe. During my confinement here I shall ask for nothing."

He was now much calmer, feverish symptoms steadily decreasing, pulse already down to seventy-five, his brain less excitable, and his mind becoming more resigned to his condition. Complained that the foot-falls of the two sentries within his chamber made it difficult for

*marginal note:* Inaccurate in detail & fanciful in recital. The pipe with smoking and chewing tobacco was in my valise of which Genl Miles had taken possession. One of his staff officers sent me a piece of the chewing tobacco and when I subsequently stated that I wished my pipe and the smoking tobacco he said he thought I preferred the chewing tobacco. I offered to return the chewing tobacco but Genl Miles decided I could have both. The delay in bringing the pipe Dr. C. considered significant & it was remembered when I subsequently offered the pipe to him.

---

*Edwin A. Evans.

†Captain Will E. Church was assistant adjutant general of volunteers.

‡The ship that had taken Davis from Savannah to Virginia.

him to collect his thoughts, but added cheerfully that, with this—touching
*bah!* his pipe—he hoped to become tranquil.

This pipe, by the way, was a large and handsome one, made of
meerschaum, with an amber mouth-piece, showing by its color that it
had seen "active service" for some time—as indeed was the case, hav-
*not so, it had been* ing been his companion during the stormiest years of his late titular
*only recently used* Presidency. It is now in the Writer's possession, having been given to
him by Mr. Davis, and its acceptance insisted upon as the only thing
*the reason given was the* he had left to offer.
*expectation that it would*
*be stolen, perhaps I should*  _____
*have said "confiscated" as*
*the expressions of Capt.*  *Davis here is referring to Captain Charles T. Hudson, who captured the
*Hudson and the evasion of* Davis party and ransacked their personal possessions, and Chaplain Mans-
*Col. French even more* field French, whom he met when the steamer taking him to Fort Monroe
*than the pillage I had suf-* stopped at Beaufort, South Carolina.
*fered suggested*
*the danger.**

# •CHAPTER 4•

*Conversation with Mr. Davis on many Points.—The Removal of his Shackles demanded as a Medical Necessity.*

Morning of 25th May. My patient much easier and better. Had slept a little, and thanked me for the additional mattress.

"I have a poor, frail body," he said; "and though in my youth and manhood, while soldiering, I have done some rough camping and campaigning, there was flesh then to cover my nerves and bones; and that makes an important difference."

He then spoke of his predisposition to bilious fever at this period of the year, stating that it usually began with a slight chill, then ran into a remittent condition. Had also suffered much from neuralgia, by which the sight of one eye had been destroyed; and had been a victim to what he called "the American malady," dyspepsia, ever since quitting the active, open-air life of the army.

Having ordered him a preparation of Calisaya bark after each meal to assist digestion, Mr. Davis spoke familiarly of all the various preparations of this medicine; then digressed into some reminiscence of a conversation he once had with an eminent English physician in regard to anti-periodics.

He took the ground, said Mr. Davis, that Peruvian bark in its various forms was the only reliable therapeutic agent of this kind—and it may be so with the practice in England. Here, however (I told him), we have a number perfectly reliable, such as Salicine, from the willow, a preparation of arsenic (in solution), and so forth.

He appeared anxious to know what agents could be used for adulterating quinine and the other preparations of bark, for that they are grossly adulterated he knew. Taking all the risks of running the blockade, these preparations, or preparations purporting to be such, had been sold at Wilmington and Charleston during the war, at prices in gold for which the genuine articles could scarcely have been procured in London. They were the best his people could get, however, and *not me* very thankful they were when they could be had. Then spoke of the crime of adulterating medicines as heinous in the extreme, and referred to a speech he had made on the subject in the Senate of the United States, asking legislative interference, and that no adulterated drugs should be allowed to pass the Custom-House. His action had been based, partly on his own acquaintance with the facts, but more especially on a report from an eminent chemist in New York city, set- *all about,* ting forth the magnitude of the abuse, with tabular statements. *but never at the facts*

*it was also prohibited on land*

"There was one restriction of the war," he went on to say, "imposed by the overwhelming superiority of your navy, which I do not believe an enlightened and Christian civilization can approve. I refer to that making medicines contraband of war. This inflicted much undeserved suffering on women and children and the whole non-combatant class, while comparatively but little affecting the combatants. For our soldiers we had to procure the requisite medicines, at whatever cost or sacrifice; so that the privation fell chiefly upon those who were not engaged in the war, save as helpless spectators. I am far from saying this restriction was not justified by the laws of war, as heretofore acknowledged and practised; but whenever these laws come to be revised in a spirit more harmonizing with the advanced intelligence of our times, some friend of humanity should plead that cargoes duly vouched as only containing medicines should not be liable to stoppage."

*I did not say so, the apology is the writer's and historically incorrect.*

Happening to notice that his coffee stood cold and apparently untasted beside his bed in its tin cup, I remarked that here was a contradiction of the assertion implied in the old army question, "Who ever saw cold coffee in a tin cup?" referring to the eagerness with which soldiers of all classes, when campaigning, seek for and use this beverage.

"I cannot drink it," he remarked, "though fond of coffee all my life. It is the poorest article of the sort I have ever tasted; and if your government pays for such stuff as coffee, the purchasing quartermaster*{?} must be getting rich. It surprises me, too, for I thought your soldiers must have the best—many of my Generals† {?} complaining of the difficulties they encountered in seeking to prevent our people from making volunteer truces with your soldiers whenever the lines ran near each other, for the purpose of exchanging the tobacco we had in abundance against your coffee and sugar."

Replied that the same difficulty had been felt on our side, endangering discipline and calling for severe measures of repression. The temptation to obtain tobacco was uncontrollable. One of our lads would pop his head up from his rifle-pit and cry: "Hey, Johnny, any tobacco over your way?" to which the reply would instantly come, "Yes, Yank, rafts of it. How is it with you on the coffee question?" A satisfactory reply being given, the whisper would run along each line, "Cease firing, truce for coffee and tobacco;" and in another moment scores of the combatants, on either side, would be scrambling over their respective earthworks, and meeting on the debatable land between, for commercial dicker and barter on true Yankee style.

This picture seemed to amuse the patient. His spirits were evidently improving. Told him to spend as little time in bed as he could; that exercise was the best medicine for dyspeptic patients. To this he answered by uncovering the blankets from his feet and showing me his shackled ankles.

---

*The commissary officer purchased food at army posts.

†Davis was sensitive to references to the Confederacy, its government, or its army as *his* own (see 92).

"It is impossible for me, Doctor; I cannot even stand erect. These shackles are very heavy; I know not, with the chain, how many pounds. If I try to move they trip me, and have already abraded broad patches of skin from the parts they touch. Can you devise no means to pad or cushion them, so that when I try to drag them along they may not chafe me so intolerably? My limbs have so little flesh on them, and that so weak, as to be easily lacerated."

At sight of this I turned away, promising to see what could be done, as exercise was the chief medical necessity in his case; and at this moment the first thrill of sympathy for my patient was experienced.

That afternoon, at an interview sought with Major-General Miles, my opinion was given that the physical condition of State-prisoner Davis required the removal of his shackles, until such time as his health should be established on some firmer basis. Exercise he absolutely needed, and also some alleviation of his abnormal nervous excitement. No drugs could aid a digestion naturally weak and so impaired, without exercise; nor could anything in the pharmacopœia quiet nerves so over-wrought and shattered, while the continual irritation of the fetters was counter-poising whatever medicines might be given.

"You believe it, then, a medical necessity?" queried General Miles.

"I do most earnestly."

"Then I will give the matter attention;" and at this point for the present the affair ended.

*May 26th.*—Called with the Officer of the Day, Captain James B. King, at 1 P.M. Found Mr. Davis in bed, complaining of intense debility, but could not point to any particular complaint. The pain in his head had left him last night, but had been brought back this forenoon and aggravated by the noise of mechanics employed in taking down the wooden doors between his cell and the exterior guard-room, and replacing these with iron gratings, so that he could at all times be seen by the sentries in the outside room, as well as by the two "silent friends," who were the unspeaking companions of his solitude.

Noticed that the prisoner's dinner lay untouched on its tin plate near his bedside, his meals being brought in by a silent soldier, who placed food on its table and then withdrew. Had remarked before that he scarcely touched the food served to him, his appetite being feeble at best, and his digestion out of order.

Quitting him, called on General Miles, and recommended that I be allowed to place the prisoner on a diet corresponding with his condition, which required light and nutritious food. Consent was immediately given, and I had prepared and sent over from my quarters some tea and toast for his evening's meal.

Calling about 7 P.M., found Mr. Davis greatly improved, the tea and toast having given him, he said, new life. Though he had not complained of the fare, he was very thankful for the change. Remarked in reply that I had observed the food given was not fit for an invalid in his condition, and was happy to say permission had been given me to supply from my own table such diet as he might seem to need. On this he repeated that I had an unequal and perplexing task.

"As a soldier you could soon dispose of me," he said; "but as a master of the healing art all your energies will be taxed; and I sometimes hope—sometimes fear—in vain. You have in me a constitution completely shattered, and of course all its maladies aggravated by my present surroundings."

He then commenced talking—and let me here say that I encouraged him in this, believing conversation and some human sympathy the best medicines that could be given to one in his state—on the subject of the weather.

How has the weather been—rough or fair? In this huge casemate, and unable to crawl to the embrasure, he could not tell whether the weather was rough or smooth, nor how the wind was blowing.

"All my family are at sea, you are aware, on their way to Savannah; and I know the dangers of going down the coast <u>at this season of the year</u> {?} too well to be without intense alarm. My wife and four children, with other relatives, are on board the *Clyde,* and these propellers roll dreadfully and are poor sea-boats in rough weather."

He then explained with great clearness of detail, and evidently having studied the subject, why the dangers of going down the coast in rough weather were so much greater than coming north. Going down, ships had to hug the shore—often running dangerously near the treacherous horrors of Cape Hatteras; while in running north they stood out from land to catch the favoring gulf stream, to avoid which they had to run in shore as close as they could when steering south.

He appeared intensely anxious on this subject, recurring to it frequently and speculating on the probable position of the *Clyde* at this time. "Should she be lost," he remarked, "it will be '<u>all my pretty chickens and their dam</u> at one fell swoop.'* It will be the <u>obliteration of my name and house</u>."

*false*

"Mrs. Davis, too," he continued, "has much to contend with. Her sister has been very ill, and her two nurses left her while here, and she could procure no others.† My only consolation is, that some of my paroled people are on board, and soldiers make excellent nurses. Soldiers are fond of children. Perhaps the roughness of their camp-life makes the contrasted playfulness of infancy so pleasant. Charles of Sweden, Frederick the Great, and Napoleon, were illustrations of this peculiarity. The Duke of Wellington is the only eminent commander of whom no trait of the sort is recorded."

*did not then know of all the brutality*

Talking of propellers, and how badly they rolled in a rough sea, I spoke of one called the *Burnside,* formerly stationed at Port Royal, of which the common remark was, that in every three rolls she went clean round.

---

*Macbeth, iv.i.216.

†Margaret Howell (later wife of the Chevalier Charles [Carl] de Wechman-Stoëss), like her sister, suffered from nerves throughout her long life.

"Once," I added, "when her Captain was asked what was her draught of water, he replied that he did not know to an inch the height of her smoke-stack, but it was from the top of that to her keel."

This, and other anecdotes, amused the patient for some quarter of an hour; and whatever could give his mind a moment's repose was in the line of his cure.

As I was leaving, he asked had I been able to do nothing to pad or cushion his shackles? He could take no exercise, or but the feeblest, and with great pain, while they were on.

To this gave an evasive answer, not knowing what might be the action of General Miles, and fearing to excite false hopes. No such half-way measures as padding would suffice to meet the necessities of his case; while their adoption, or suggestion, might defer the broader remedy that was needed. On leaving, he requested me in the morning to note how the wind blew, and the prospects of the weather, before paying him my visit. Until he heard of his family's arrival in Savannah he could know no peace.

# •CHAPTER 5•

*Conversations of some Interest.—The Shackles Removed.—Mr. Davis on Various Scientific Subjects.*

**M**ay 27th.—Called in the morning with the Officer of the Day, Captain Titlow. Found Mr. Davis in bed, very weak and desponding. He had not slept. Had been kept awake by the heavy surging of the wind through the big trees on the other side of the moat. Appeared much relieved when I told him the breeze was nothing like a storm, though it blew north-easterly, which was favorable to the ship containing his family.

*The account is that there were other noises, the wind was effective only in causing anxiety*

He expressed great concern lest his wife should hear through newspapers of the <u>scene in his cell</u> when he was ironed. Would it be published, did I think? And on my remaining silent—for I knew it had been sent to the newspapers on the afternoon of its transpiring—he interlaced his fingers across his eyes, and ejaculated: "Oh, my poor wife, my poor, poor girl! How the heart-rending narrative will afflict her!"

*not the scene but the fact*

*Too vulgar to comprehend a gentleman*

He remained silent for some moments as I sat beside his bed; and then continued, extending his hand that I might feel his pulse:

"I wish she could have been spared this knowledge. There was no necessity for the act. My physical condition rendered it obvious that there could be no idea that fetters were needful to the security of my imprisonment. It was clear, therefore, that the object was to offer an indignity both to myself and the cause I represented—not the less sacred to me because covered with the pall of a military disaster. It was for this reason I resisted as a duty to my faith, to my countrymen, and to myself. It was for this reason I courted death from the muskets of the guard. The Officer of the Day prevented that result, and, indeed,"—bowing to Captain Titlow—"behaved like a man of good feeling. But, my poor wife! I can see the hideous announcement with its flaming capitals, and cannot but anticipate how much her pride and love will both be shocked. For myself I am resigned, and now only say, 'The Lord reprove them!' The physical inconvenience of these things I still feel (clanking his ankles together slightly under the bedclothes), but their sense of humiliation is gone. Patriots in all ages, to whose memories shrines are now built, have suffered as bad or worse indignities."

*not true*

He thanked me for the breakfast that had been sent him, expressing the hope that I would not let my wife be put to too much trouble making broth and toast for one so helpless and utterly wretched.

"I wish, Doctor," said he, "I could compensate you by getting well; but my case is most unpromising. Your newspapers," he {†} went on—this with a grim smile—"should pray for the success of your skill.* If you fail, where will their extra editions be—their startling head-lines? My death would only give them food for one or two days at most; while my trial—for I suppose I shall be given some kind of trial— would fatten for them a month's crop of lucrative excitement."

†Thus might speculate a newspaper man, thus could not I.

Finding the conversation, or rather his monologue, running into a channel more likely to excite than soothe him—the latter being the object for which I was always willing to listen during the fifteen or twenty minutes these interviews usually lasted while he was seriously ill—I now rose to take my leave, gently hinting that he should avoid such thoughts and topics as much as possible.

He took my remark in a wrong sense, as if I had been hurt at his saying anything that might cast a reflection on the justice that would be dealt to him by my government, or upon the style of journalism in Northern newspapers. But I explained that nothing could be farther from my thoughts: that my counsel was purely medical, and to divert him from a theme that must re-arouse the cerebral excitement we were seeking to allay.

"For the rest, Mr. Davis," I went on, "that Doctor should go to College again who is not ready to listen with interest and attention to whatever subject may be uppermost in his patient's mind, unless convinced that the mind's brooding upon it will do harm, not good. We need ventilation in the world of mind not less than in that of physics. Our thoughts need to go abroad in the minds of other men, and take their exercise in the sunlight and free air of language. The doctrine of confession in the Catholic church is based on the soundest principles of moral and intellectual hygiene. It is throwing open the doors and windows of the soul, changing the atmosphere, and disinfecting every crevice of the mind of the foul vapors engendered by the close dampness and darkness of secresy. The physician who has not learned to act in this faith should re-commence his education."

Called again at 8 P.M. same day. Mr. Davis still very weak, and had been troubled with several faint, not exactly fainting, spells, his pulse indicating extreme debility. He said the nights were very tedious and haggard. During the day he could find employment reading (the Bible or prayer-book being seldom out of his hand while alone), but during the night his anxieties about his family returned; and the footh-falls [sic] of the sentries in the room with him—their very breathing or coughing—continually called back his thoughts, when otherwise and for a moment more pleasantly wandering, to his present situation. He had watched the weather all day with intense interest; and had been cheered to observe from the slant of the rain that the wind appeared

---

*Davis recognized from the first that the *Prison Life* was not the work of Craven but of Charles G. Halpine, whom he called by his pseudonym of Miles O'Reilly. Halpine was a New York City "newspaper man."

to continue north-east, so that he hoped his family were by this time in Savannah.

Then went on to say that he feared, after he had been removed from the *Clyde,* his wife must have suffered the annoyance of having her trunks searched—an unnecessary act, it seemed to him, as, of course, if she had anything to conceal, she could have got rid of it on the passage up.*

On my remarking, to soothe him, that no such search was probable, he said it could hardly be otherwise, as he had received a suit of heavy clothes from the propeller; and Gen. Miles, when informing him of the fact, had mentioned that there were quite a number of suits there.

"Now I had none with me but such as my wife placed in her own trunks when she left Richmond, so that her trunks have probably been opened; and I suppose," he added with another grim smile, "that the other clothes to which Gen. Miles referred, are now on exhibition or preserved as 'relics.' My only hope is, that in taking my wardrobe they
X did not also {"}confiscate{"} that of my wife and children; but I realize that we are like him of old who fell amongst a certain class of people and was succored by the good Samaritan."†

"And so, Doctor," he went on, "you think all the miserable details of my ironing have been placed before the public? It is not only for
X the hurt feelings of my wife and children, but for the honor of Americans {?} that I regret it. My efforts to conceal from my wife the knowledge of my sufferings are unavailing; and it were perhaps better that she should know the whole truth, as probably less distressing to her than what may be the impressions of her fears. Should I write such a letter to her, however, she would never get it."

*Sunday, May 28th.*—At 11 A.M. this morning was sitting on the porch in front of my quarters when Captain Frederick Korte, 3d Pennsylvania Artillery, who was Officer of the Day, passed towards the cell of the prisoner, followed by the blacksmith. This told the story, and sent a pleasant professional thrill of pride through my veins. It was a vindication of my theory, that the healing art is next only in its sacredness and power to that of the healers of the soul—an instance of the doctrinal toga forming a shield for suffering humanity, which none were too exalted or powerful to disregard. I hastily followed the party, but remained in the outer guardroom while the smith removed the shackles. Did not let Mr. Davis see me then, but retired, thinking

---

*After Jefferson Davis had been taken to the fort, the remaining members of the party not only had their baggage searched, but Varina and her sister were forced to strip down to their undergarments and be searched by two female detectives.

†It was at this time that Col. Pritchard and Capt. Hudson obtained from Varina the shawl and raincoat or raglan Jefferson had used at the time of his capture. These "female garments" often were incorrectly shown as a dress and petticoats in illustrations of the capture; these immeasurably galled the proud Davises.

it better the prisoner should be left alone in the first moments of regaining so much of his personal freedom.

Called again at 2 P.M. with the Officer of the Day. Immediately on
entering, Mr. Davis rose from his seat, both hands extended, and his
eyes filled with tears. {?} He was evidently about to say something, | *no*
but checked himself; or was checked by a rush of emotions, and sat
down upon his bed. That I was gratified by the change I will not deny—
and let those in the north into whose <u>souls the iron</u> of Andersonville | *bah, rather into whose ears*
has entered, think twice before they condemn me. The war was over; | *the slander*
the prisons on both sides were empty. If by rigor to Davis we could
have softened by a degree the sufferings of a single Union prisoner, I,
for one, would have said let our <u>retaliation be</u> so terrible as to bring | *oh! the power of falsehood*
the <u>South</u> to justice. But now, no sufferings of his could recall the souls
that had fled, or the bodies that were wasted and fever-stricken. It
would not be retaliation to secure justice, but mere ignoble vindic-
tiveness to further torture this unhappy and shattered man. Besides,
as his medical adviser, I could know him in no other capacity; and it
then remained to be proved—remains yet to be proved—that he was
in any manner of volition or wish responsible for the horrors we de-
plore. Even Napoleon complained that Virion, and his other commissaries of prisoners, stole the food and other stores furnished for
their use; and time must develop whether, and how far, Mr. Davis was
responsible for the <u>cruel treatment of our boys.</u> | *paltry*

Thus feeling, I congratulated him on the change, observing that my
promise of his soon feeling better was being fulfilled; and he must now
take all the exercise that was possible for him, for on this his future
health would depend. Captain Korte, too, joined in my congratula-
tions very kindly, and spoke with the frank courtesy of a gentleman
and soldier.

In speaking of his present state of health, and the treatment he had
formerly been under for the same symptoms, Mr. Davis referred very
kindly, and in terms of admiration, to his former friend and medical
attendant, Dr. Thomas Miller, of Washington. Also to Dr. Stone,*of
Washington, who had made a specialty of the eye and its diseases.
From him he had received clearer ideas of the power of vision, and | *not so*
the adaptation of the eye to various distances and degrees of light, than
from any other source. Referring to his own loss of sight in one eye
from leucoma, or an ulceration of the cornea, he said he could discern
light with it, but could not distinguish objects.

Entering then into conversation upon optics and acoustics, Mr. Davis spoke on both subjects, but more especially the former, with great
familiarity. Referring to the undulating waves by which both light and
sound are conveyed, he remarked:

---

*Apparently Craven believed Davis's physician to be Robert King Stone,
M.D., a specialist in eye diseases who was the Lincoln family's physician. Davis's physician in Washington was Dr. William Stone.

"With what admirable perversity nature has avoided all straight lines and angles—the curve, or waving 'line of beauty,' first discovered to men by Hogarth, being the rule with her in every variety of production. In no leaf, flower, tree, rock, animal, bird, fish or shell that nature has produced, can a straight line, angle, or two lines exactly parallel be found."

Speaking of how greatly the powers of the sight may be increased by practice, Mr. Davis upheld the theory that the brain, too, was also enlarged in its capacities, both physically and intellectually, by continual labor. He pointed to the large brains of nearly all who have been eminent in pursuits involving mental labor, contending that as the labor of the tailor develops the muscles of the right thumb and forefinger, those of the delver the muscles of the leg, and so forth, so the increased exercise of the brain increased its size. There was a fault in his parallel, he knew, or rather what appeared to be a fault—that we can establish no analogy between the mental and physical phases of existence. Still it was certain that labor enlarged all organs involved in it, so far as we had means of judging; and that while we did not know how the brain acted in its reception or emission of ideas—whether purely passively, or with some physical action, however slight—we did know for certain that the brains of all great intellectual workers were much larger, on the average, than were those of men pursuing different callings.

Remarked that with these ideas, he must to a great extent be a believer in phrenology; to which he assented, while at the same time protesting against the charlatanisms which had overlapped, for selfish purposes of gain, what of truth there was in the science.* Before the matter could be properly tested, the anatomy of the brain should be made a specialty, and studied with all the assistance of innumerable subjects for many years. But the men who now put themselves forward as professors of the science, had probably never seen the inside of any brain—certainly not of half a dozen—in their lives.

Referring to the stories that were probably being circulated about him in the Northern papers, and the falseness of such stories in general, Mr. Davis instanced what he called the foul falsehood that he had preached and effected the repudiation of the Mississippi bonds.

"There is no truth in the report," he said. "The event referred to occurred before I had any connection with politics—my first entrance into which was in 1843; nor was I at any time a disciple of the doctrine of repudiation. Nor did Mississippi ever refuse to acknowledge as a debt more than one class of bonds—those of the Union State Bank only.

"To show how absurd the accusation is," continued Mr. Davis, "although so widely believed that no denial can affect its currency, take

---

*Phrenology, a popular pseudoscience of the nineteenth century, claimed to be able to tell a person's character and abilities by examining the external bumps on the skull.

the following facts. I left Mississippi when a boy to go to college; thence to West Point; thence to the army. In 1835 I resigned, settled in a very retired place in the State, and was wholly unknown, except as remembered in the neighborhood where I had been raised. At the time when the Union Bank bonds of Mississippi were issued, sold and repudiated—as I believe justly, because their issue was in violation of the State Constitution—I endeavored to have them paid by voluntary contributions; and subsequently I sent agents to England to negotiate for this purpose."

*A jumble in the order of events &, very, very inaccurate as to mode of proceeding*

Recurring then to the subject of optics and diseases of the eye—which appeared a favorite with him—Mr. Davis descanted on the curious effects of belladonna on the iris and crystalline lens; stating that, though a valuable remedy when only used as such, it tended to coagulate and produce cataract in the latter when used in excess—as witness the number of cases of this kind of injury amongst the ladies of Italy and Spain, where the article was much used as a toilet adjunct. He spoke of the beautiful provisions of nature for the protection of this organ, illustrating by the third transparent eyelid or membrane which all diving birds drop over the eye when darting swiftly through the air or water, thus protecting the delicate organ from being hurt, while allowing a sufficiency of light to guide them. He could not believe that any living things as a class were deprived of the joy of sunlight; and while the microscope had thus far found no organs that we could recognise as of sight in many classes of living things—shell-fish, worms, and so forth—he believed that they must in some manner be impressible with the alterations of light and darkness. It had so long appeared a question with him whether his own eyesight could be saved, that he had given this subject much attention—or rather reflection; and <u>he</u> quoted from Milton with great pathos several passages on the subject:

*no, "he" did not.*

> Oh dark, dark, dark, amid the blaze of noon;
> Irrevocably dark! total eclipse without the hope of day.*

And again:

> Nor to these idle orbs doth sight appear
> Of sun, or moon, or stars, throughout the year,
> Or man, or woman. Yet I argue not
> Against Heaven's hand or will, nor bate a jot
> Of heart or hope; but still bear up and steer
> Right onward.†

---

*Sampson Agonistes, 1.86.
†"Sonnet 22."

# •CHAPTER 6•

*Operations on the Southern Coast.—Davis Hears that he is Indicted and to be Tried.—His Joy.—Views of his own Defence.*

**M**ay 29th.—Called with Captain Bispham,* 3d Pennsylvania Artillery, Officer of the Day. Found Mr. Davis walking up and down the floor, apparently better—but still laboring under some excitement. He said exercise had already done him good; had slept much better last night; and rejoiced to see clear and bright weather again, though little sunshine entered his cell. Thought though it did not shine on him, it was shining on his dear wife and children, safely havened from the dangers of the ocean.

Complained of the dampness of his cell, as one probable cause of his illness. The sun could never dart its influence through such masses of masonry. Surrounded as the fort was with a ditch, in which the water rose and fell from three to four feet with the tide, it was impossible to keep such places free from noxious vapors.

*no |* "I am something of <u>an engineer</u>," he said, "and the causes are obvious. Builders fill in the backs of walls with stone-chips and rubble, insufficiently mortared, through which the tidal water ebbs and falls. When it falls it leaves vacuums of damp air, and when it rises again, this mephitic air, with its gases engendered in closeness, dampness and darkness, is forced upward into the casemates, for no masonry is so perfect as to exclude the permeation of gases.

"I am aware," he went on, "that officers and soldiers and their families have been in the habit of occupying these casemates; but when *never said that |* Secretary of War† I issued an order forbidding the practice. Huts or tents are much healthier, more especially for children. The casemates of Fort <u>Pulaski</u> {?} were peculiarly unhealthy, that place being erected on what might be called a shaking-scraw, or sponge of miasmatic vegetation, thoroughly permeated by tidal action. Its foundations had to be pile-driven at an enormous expense of money and labor, and only from the necessities of the coast could such a selection of a site have been justified."

Mentioned that I had been at the siege, and gave him some partic- *Not true I did not know* ulars explanatory of the actual situation at the time of the surrender *who was in command. |* of Col. Olmstead‡ of the 2d Georgia Volunteers, <u>whom</u> he appeared

---

*Joseph P. Bispham.
†1853-1857.
‡Charles H. Olmsted.

at first inclined to blame as guilty of a premature capitulation. After all, however, he thought the Colonel was excusable, as further holding-out promised no advantages to compensate its loss, the up-river batteries of our forces making it certain that Tatnall's fleet could render no assistance. The surrender of Port Royal he did not think premature, under the circumstances, because if his people had not retreated when they did, our gunboats, running round the creeks in rear of Hilton Head, Port Royal and St. Helena Islands, would have made retreat impossible; while the troops of our Sherman expedition when landed were more than sufficient to overpower the garrisons. The mistake was that powerful works had not been erected in rear of the islands to cover the ferries, and thus secure uninterrupted communication with the mainland. Had this been attended to in the first instance, there would then have been no excuse for the abandonment of the powerful works designed to protect Port Royal—at least none unless preceded by a more protracted resistance.

*It is evident that the writer never heard my opinion & is ignorant of the case.*

Recurring to the subject of his family, Mr. Davis asked me had I not been called upon to attend Miss Howell, his wife's sister, who had been very ill at the time of his quitting the *Clyde.* Replied that Col. James,* Chief Quartermaster, had called at my quarters, and requested me to visit a sick lady on board that vessel; believed it was the lady he referred to, but could not be sure of the name. Had mentioned the matter to Gen. Miles, asking a pass to visit; but he objected, saying the orders were to allow no communication with the ship.

Mr. Davis exclaimed this was inhuman. The ladies had certainly committed no crime, and there were no longer any prisoners on board the ship when the request was made, he and Mr. Clay having been the last removed. The lady was very seriously ill, and no officer, no gentleman, no man of Christian or even human feeling, would have so acted.† Gen. Miles was from Massachusetts, he had heard, and his action both in this and other matters appeared in harmony with his origin. It was much for Massachusetts to boast that one of her sons had been appointed his jailor; and it was becoming such a jailor to oppress helpless women and children.* * * * * *

*June 1st.*—Called with Captain Korte, Officer of the Day, about noon. Had been sent for at 8 P.M., but was away fishing. Mr. Davis was suffering from a numbness of the extremities, which he feared was incipient paralysis. Told him it was merely due to an enfeebled circulation, and recommended bathing and friction.

He asked me what luck fishing, and appeared in better spirits than usual. Had just heard, he said, through an irregular channel, that he

---

*William L. James.

†Despite their long lives, illness was a constant source of trouble for the Davises and their families. One can only conclude that these illnesses fulfilled some psychological needs.

had been indicted with Mr. Breckinridge* in the District of Columbia, and hoped therefore that he was about to have a constitutional trial— not one by military commission, to which he would not have pleaded, regarding it as foregone murder. The news had reached him through the conversation of some soldiers in the guard-room, who sometimes spoke to each other in loud tones what they wished him to overhear. It was probably in no friendly spirit they had given him this news; but to him it was as welcome as air to the drowning.

He then referred to the severity of his treatment, supposing himself at present to be merely held for trial, and not already undergoing arbitrary punishment. As this conversation was a very important one, I took full note of it almost immediately on quitting his cell, and it is now given in very nearly, if not precisely, his own words:

"Humanity supposes every man innocent," urged Mr. Davis, "until the reverse shall be proven; and the laws guarantee certain privileges to persons held for trial. To hold me here for trial, under all the rigors of a condemned convict, is not warranted by law—is revolting to the spirit of justice. In the political history of the world, there is no parallel to my treatment. England and the despotic governments of Europe have beheaded men accused of treason; but even after their conviction no such efforts as in my case have been made to degrade them. Apart, however, from my personal treatment, let us see how this matter stands.

"If the real purpose in the matter be to test the question of secession by trying certain persons connected therewith for treason, from what class or classes should the persons so selected be drawn?

"From those who called the State Conventions, or from those who, in their respective conventions, passed the ordinance of secession? Or, from the authors of the doctrine of State rights? Or, from those citizens who, being absent from their States, were unconnected with the event, but on its occurrence returned to their homes to share the fortunes of their States as a duty of <u>primal</u> allegiance? Or from those officers of the State, who, being absent on public service, were called home by the ordinance, and returning, joined their fellow-citizens in State service, and followed the course due to that relation?

"To the last class I belong, who am the object of greatest rigor. This can only be explained on the supposition that, having been most honored, I, therefore, excite most revengeful feelings—for how else can it be accounted for?

"I did not wish for war, but peace. Therefore sent Commissioners to negotiate before war commenced; and subsequently strove my uttermost to soften the rigors of war; in every pause of conflict seeking,

---

*John C. Breckinridge of Kentucky had been a Confederate general and Davis's last secretary of war (appointed 4 February 1865). He fled to Florida, from where he escaped to Cuba, England, and Canada. Thus he had been charged in absentia; when he returned to Kentucky four years later to resume his practice of law, the charges were not pressed.

if possible, to treat for peace. Numbers of those already practically pardoned are those who, at the beginning, urged that the black flag should be hoisted, and the struggle made one of desperation.

"Believing the States to be each sovereign, and their union voluntary, I had learned from the Fathers of the Constitution that a State could change its form of government, abolishing all which had previously existed; and my only crime has been obedience to this conscientious conviction. Was not this the universal doctrine of the dominant Democratic party in the North previous to secession? Did not many of the opponents of that party, in the same section, share and avow that faith? They preached, and professed to believe. We believed, and preached, and practised.

"If this theory be now adjudged erroneous, the history of the States, from their colonial organization to the present moment, should be rewritten, and the facts suppressed which may mislead others in a like manner to a like conclusion.

"But if—as I suppose—the purpose be to test the question of secession by a judicial decision, why begin by oppressing the chief subject of the experiment? Why, in the name of fairness and a decent respect for the opinions of mankind, deprive him of the means needful to a preparation of his defence; and load him with indignities which must deprive his mind of its due equilibrium? It ill comports with the dignity of a great nation to evince fear of giving to a single captive enemy all the advantages possible for an exposition of his side of the question. A question settled by violence, or in disregard of law, must remain unsettled for ever.

"Believing all good government to rest on truth, it is the resulting belief that injustice to any individual is a public injury, which can only find compensation in the reaction which brings retributive justice upon the oppressors. It has been the continually growing danger of the North, that in attempting to crush the liberties of my people, you would raise a Frankenstein of tyranny that would not down at your bidding. Sydney, and Russell, and Vane, and Peters, suffered; but in their death Liberty received blessings their lives might never have conferred.*

"If the doctrine of State Sovereignty be a dangerous heresy, the genius of America would indicate another remedy than the sacrifice of one of its believers. Wickliffe died, but Huss took up his teachings; and when the dust of this martyr was sprinkled on the Rhine, some essence of it was infused in the cup which Luther drank.

"The road to grants of power is known and open; and thus all questions of reserved rights on which men of highest distinction may differ, and have differed, can be settled by fair adjudication; and thus only can they be finally set at rest."

---

*Algernon Sidney (Sydney, 1622-1683), William, Lord Russell (1639-1683), Sir Henry Vane the Younger (1613-1662), and Hugh Peter (Peters, 1598-1660) were English political martyrs.

He then apologized for talking politics to one who should not hear such politics as his; but out of the fulness of the heart the mouth speaketh, and in his joy at the unhoped for news that he had been indicted, and was to have a trial which he supposed must be public, and which publicity would compel to be not wholly one-sided, there was some excuse for his indiscretion.

To change the subject, he returned to fishing, of which we had been speaking. Was a follower and admirer of the sport, but more in theory than practice. His life had been too busy for the past thirty years to allow his indulging even his most cherished inclinations, except at rare intervals. Izaak Walton had been one of his favorite authors; and one of the counts he had against Benjamin Franklin, was the latter's fierce attack on the gentle fisherman. Indeed Franklin had said many things not of benefit to mankind. His soul was a true type or incarnation of the New England character—hard, calculating, angular, unable to conceive any higher object than the accumulation of money. He was the most material of great intellects. None of the lighter graces or higher aspirations found favor in his sight; and with true New England egotism, because he did not possess certain qualities himself, they were to be ignored or crushed out of existence everywhere. The hard, grasping, money-grubbing, pitiless and domineering spirit of the New England Puritans found in Franklin a true exponent. Noble qualities he had, however—courage, truth, industry, economy and honesty. His school of common sense was the apotheosis of selfish prudence. He could rarely err, for men err from excess of feeling, and Franklin had none. The homely wisdom of his writings, judged from the material stand-point, could never be surpassed; and while he confessed to disliking him, he was compelled to admire his "Poor Richard" from its sinewy force.

Mr. Davis then spoke of the restrictions placed upon his reading, which he supposed must soon terminate if he was to be placed on trial. Books would be indispensable to preparing his defence, nor did he see how he could be denied free intercourse with counsel.

Books, if he could get them, would be a great consolation. True, he had the two best—pointing to his Bible and prayer-book; but the mind could not keep continually at the height and strain of earnestness required for their profitable reading. That the papers and other publications of the day should be denied him, he could understand—though even this would not be right when he was preparing for trial. He would then require to know what phase of public opinion he addressed; for in all such trials—and in this age of publicity there must be two tribunals—one inside, but infinitely the vaster one outside the courtroom. To old English or other books for his perusal, what objection could be urged? Such indulgences were given to the worst criminals before trials; and even after conviction the prison libraries were open for their use. A mind so active as his had been for forty years, could not suddenly bring its machinery to a pause. It must either have food, or prey upon itself, and this was his case at present. Except for the purpose of petty torture, there could be no color of reason for withholding from him any books or papers dated prior to the war.

*June 7th.*—I received the following letter from Mrs. Davis, dated Savannah, June 1st, 1865, to Dr. J. J. Craven, Chief Medical Officer, Fort Monroe, Va.

> SAVANNAH, GA.,
> June 1st, 1865.
>
> DR. J. J. CRAVEN, *Chief Med. Officer, Fort Monroe, Va.:*
>
> SIR,—Through the newspapers I learn that you are the Surgeon of the post, and consequently in attendance upon Mr. Davis. Shocked by the most terrible newspaper extras issued every afternoon, which represent my husband to be in a dying condition, I have taken the liberty, without any previous acquaintance with you, of writing to you. Perhaps you will let me know from your own pen how he is. Would it trouble you too much to tell me how he sleeps—how his eyes look—are they inflamed?—does he eat anything?—may I ask what is the quality of his food? Do not refuse my request. It seems to me that no possible harm could accrue to your government from my knowing the extent of my sorrow. And if, perchance, actuated by pity, you do not tell me the worst, the newspapers do, and then the uncertainty is such agony! You will perceive, my dear sir, that I plead with you upon the supposition that you sympathize with our sorrows, and in the sufferings of the man have lost sight of the political enemy, who no longer has the power to do aught but bear what is inflicted.
>
> I will not believe that you can refuse my petition. If you are only permitted to say he is well, or he is better, it will be a great comfort to me, who has {*have*} no other left. If you are kind to him, may God have you in His holy keeping, and preserve all those sources of happiness to you which have, in one day, been snatched away from,
>
> > Yours very respectfully,
> > VARINA DAVIS.*

---

*Davis felt that Craven's worst violation of his professional ethics was the revelation of Mrs. Davis's personal letters. Long before he had ever heard of the *Prison Life*, Davis assured his wife that the revelation of one of her letters in a newspaper article should not be a concern. "You attach over much importance to the publication of your letter. Those who know you will need no assurance that it was not written with such expectations and no one will find any thing in it inconsistent with a proper feeling or inappropriate to the occasion." (Davis to Mrs. Davis, 24 January 1866, Jefferson Davis Collection.)

# •CHAPTER 7•

*Mr. Davis on the New England Character.—Dissensions of the Confeder-ate Leaders.—Future of the South and Southern Blacks.*

June 8th.—Was called to the prisoner, whom I had not seen for a week. Entered with Captain E. A. Evans, Officer of the Day. Found Mr. Davis relapsing and very despondent. Complained again of intolerable pains in his head. Was distracted night and day by the unceasing tread of the two sentinels in his room, and the murmur or gabble of the guards in the outside cell. He said his casemate was well formed for a torture-room of the inquisition. Its arched roof made it a perfect whispering gallery, in which all sounds were jumbled and repeated. The torment of his head was so dreadful, he feared he must lose his mind. Already his memory, vision, and hearing, were impaired. He had but the remains of one eye left, and the glaring, white-washed walls were rapidly destroying this. He pointed to a <u>crevice in the wall</u> where his bed had been, explaining that he had changed to the other side to avoid its mephitic vapors.

Of the trial he had been led to expect, had heard nothing. This looked as if the indictment were to be suppressed, and the action of a Military Commission substituted. If so, they might do with him as they pleased, for he would not plead, but leave his cause to the justice of the future. As to taking his life, that would be the <u>greatest boon they could confer on</u> him, though for the sake of his family he might regret the manner of its taking.

Talked with Mr. Davis for some time, endeavoring to allay his <u>irritation</u>. ❴?❵ The trouble of his head did not arise from the causes he supposed, but from a torpid condition of the liver, and would be at once relieved by a bilious cathartic which I prescribed. It was impossible that any malarial poisons at this season of the year could have influence in his casemate. The ventilation was thorough, the place scrupulously clean; and the very whitewash of which he complained as hurting his eyes, was a powerful disinfectant, if such poisons existed. ❴†❵ After the action of the medicine he would look on the world with a more hopeful view. In regard to his expected trial, knew nothing, never had known anything, and even knowing would be forbidden to speak.

He said he had not mentioned the matter to question me, but as an ejaculation of impatience, for which his intolerable pain must bear the blame. He was no stranger to pain, nor easily overcome by it. At Buena Vista, though severely wounded, he kept saddle until the close of the

*the loud calling of the numbers of relief sentinels*

*it was a large space of green masonry*

*somebody's idea no doubt but not mine*

*†strange inconsistency—Dr. C. explained on several occasions his theory of the tides like a force pump driving the mephitic gas up into the room, and found in the settling of the vertical wall evidence of a bad foundation favorable to the pumping process—He also noticed and objected to the new plastering.*

day; but the pain of no wound could compare to this aching fury of the brain.

*June 9th.* Called, accompanied by Captain Korte, Officer of the Day. Mr. Davis very well—almost entirely relieved. Said he would believe after this that disquietude could be best reached through the stomach. Had slept <u>well</u> and was greatly refreshed; his head almost free from pain.    *not "<u>well</u>"*

Calling me to the embrasure, he pointed out some dark spots on the slope of the moat opposite, and asked me what they were. Told him they were oysters. He had thought so, but was not sure. Had seen them growing in a stranger place—the branches of trees so <u>heavily fruited</u> with them as <u>almost to break</u>. Told him I had seen the same   *never said so* thing, but only along the coasts of South Carolina, Georgia, and Florida. In the South the oysters cling to high rocks and drooping branches of trees, only requiring to be submerged for a few hours at high tide; while with us, the frosts of winter compel them to keep in deep water.

Mr. Davis spoke of the Coon oysters of the Southern coast—the long, razor-shaped oysters, growing on high ledges, and referred to the negro version of how the coons obtained their flesh. Their story is, that the coon takes in his mouth a blade of bluebent, or meadow grass, and when the oyster opens his shell, drives the stiletto point of the grass into his flesh, killing him instantly, so that he has no power to close his defences. This, though ingenious, is not true. The coon bites off the thin edges of the shell at one point, and then sucks out all the softer parts of the body.

In regard to the propagation of oysters, had some talk, Mr. Davis thinking the spawn drifted in the water unable to control itself and adhered to the first solid substance—rock, bank, or branch—with which it was brought in contact. This, I explained, was not so; the oyster, for the first three or four days of his life, being a tunicated pteropod, able to swim in any direction he may please. At the end of this first period, when he finds a congenial object to fasten upon, he literally settles down in life and commences building himself a house from which there is no annual "May moving"—no process of ejectment short of death.

Talking of the shell-fish and snails of the Southern coast, Mr. Davis referred to the beautiful varieties of helix (*bullima immaculata*, very rare, and *bullima oblongata*) that may be seen feeding on the wild orange-trees of Florida. Also to the sport of harpooning devil-fish by night, first attracting them to the surface by a fire of pine-knots kindled in a   *new to me* cresset over the bow of the boat. The skin of the largest devil-fish ever known, he said, had been preserved in Charleston, its weight when caught being fourteen hundred pounds. Told him I had seen one caught about two years before weighing over six hundred pounds, and the old negroes of the island said it was the heaviest they had seen. He talked of the molluscs and crustacea of the coast, this appearing a favorite subject, and his remarks being much pleasanter, though of less interest, than when given a political complexion. He possesses a large, varied, and practical education; the geology, botany, and all products of his section appearing to have in turn claimed his attention. Not the superficial study of a pedant, but the practical acquaintance of a man who has turned every day's fishing, shooting, riding, or pic-nicking, to scientific account.

*June 10th.*—Mr. Davis out of sorts, very ill-tempered. Complained that his clean linen, to be sent over twice a week by General Miles, had not been received. General Miles had taken charge of his clothing, and seemed to think a change of linen twice a week enough. It might be so in Massachusetts. But now even this wretched allowance was denied. The general might know nothing of the matter; but if so, some member of his staff was negligent. It was pitiful they could not send his <u>trunks</u> to his cell, but must insist on thus doling out his clothes, as though he were a convict in some penitentiary. If the object were to degrade him, it must fail. None could be degraded by unmerited insult heaped on helplessness but the perpetrators. The day would come that our people would be ashamed of his treatment. For himself, the sufferings he was undergoing would do him good with his people (the South). Even those who had opposed him would be kept silent, if not won over, by public sympathy. Whatever other opinions might be held, it was clear he was selected as chief victim, bearing the burden of Northern hatred which should be more equally distributed.

Speaking of the negroes, Mr. Davis remarked, as regards their future, he saw no reason why they must die out, unless remaining idle. If herded together in idleness and filth, as in the villages established by our military power, the small-pox, licentiousness, and drunkenness would make short work of them. Wherever so herded, they had died off like sheep with the murrain. But remaining on the plantations, as heretofore, and employed for wages, they were a docile and procreative people, altogether differing from the Indians, and not likely to die out like the latter. Their labor was needed; and though they could not multiply so fast in freedom as under their former wholesome restraints, he saw no good argument for their dying out.

In ten years, or perhaps less, the South will have recovered the pecuniary losses of the war. It has had little capital in manufactures. Its capital was in land and negroes. The land remains productive as ever. The negroes remain, but their labor has to be paid for. Before the war, there had been 4,000,000 negroes, average value, $500 each, or total value, two thousand millions of dollars. This was all gone, and the interest upon it, which had been the profits of the negro's labor in excess of his cost for food, clothing, and medicines. Still their labor remains; and with this, and such European labor as will be imported and such Northern labor as must flow South, the profits of the Southern staples will not be long in restoring material prosperity.

The profits of the cotton crop are enormous. {?} Good bottom lands, such as on the Mississippi and Yazoo rivers, yield a bale of 400 lbs. per acre, and some as high as a bale and a quarter; but this is rare. The uplands throughout Georgia, South Carolina, Alabama, etc., yield about from half to three-quarters of a bale; and under the old system of labor,

*had but one small trunk*

*not my expressions, but the writers.*

a good negro averaged ten bales a season. The land of the Sea Islands ran about 200 lbs. to the acre; but its fine, long, silky, and durable staple made it from twice to four times the value of other cotton.

In his freedom, if capable of being made to labor at all, the negro will not average more than six bales a year; but as the price of cotton has more than doubled, and is not likely to recede, even this will yield an enormous profit. {?} Six bales, of 400 lbs. each, will be worth $600 at twenty-five cents per pound, while the cost of this species of labor will be about $150 a year per hand and found—a profit of certainly not less than $300 a year on each black laborer employed. {?}

The land will not pass to any great extent from its former proprietors. They will lease it for a few years to men with capital, and then resume working it themselves; or sell portions of it with the same object, not materially decreasing their own possessions. When the country is quiet and the profits of the crop come to be known, there will be a rush southward from the sterile New England regions and from Europe, only equalled by that to California on the discovery of gold. Men will not stay in the mountains of Vermont and New Hampshire cultivating little farms of from fifty to a hundred acres, only yielding them some few hundreds a year profit for incessant toil, when the rich lands of the South, under skies as warm and blue as those of Italy, and with an atmosphere as exhilarating as that of France, are thrown open at from a dollar and a half to three dollars per acre. The water-power of the South will be brought into use by this new immigration, and manufactures will spring up in all directions, giving abundant employment to all classes. The happy agricultural state of the South will become a tradition; and with New England wealth, New England's grasping avarice and evil passions will be brought along.*

*views on agricultural prospects of the South much misapprehended.*

The estimate that a million negroes have died off during the war, he considered excessive. They had fled or been dragged away from their old homes in great numbers; but much less than a million, he thought, would cover their casualties. As to any general mingling of the races, nature had erected ample barriers against the crime. Depraved white men occasionally had children by black women; but it was comparatively rare for mulattoes to have large or healthy families; and quadroons, though extremely amorous, rarely had children at all. There could be no danger that Southern white women of the poorer class, though left greatly in excess of the white male population by the war, would either cohabit with or marry negroes. Public sentiment on the point is so strong they dare not do it; nor had they any inclination. It would be regarded South as crimes against nature are regarded in all civilized communities.

The blacks were a docile, affectionate, and religious people, like cats in their fondness for home. The name of freedom had charms for them;

---

*Economic aid and development of the South would be an important part of the New South myth.

but until educated to be self-supporting, it would be a curse. If herded together in military villages and fed on rations gratuitously distributed, rum, dirt, and venereal diseases would devour them off the face of the earth in a few years. With peace established, they would return, in ninety-five cases out of the hundred, to their old plantations, and work for their old masters. Freedom was to them an orgie, of which such as had enjoyed it were rapidly sickening. While health lasted, and idleness was saved its penalty by government support, they might get along well enough. But when sick, starving, and ill-treated, their first wish was a longing to be back with their old masters, and redomiciled on their old plantations. Of this, even during the war, and at penalty of returning to slavery, he had seen many instances—enough to convince him that with freedom assured, or rather its evils to them in their unprepared state better understood—the great majority of the blacks would flock back eagerly.

Mr. Davis said he heard my little daughter had undertaken to be his housekeeper, and sent over his meals. He knew the kind hand of woman was always tenderest in the greatest grief. It only needed they should see misery to wish and labor for its relief, unless some great moral turpitude repelled. He begged me to carry the assurance of his gratitude, and hoped—if he might never see her himself—that his children would some day have opportunity to thank the young lady who had been so kind to their father.*

*Sweet girl*
*your kindness*
*is gratefully remembered.*

*This is the *only* Davis comment that offers positive reinforcement for the textual account.

# •CHAPTER 8•

*Mr. Davis on Cruelty to Prisoners.—Mexico.—Turtle on the Southern
Coast.—The Southern Leaders an Aristocracy.—Lecture on the Fine Arts,
by a Strange Man in a Strange Place.*

June 11th.—Called with Captain R. W. Bickley,* 3d Pennsylvania
Artillery, Officer of the Day. Mr. Davis still improving, febrile symptoms abated, and had slept, <u>for him</u>, very well the night before.
Thanked me for some fruit sent with his breakfast, and then spoke of
the fruits of the tropics and their beautiful adaptation to the wants of
the inhabitants. Also of Mexico, its climate and productions; a land
for which God had done everything, and "where only man was vile."
Considered the Mexicans not capable of self-government; they must
be cared for, and it belonged to America to protect them. Had the
South succeeded without the help of France, this would have been one
of his first cares, and he should not have hesitated a moment. The
South having failed, leaving the North more powerful than ever, the
duty of establishing a continental protectorate was imperative, and
could not long be evaded.

*Thought not so, and cer-
tainly never said anything
like this*

Mr. Davis remarked that when his tray of breakfast had been
brought in that morning, he overheard some soldiers in the guard-room
outside commenting on the food given our prisoners during the late
war. To hold him responsible for this was worse than absurd—crim-
inally false. For the last two years of the war, Lee's army had never
more than half, and was oftener on quarter rations of rusty bacon and
corn. It was yet worse with other Southern armies when operating in
a country which had been campaigned over any time. Sherman, with
a front of thirty or forty miles, breaking into a new country, found no
trouble in procuring food; but had he halted anywhere, even for a single week, must have starved. Marching every day, his men eat out a
new section, and left behind them a starving wilderness.

Colonel Northrop,† his Commissary-General, had many difficulties to contend with; and, not least, the incessant hostility of certain
opponents of his administration, who, by striking at Northrop, really
meant to strike at him. Even General ———, otherwise so moderate
and conservative, finally was induced to join this injurious clamor.‡

---

*Robert W. Bickley.

†Lucius B. Northrop was a favorite of Davis.

‡Halpine here refers to Robert E. Lee. He had maintained a gentlemanly
but bitter contempt for Northrop, who was Lee's only outspoken critic in the
Davis administration.

There was food in the Confederacy, but no means for its collection, the holders hiding it after the currency had become depreciated; and, if collected, then came the difficulty of its transportation. Their railroads were overtaxed, and the rolling-stock soon gave out. They could not feed their own troops; and prisoners of war in all countries and ages have had cause of complaint. Some of his people confined in the West and at Lookout Point, had been nearly starved at certain times, though he well knew, or well believed, full prison-rations had been ordered and paid for in these cases.

*no! I heard they were stinted on the pretext of retaliation*

Herd men together in idleness within an inclosure, their arms taken from them, their organization lost, without employment for their time, and you will find it difficult to keep them in good health. They were ordered to receive precisely the same rations given to the troops guarding them; but dishonest Commissaries and Provost-Marshals were not confined to any people. Doubtless the prisoners on both sides often suffered that the officers having charge of them might grow rich; but wherever such dishonesty could be brought home, prompt punishment followed. General Winder* and Colonel Northrop did the best they could, he believed; but both were poorly obeyed or seconded by their subordinates. To hold him responsible for such unauthorized privations was both cruel and absurd. He issued order after order on the subject, and, conscious of the extreme difficulty of feeding the prisoners, made the most liberal offers for exchange—almost willing to accept any terms that would release his people from their burden. Nonexchange, however, was the policy adopted by the Federal Government—just as Austria, in her later campaigns against Frederick the Great, refused to exchange; her calculation being, that as her population was five times more numerous than Prussia's, the refusal to exchange would be a wise measure. That it may have been prudent, though inhuman, situated as the South was, he was not prepared to deny; but protested against being held responsible for evils which no power of his could avert, and to escape from which almost any concessions had been offered.†

*never said so don't believe it now, despite the tales which have been told*

*restore his suffering countrymen who pined in northern prisons*

Anxious to hear the opinion of Mr. Davis about the future of Mexico, I brought back the conversation to that point, suggesting that when the country became quiet, and with our continual influx of European immigration, we might have men and enterprise enough to resettle Mexico, and colonize out the present indolent and inefficient race.

---

*John Henry Winder as provost marshal was responsible for the care and feeding of federal prisoners and, for a time, the entire Confederate capital. His thankless obligations made him countless enemies on both sides. Only his natural death on 7 February 1865 saved him from a prison term and possible execution.

†While Halpine was eager to present his view of Confederate prisons as justification for the kind treatment afforded Davis, Davis himself was understandably reticent about its discussion. Captain Henry Wirz had been executed in November 1865, and talk of wartime prisons could only exacerbate Northern animosity toward Davis.

"The programme might answer," he thought, "for the thinly peopled parts, though even there its fulfillment must be in the remote future. When the Valley is reached, however, the population is comparatively dense—twenty to the square mile; and political economy teaches that no people so numerous can be crushed out by colonization. A new race must come in to master and guide them, using the present generation as hewers of wood and drawers of water, while educating the next generation for a happier and more intelligent future. It was on a recognition of this necessity the French Emperor **{?}**  *might or could*  based his scheme of European protection; but in failing to make terms with the seceded States, and support them in their struggle, he proved that his comprehension was not equal to the problem. The failure of the South rendered a future of European rule for Mexico impossible."  *The prophecy is not mine.*

*June 14th.*—Visited prisoner in company with Captain Evans, Officer of the Day. Prescribed for some slight return of nervous headache and sleeplessness. Referring to our previous conversation about the shell-fish, etc., of the Southern coast, Mr. Davis said that books of a scientific nature, if allowed him, would keep his attention occupied, and could do no harm. Would be glad to have a few volumes on the conchology, geology, or botany of the South, and was at a loss to think how such volumes could endanger his safe-keeping.

Said that the loggerhead-turtle appeared a contradiction of the rule that nature makes no vain effort—nothing that had not a perceivable use. Here, however, was an animal averaging from one to three hundred pounds weight, very plentiful from Hatteras to the Gulf, for which human ingenuity had yet found no use. But what part it may perform in the economy of the ocean must of course remain a mystery. That it had some useful mission amongst the denizens of the deep, all analogy would lead us to believe. Early in the spring they come up from the Caribbean Sea and Gulf of Mexico, only approaching the shore to lay their eggs when the high tide serves just after dusk of the evening. The male then remains at the edge of the surf, while the female crawls up the beach to find a proper place for laying. The place being selected, she first makes a hole with her head; then increases its size to about that of a peck measure, by putting one of her forefins into it, and twisting herself around until the required space has been scooped out. The eggs are then laid, about 200 in number, nearly the bulk of a hen's egg each, but with a soft, pliable, and very tough white skin. This done, she packs sand over them to the proper depth, and smoothes the place by crawling over it several times with heavy pressure.

Of these eggs, when undisturbed, about eighty per cent are hatched; in some four or five weeks swarms of little turtle suddenly breaking out, each about the size and color of a ginger-snap, and hurrying toward the water with infallible instinct. The eggs have three active and powerful enemies—the coon, the crow, and the negro. The coon hunts the turtle-nest by smell, as a certain breed of dogs in France hunt the truffle, and having taken his first meal, leaves the nest open to the crows, who are not long in finishing what may be left. The negroes search the shores every morning at daylight in this season, and when they find the track made by a turtle's flippers follow it up to where the nest is buried, prodding into the sand with a long stick until it is found, and carrying off the contents. The loggerhead is famous for its longevity, and occasionally weighs from four to six hundred pounds.

*the pronoun in the possessive was "our" it may have fitted the writers sentence, but he should have omitted the parenthesis—which does not fit the fact.*

Speaking of the peculiarities of his people—as he always styled the late Confederate States—Mr. Davis said they were essentially aristocratic, their aristocracy being based on birth and education; while the men of the North were democratic in the mass, making money the basis of their power and standard to which they aspired. It always commanded a premium socially, and was accepted in lack of other qualities. No matter how ill-bred or base, no man possessed of wealth who had not been made judicially infamous, was excluded from northern society. This money-element entered into the politics of the North, while at the South it was, and always had been, powerless. At northern primary elections and nominating conventions, the reins were for him who had money to pay for being allowed control; and the power thus obtained by money was used to get back what it had cost, and to treble that sum during its tenure.

Birth is a guarantee we do not ignore in raising stock, nor should we in growing men. Which should be more important—the pedigree of a horse on which we stake our money, or that of a man we are asked to select for some position of control? The basis of political prominence at the North has been money first, and secondly loquaciousness, effrontery, the arts of the demagogue; while at the South—except in the case of shining talents lifting some individual to eminence by their force—birth, education, and representative rather than noisy or showy qualities, formed the ladder to distinction. No one could fail to be impressed with this difference while attending our National Conventions, Congress, or any other body in which the two sections were represented. He must not be misunderstood as wishing to imply that we had no good blood, no education, no culture at the North—far from it, for he knew we had all in abundance; but under our political system, and owing to the vast influx of a foreign population, they were excluded from our public or representative life. In a word, prominence at the North has, of late, been obtained either by money of the man made prominent, or that he served the money interests of those who pushed his elevation. This evil must continually increase with the increase of immigration; while at the South, birth, education, and intelligence had been the chief usual elements of political distinction—the first necessity being, however, that the man selected should be a true representative of the views of his constituency, whether those views were right or wrong according to northern notions.

To this representative quality, Mr. Davis went on, were due the various positions with which the South had honored him. His selection to the chief office of the Confederacy was in no manner sought. The reasons inspiring the choice were obvious. He was a Mississippian; had graduated at the Military Academy; served with some distinction in the

Mexican war; had large experience in the military committee of the Senate, and in the War Department. But one of his chief recommendations lay in this, that after the removal of Calhoun and General Quitman* by death, he became the chief exponent or representative of those principles of State Sovereignty which the South cherished, and of which, as he claimed, the Fathers of the country had been the founders, Thomas Jefferson the inspired prophet, and they the eloquent apostles. He was certainly not more responsible for his own elevation than any of those who had voted to make him President.

*made no such vain pretension for myself, nor assigned such position to Genl Quitman*

*June 17th.*—Visited Mr. Davis with Captain Korte, Officer of the Day. General Miles, learning that the pacing of the two sentinels in his room at night disturbed Mr. Davis and prevented his sleeping, gave orders that the men should stand at ease during their two hours of guard, both night and day, instead of pacing their accustomed beat. This, Mr. Davis said, was much pleasanter for him, but cruel {?} for the men obliged to stand so long in one position, as if they had been bronze or marble statues. Feared, as it cost them suffering, {?} it would make them hate him more, as the cause—though innocent—of their inconvenient attitude; and there were plenty of men wearing uniforms of that color who hated him more than enough already.

*A volunteer standing "at ease" is not very like a statue; he may have misunderstood the remarks made about the Sentinels at the "Horse Guards" who stand "at attention" & have been likened to statues.*

From this point Mr. Davis glided off to some considerations of statuary, commenting on the growing taste for representing animals, birds and men, in painful or impossible attitudes in the *basso-relievos,* bronzes, and other ornaments of modern sculpture. Stricken deer contorted by death-wounds; horses with sides lacerated by the claws of a clinging tiger; partridges, or other birds, choking in snares or pierced with arrows; dying Indians, wounded gladiators, dying soldiers—pain or death in every variety of grade, seemed to form the present staples for popular bronze and Parian ornament. Our sculptors made their horses stand eternally with fore-paws poised in air in an attitude only possible for a moment to the living animal. Such works were not pleasing, but the reverse. They fretted the sensibilities with petty pain, and lacked the repose which should form the chief charm of sculpture. The groups of the Laocoon and Dying Gladiator were the <u>only</u> eminent works of antiquity of which he had heard or seen casts, in which pain or horror had been the elements depicted; and in these the treatment had been so overwhelmingly grand as to numb the sense of suffering by the splendor of their beauty. For modern sculpture, however—the statuary designed for parlor ornaments—he wished to see more pleasant themes. The agony of a wounded deer or bird could have nothing to recommend it but the fidelity of imitation with which the agony was portrayed; while in the Laocoon, there was the titanic struggle of the father to free his children from the coils of the serpent, and behind the Dying Gladiator rose up the gazing circles of the

*?*

---

*John C. Calhoun and John A. Quitman.

amphi-theatre—each subject wakening trains of thought and emotion which concealed our sense of physical pain, or only allowed it to obtrude as a sort of undertone, or diapason, to the awful beauty of the picture.

Mr. Davis, on this subject, was really eloquent, showing a keen appreciation of art, and I only regret that my notes report him so imperfectly. It struck me as a strange place for such a dissertation, a strange man strangely circumstanced to be its author, and a strange incident—two armed soldiers standing like statues within a cell, to have given origin in such a mind to a lecture on the aesthetics of repose applied to modern sculpture.

# •CHAPTER 9•

*Mr. Davis on Gen. Butler and Dutch Gap.—He denies that Secession was Treason.—His Opinion of Grant, McClellan, Pope, and other Union Officers; also of Bragg, Lee and Pemberton.—His Flight from Richmond and Arrest.*

June 18*th*—Called on Mr. Davis with Captain Jerome E. Titlow, Officer of the Day. Found him continuing to improve in general health— much stronger than he had been on his arrival. Complained of a stricture or tightening of the chest, accompanied by a dry cough. Ordered him to exercise his arms by swinging them back and forth horizontally twice or thrice a day.

*the writer acknowledges not to have seen him then.*

Standing at the embrasure, the white sails of a passing vessel suggested the trade and commerce of the James, for the mouth of which it appeared steering. Together in fancy we reascended the banks of the river, with which Mr. Davis was familiar. He asked the fate of all the beautiful plantations along its shores; of Brandon belonging to the Harrisons on the south bank, a place Gen. Butler had harried; of Westover; and beautiful Shirley on the north bank, just opposite Bermuda Hundreds, belonging to that noble Virginian of the old school, Mr. Hill Carter. Told Mr. Davis it was the only one left standing, in all its beautiful antiquity, of the palaces that once lined the James. Carter had been kind to the wounded of McClellan's soldiers and had taken no part in the war, though very possibly a Southern man in sentiment. His place consequently had been not only spared from incursion, but guarded with jealous care by daily details, and was the green spot in the desert made by the movements of contending armies.

Talking of Gen. Butler, said Mr. Davis, with a smile, Richmond owes him something, if only for giving it the best joke of the war. He referred to the Dutch Gap Canal,* considered as a war-measure, for as a commercial one, improving the navigation of the James, it was full of advantage. It was a task imposing great hardships upon many thousand soldiers; and must have been inspired by Grant's similar attempt to change the course of the Mississippi at Vicksburg. If successful, the canal only avoided one battery, Fort Howlett, which might have been carried by a resolute

*the reverse of my opinion*

---

*The Dutch Gap Canal was constructed mostly by black soldiers in Butler's Army of the James beginning in August 1864 under the direction of Capt. Peter S. Michie. Designed to avoid Confederate batteries along the south bank of the James River, it was not completed until April 1865. Since then it has become the navigation channel of the river.

effort; nor could any of us understand what adequate object could be gained by it when completed. The James, from Dutch Gap to Richmond, was too shallow for gun-boats; was paved with torpedoes, and obstructed in every conceivable manner. Besides, the works at Chapin's and Drury's Bluffs would still remain.

*not mine*

Commercially, the canal might be of great value to Richmond. The loop of the river which it cut off—about seven miles in length—formed the shallowest and most intricate part of its navigation, from Rockett's to the sea. By making a lock of the Dutch Gap Canal, and throwing a dam across the river just below the higher lock, the water up to Richmond might be permanently raised two feet and placed beyond tidal influence, thus allowing vessels of ten or eleven feet draft to reach the city in all stages of the tide, while at present vessels drawing even eight or nine feet can only with extreme difficulty be brought up at high tide. Commercially, the canal was good; but as a war-measure, of no value.

*The Dr. deals boldly with a question which Engineers approach most cautiously, but I must object to his transfer of authorship of the plan. It is not mine.*

Mr. Davis said it was contrary to reason, and the law of nations, to treat as a rebellion, or lawless riot, a movement which had been the deliberate action of an entire people through their duly organized State governments. To talk of treason in the case of the South, was to oppose an arbitrary epithet against the authority of all writers on international law. Vattel* deduces from his study of all former precedent—and all subsequent international jurists have agreed with him—that when a nation separates into two parts, each claiming independence, and both or either setting up a new government, their quarrel, should it come to trial by arms or by diplomacy, shall be regarded and settled precisely as though it were a difference between two separate nations, which the divided sections, *de facto,* have become. Each must observe the laws of war in the treatment of captives taken in battle, and such negotiations as may from time to time arise shall be conducted as between independent and sovereign powers. Mere riots, or conspiracies for lawless objects, in which only limited fractions of a people are irregularly engaged, may be properly treated as treason, and punished as the public good may require; but Edmund Burke had exhausted argument on the subject, in his memorable phrase, applied to the first American movement for independence: "I know not how an indictment against a whole people shall be framed."

But for Mr. Lincoln's untimely death, Mr. Davis thought, there could have been no question raised upon the subject. That event—more a calamity to the South than North, in the time and manner of its transpiring—had inflamed popular passions to the highest pitch, and made the people of the section which had lost their chief now seek as an equivalent the life of the chief of the section conquered. This was an impulse of passion, not a conclusion which judgment or justice could support. Mr. Lin-

---

*Emeric de Vattel, an eighteenth-century Swiss jurist, was renowned for his *Law of Nations,* which was the standard work on international law.

coln, through his entire administration, had acknowledged the South as a belligerent nationality, exchanging prisoners of war, establishing truces, and sometimes sending, sometimes receiving, propositions for peace. On the last of these occasions, accompanied by the chief member of his cabinet, he had personally met the Commissioners appointed by the Southern States to negotiate, going half way to meet them not far from where Mr. Davis now stood; and the negotiations of Gen. Grant* with Gen. Lee, just preceding the latter's surrender, most distinctly and clearly pointed to the promise of a <u>general amnesty</u>; Gen. Grant, in his final letter, expressing the hope that, with Lee's surrender, "all difficulties between the sections might be settled without the loss of another life," or words to that effect.  *?*

To my question what he thought of General Grant, Mr. Davis replied that he was a great soldier beyond doubt, but of a new school. If he had not started with an enormous account in bank, his checks would have been dishonored before the culmination was reached. At Shiloh he was defeated the first day, and would have been destroyed or compelled to surrender next morning, but for Buell's† timely arrival with a fresh and well-disciplined reinforcement, the strength of which had been variously stated.  *Imperfectly stated*

When Secretary of War, he thought McClellan <u>the ablest</u> **{?}** *not so* officer in the army, and had employed him on two important services—as Military Commissioner in the Crimea, and to explore a route for the Pacific railroad—both of which duties had been discharged in a manner to increase his reputation.‡ He organized the Army of the Potomac admirably, but it required a commander of more dash to wield the weapon in the field. McClellan's caution amounted very closely to timidity—moral timidity, for he was personally brave. On his first landing in the Peninsula there had been only 7,000 troops to meet him, and these he should have rushed upon and overwhelmed at whatever cost. Cautious, and wishing to spare the blood of his men, he commenced a regular siege at Yorktown, giving his enemies time to concentrate sufficient numbers and drive him back. As a magnanimous enemy he respected McClellan, but thought he had been promoted too rapidly for his own good—before he had ripened in command and gained the experience requisite for the supreme position. Had he been kept in a subordinate capacity the two first years of the war, rising from a division to a corps, and thence to command in chief, he would have been <u>the greatest</u> **{?}** of our soldiers. He had the best natural gifts  *?* and highest intellectual training, and was just becoming fitted, and the best fitted, for his position when removed. Had he been <u>supported by</u>  *inaccurate* <u>the government</u> he might have taken Richmond two years earlier, and it was with joy Mr. Davis heard of his removal **{?}** after the battles  *?*

---

*Ulysses S. Grant.

†Don Carlos Buell.

‡Although Davis had never been fond of McClellan, this 1864 Democratic presidential candidate found a warm supporter in Halpine.

of South Mountain and Antietam. Such sacrifices of officers to the ignorance of an unwarlike people, anxious to find in him a scapegoat for
their own lack of discipline or endurance, were unavoidable in the early
stages of every popular war.

Pope, while Secretary of War, he had never been able to make ser-
viceable, and Pope held his own gallantly. His mind was not less in-
flated than his body. He was a kind of American gascon, but with good
scientific attainments. Sumner and Sedgwick* were gallant and able
soldiers—excellent commanders in action, courteous and reliable in
all the relations of life. Hunter,† of whom I asked him specially as one
of my old commanders, was his beau ideal of the military gentleman—the soul of integrity, intrepidity, true Christian piety and honor.
Mr. Davis had long been associated with him, both in the service and
socially, and believed Hunter's want of success due in a great measure
to his unwillingness to bend to anything mean or sinister. He was rash,
*All this of a man whose* impulsive; a man of action rather than thought; yielding to passions
*atrocities had caused him* which he regarded as divine instincts or intuitions—the natural tem-
*to be put under ban* per of a devotee or fanatic.

Of the officers on the Confederate side, Mr. Davis spoke in high
terms of General Lee, as a great soldier and pure, Christian gentleman; also, in praise of Bragg and Pemberton,‡ though the two latter,
from unavoidable circumstances and the hostility of the party opposed to Mr. Davis, had not been accorded the position due to their
talents by public opinion in either section. Pemberton made a splendid defence of Vicksburg, and might have been relieved if the officer
commanding the army sent to relieve him (General Johnson)§ had not
failed to obey the positive orders to attack General Grant which Mr.
Seddon,★ then Secretary of War, had sent. If the same officer, who
was upheld in command by the anti-administration party, had vig-
orously attacked Sherman at Atlanta when directed, the fortunes of
the war would have been changed, and Sherman hurled back to Nashville, over a sterile and wasted country—his retreat little less disas-

---

*Edwin V. Summer and John Sedgwick.

†David Hunter was an old friend of Halpine. The general, a native of
Washington, D.C., and a descendant of one of Virginia's leading families,
had freed the slaves on the Sea Islands. On 12 April 1862, Hunter, as commander of the Department of the South, formed the first official regiment of
black troops made up of freedmen from South Carolina, Georgia, and Florida. Due to this, four months later Davis labeled Hunter an "outlaw," permitting his immediate execution if caught by Confederate troops. Halpine's
misunderstanding of Davis's true opinions are most glaring in references to
David G. Hunter.

‡Braxton Bragg was a special favorite of Davis. John C. Pemberton had
defended Vicksburg to the end, thus following Davis's orders and ignoring
those of Gen. Joseph E. Johnston, who had ordered him to flee from the
doomed city with his army.

§Joseph E. Johnston; Halpine consistently misspelled his name.

★James A. Seddon.

trous than Napoleon's from Moscow. He did not do so, and was relieved—General Hood,* a true and spirited soldier, taking his place—but the opportunity was then gone; and to this delay, more than to any other cause, the Southern people will attribute their over- *misconception* throw, whenever history comes to be truly written.

Bragg's victory over Rosecrans at Chickamauga, Mr. Davis regarded as one of the most brilliant achievements of the war, considering the disparity of the forces. The subsequent concentration of Grant and Hooker with Rosecrans, and the victory of their combined forces at Lookout Mountain, was the result of an audacity or desperation which no military prudence could have foreseen. So confident was Bragg in the impregnability of his position, that immediately after Chickamauga he detached Longstreet,† with 16,000 men—about a third of his entire force—to make a demonstration against Knoxville, *too ignorant to understand* thus indirectly threatening Grant's communications with Nashville. *the statement is a map of* Bragg's position was finally carried by the overwhelming numbers of *errors.* the enemy. The opponents of his administration censured Bragg for detaching Longstreet, but the subsequent events which made that movement unfortunate were of a character which no prudence could have foreseen, no military calculation taken into view as probable.

All such reflections were idle, however, concluded Mr. Davis, and he must not be again betrayed into their indulgence. Success is virtue and defeat crime. This is the philosophy of life—at least the only one the great masses of mankind feel ready to accept. Woe to the conquered is no less a popular cry in the nineteenth century than when the barbarians first yelled it as they swarmed with dripping swords to the sack of Rome.

Mr. Davis then spoke of the circumstances attending his <u>flight</u> from *?* Richmond.

On leaving Richmond he went first to Danville, because it was intended that Lee should have moved in that direction, falling back to make a junction with Johnson's force in the direction of Roanoke River. Grant, however, pressed forward so rapidly, and swung so far around, that Lee was <u>obliged</u> to retreat in the direction of Lynchburg with his main force, *?* <u>while his vanguard,</u> which arrived at Danville, insisted on falling back and *another error* making the rallying-point at Charlotte in North Carolina.

In Danville Mr. Davis learned of Lee's surrender. <u>Immediately</u> started for <u>Goldsboro</u>, where he met and had a consultation with Gen. *Greensboro* Johnson, thence going on south. At Lexington he received a dispatch *not so, but after much de-* from Johnson requesting that the Secretary of War (Gen. Breckin- *lay.* ridge) should repair to his headquarters near Raleigh—Gen. Sherman having submitted a proposition <u>for laying down arms</u> which was too *the writer's own* comprehensive in its scope for any mere military commander to decide upon. Breckinridge and Postmaster-General Reagan immedi-

---

*John B. Hood.
†William S. Rosecrans, Joseph Hooker, and James Longstreet.

ately started for Johnson's camp, where Sherman submitted the terms of surrender on which an armistice was declared—the same terms subsequently disapproved by the authorities at Washington.

One of the features of the proposition submitted by General Sherman was a declaration of amnesty to all persons, both civil and military. Notice being called to the fact particularly, Sherman said, "I mean just that;" and gave as his reason that it was the only way to have perfect peace. He had previously offered to furnish a vessel to take away any such persons as Mr. Davis might select, to be freighted with whatever personal property they might want to take with them, and to go wherever it pleased.

General Johnson told Sherman that it was worse than useless to carry such a proposition as the last to him. Breckinridge also informed General Sherman that his proposition contemplated the adjustment of certain matters which even Mr. Davis was not empowered to control. The terms were accepted, however, with the understanding that they should be liberally construed on both sides, and fulfilled in good faith—General Breckinridge adding that certain parts of the terms would require to be submitted to the various State governments of the Confederacy for ratification.

These terms of agreement between Johnson and Sherman were subsequently disapproved by the authorities at Washington, and the armistice ordered to cease after a certain time. Mr. Davis waited in Charlotte until the day and hour when the armistice ended; then mounted his horse, and, with some cavalry of Duke's brigade (formerly Morgan's),* again started southward, passing through South Carolina to Washington, in Georgia. At an encampment on the road, he thinks, the cavalry of his escort probably heard of the final surrender of General Johnson, though he himself did not until much later. Being in the advance, he rode on, supposing that the escort was coming after.

As with his party he approached the town of Washington, he was informed that a regiment, supposed to belong to the army of General Thomas,† was moving on the place to capture it, in violation, as he thought, of General Sherman's terms. On this he sent back word to the General commanding the cavalry escort to move up and cover the town—an order which probably never reached its destination—at least the cavalry never came; nor did he see them again, nor any of them. Thinking they were coming, however, and not apprehending any molestation from the Federal troops, even if occupying the same town, he entered Washington, and remained there over night—no troops of the United States appearing. Here he heard of his wife and family, not having seen them since they had left Richmond, more than a month before his own departure. They had just left the town before

---

*Basil W. Duke and John H. Morgan were brothers-in-law.
†George H. Thomas.

his arrival, moving South in company with his private secretary, Colonel Harrison,* of whose fidelity he spoke in warm terms, and accompanied by a small party of paroled men, who, seeing them unprotected, had volunteered to be their escort to Florida, from whence the family, not Mr. Davis himself, intended to take ship to Cuba.

Mr. Davis regarded the section of country he was now in as covered by Sherman's armistice, and had no thought that any expedition could or would be sent for his own capture, or for any other warlike purposes. He believed the terms of Johnson's capitulation still in force over all the country east of the Chattahoochie, which had been embraced in Johnson's immediate command; citing as an evidence of this, that while he was in Washington, General Upton,† of the Federal service, with a few members of his staff, passed unattended over the railroad, a few miles from the place, *en route* for Augusta, to receive the muster-rolls of the discharged troops, and take charge of the immense military stores there that fell into General Sherman's hands by the surrender. General Upton was not interfered with, the country being considered at peace, though nothing could have been easier than his capture, had Mr. Davis been so inclined.

At this very time, however, a division of cavalry had been sent into this district, which had been declared at peace and promised exemption from the dangers and burdens of any further military operations within its limits, for the purpose of capturing himself and party; and this he could not but regard as a breach of faith on the part of those who directed or permitted it to be done, though he did not wish to place himself in the condition of one who had accepted the terms of Johnson's capitulation or taken advantage of the amnesty which Sherman had offered. But the district in which he then found himself had been promised exemption from further incursions, and he did not think himself justly liable to capture while within its limits—though he expected to have to take the chances of arrest when once across the Chattahoochie.

Hearing that a skirmish-line, or patrol, had been extended across the country from Macon to Atlanta and thence to Chattanooga, he thought best to go below this line, hoping to join the forces of his relative, Lieutenant-General Dick Taylor,‡ after crossing the Chattahoochie. He would then cross the Mississippi, joining Taylor's forces to those of Kirby Smith§—of whom he spoke with marked acerbity—and would have continued the fight so long as he could find any Confederate force to strike with him. This, not in any hope of final success, but to secure for the South some better terms than surrender at

---

*Burton Harrison. "Colonel" in this instance is an honorary rather than military title.

†Emory Upton.

‡Richard Taylor was the son of President Zachary Taylor and brother of Sarah Knox Taylor Davis, Jefferson Davis's first wife.

§Edmund Kirby Smith.

discretion. "To this complexion," said Mr. Davis, "had the repudiation of General Sherman's terms, and the surrenders of Lee and Johnson, brought the Southern cause."

Mr. Davis left Washington accompanied by Postmaster-General Reagan, three aides, and an escort of ten mounted men with one packmule. Riding along, they heard distressing reports of bands of marauders going about the country stealing horses and whatever else might tempt their cupidity—these rumors finally maturing into information which caused him to change his course and follow on to overtake the train containing his wife and family, for whose safety he began to feel apprehensions.

This object he achieved after riding seventy miles, without halt, in a single day, joining Mrs. Davis just at daylight, and in time to prevent a party he had passed on the road from stealing her two fine carriage-horses which formed a particular attraction for their greed. "I have heard," he added, "since my imprisonment, that it was supposed there was a large amount of specie in the train. Such was not the fact, Mrs. Davis carrying with her no money that was not personal property, and but very little of that."

Having joined his family, he travelled with them for several days, in consequence of finding the region infested with deserters and robbers engaged in plundering whatever was defenceless, his intention being to quit his wife whenever she had reached a safe portion of the country, and to bear west across the Chattahoochie. The very evening before his arrest he was to have carried out this arrangement, believing Mrs. Davis to be now safe; but was prevented by a report brought in through one of his aides, that a party of guerillas, or highwaymen, was coming that night to seize the horses and mules of his wife's train. It was on this report he decided to remain another night.

Towards morning he had just fallen into the deep sleep of exhaustion when his wife's faithful negro servant, *William* Robert, came to him announcing that there was firing up the road.* He started up, dressed himself and went out. It was just at grey dawn, and by the imperfect light he saw a party approaching the camp. They were recognised as Federal cavalry by the way in which they deployed to surround the train, and he stepped back into the tent, to warn his wife that the enemy were at hand.

Their tent was prominent, being isolated from the other tents of the train; and as he was quitting it to find his horse, several of the cavalry rode up, directing him to halt and surrender. To this he gave a defiant answer. Then one whom he supposed to be an officer asked, had he any arms, to which Mr. Davis replied: "If I had, you would not be alive to ask that question." His pistols had been left in the holsters, as it had been his intention, the evening before, to start whenever the

---

*Robert was the faithful servant who accompanied the Davis children to Montreal. However, it was William who warned the Davises that federal cavalry was in the area.

camp was settled; but horse, saddle, and holsters were now in the enemy's possession, and he was completely unarmed.

Colonel Pritchard, commanding the Federal cavalry, came up soon, to whom Mr. Davis said: "I suppose, sir, your orders are accomplished in arresting me. You can have no wish to interfere with women and children; and I beg they may be permitted to pursue their journey." The Colonel replied that his orders were to take every one found in my company back to Macon, and he would have to do so, though grieved to inconvenience the ladies. Mr. Davis said his wife's party was composed of paroled men, who had committed no act of war since their release, and begged they might be permitted to go to their homes; but the Colonel, under his orders, did not feel at liberty to grant this request. They were all taken to Macon, therefore, reaching it in four days, and from thence were carried by rail to Augusta—Mr. Davis thanking Major-General J. H. Wilson* for having treated him with all the courtesy possible to the situation.

The party transferred to Augusta consisted of Reagan, Alexander H. Stevens, Clement C. Clay, two of his own aides and private secretary, Mrs. Clay, his wife and four children, four servants and three paroled men, who had generously offered their protection to Mrs. Davis during her journey. Breckinridge had been with the cavalry brigade, which had been the escort of Mr. Davis, and did not come up at Washington. He and Secretary Benjamin had started for Florida, *not so* expecting to escape thence to the West Indies. There was no specie nor public treasure in the train—{(}nothing but his private *I had no funds in the train* funds,{)} and of them very little.† Some wagons had been furnished by the quartermaster at Washington, Georgia, for the transportation of his family and the paroled men who formed their escort, and that was the only train. Mr. Davis had not seen his family for some *?* {X} months{?} before, and first rejoined them when he rode to their defence from Washington.

*June 23d.*—I received the following letter from Mrs. Davis:‡

---

*James H. Wilson.

†The question of the Confederate funds supposedly taken by the fleeing Davis government was one that Davis did not want discussed at all since even a denial might give some credence to the utterly false rumor. Mere mention of this violated Davis's rigid standard of honor and gentlemanly conduct.

‡As of this date, Mrs. Davis had not been permitted to leave Savannah, Georgia, nor to correspond directly with her husband.

DATED SAVANNAH, GA.,
June 14th, 1865.

DR. CRAVEN:

MY DEAR SIR,—Pursued by dreadful pictures thrown before me every day in excerpts from northern correspondents, and published in the daily journals, in which the agony inseparable from defeat and imprisonment is represented to have been heightened for my husband by chains and starvation, I can no longer preserve the silence which I feel should be observed by me, in your failure to answer my letter of the first inst. Can it be that these tales are even in part true? That such atrocities could render him frantic I know is not so. I have so often tended him through months of nervous agony, without ever hearing a groan or an expression of impatience, that I know these tales of childish ravings are not true— would to God I could believe that all these dreadful rumors were false as well!

But there is something about them which convinces me that they are not altogether false. You must have been kind to him, else he had not told you of his sufferings. Will you not, my dear sir, tell me the worst? Is he ill—is he dying? Taken from me, with only ten minutes' warning, I could not see any one to whom I could say that he was quite ill; indeed, suffering from fever at the hour of our separation. He has been much exposed to a Southern sun in malarial districts, and I dread everything from an attack of illness in his depressed condition, even were the humanities of life manifested to him. With a blaze of light pouring upon the dilated pupils of eyes always sensitive to it; chains fettering his emaciated limbs; coarse food, served, as the newspapers describe it, in the most repulsive manner, without knife, fork, or spoon, "lest he should commit suicide,"—hope seems denied to me; yet I cannot reconcile myself to that result, which for many years must have been his gain. Will you only write me one word to say that he may recover? Will you tell him that we are well—that our little children pray for him, and miss his fatherly care— that his example still lives for them. Please tell him not to be anxious for us; that kind friends are with us, and that those who love him have adopted us, too. Do not tell him, please, that we are not permitted to leave here; for the present, we can do very well, and then I expect, every day, a permit to leave this city for one more healthy. Please try to cheer him about us for we are kindly cared for by the Southern friends who love him here. Will you not take the trouble to write me, only this once? Can it be that you are forbidden? Else, how could a Husband and Father, as I hear you are, refuse us such a small favor, productive as it would be of such blessed comfort?

My children shall pray for you, and perhaps the prayers of "one of these little ones" may avail much with Him who said, "Suffer them to come unto me;" and that which you have done for another may be returned to you with usury in some less happy and prosperous hour. With the hope of hearing from you very soon,

   I am, sir,
    Very respectfully
     And gratefully yours,
      VARINA DAVIS.*

*Dr. Craven did not reply though he seemed to have preserved the letter of an agonized Wife and though private has published.*

---

*Publication of personal letters from Mrs. Davis to Craven struck a chord of deep anger in Davis and violated his personal code of gentlemanly honor and confidentiality (see 122).

# •CHAPTER 10•

*Diseases of the Eye.—Guards removed from the Prisoner's Room.—Mr.
Davis takes his first Walk on the Ramparts.—The Policy of Conciliation.—Mr. Davis on Improvements in Land and Naval Warfare.*

June *24th.*—Called on Mr. Davis, accompanied by Captain Titlow,
Officer of the Day. On entering found the prisoner, for the first time,
alone in his cell, the two guards having been removed from it in consequence of my report to Major-General Miles that their presence was
counteracting every effort for quieting the nerves of the patient. Mr.
Davis remarked that the change had done him good, his last night's
sleep having been undisturbed. He complained of his eyes, and a
throbbing pain in the back of his neck, asking me to give the matter
*not true* particular attention, as similar symptoms, {(}at the same season last
year, in Richmond,{)} had been followed by a severe bilious remittent fever.

Mr. Davis spoke of the injurious effects of reflected light upon the
eyes, thence diverging to the phenomena of the mirage, and the illusions of vision arising from an overexcited condition of the optic nerve,
or peculiar conditions of the atmosphere. The mirage on the deserts
of Egypt and Arabia was chiefly observable in the afternoons, when
the sands were thoroughly heated, thus producing a different medium
of atmosphere close to the earth, and causing the horizontal or vertical
refraction, or both, which produced the appearance of this so common phenomenon. Science, he remarked, was fast explaining, as the
result of natural laws, nearly all the mysteries of the earth on which
ignorance in preceding ages had founded its superstitions and magi-
cians built up a belief in their reputed power. The injurious effects of
the whitewash upon the walls of his cell to his eyes, he attributed to
the double refractive power—doubly injurious—of all salts and crys-
tallized minerals not retaining the form of the original cube, the regular octohedron, etc.; and of all these substances, the carbonate of lime
possessed the double refractive power most eminently, and was,
therefore, most injurious to the sight.

Mr. Davis said that reading continually the same type in his Bible
and Prayer-Book had become a severe tax upon his sight, of which he
had often complained to me before; but what was he to do? Utter in-
action for a mind so busy as his had been, was impossible: he must
either furnish it with external employment, or allow it to prey upon
itself. Nature had furnished all varieties of pabulum to the vision, resting it on one color when weary with another, and changing the forms

on which it had been employed with every object of nature. Even with
the most healthy, sight was a delicate organ, and with him—the sight
of one eye lost and that of the other seriously impaired—peculiarly
so. The pupil of the eye was constructed to expand or contract in harmony with each change of light, or color, or different form of object;
and to employ the vision continually on one size of type, he believed
must be injurious—at least on no other theory could he account for
the fast-growing alteration of his sight.

On this subject we had frequently conversed before, my views
agreeing with those of Mr. Davis, who, from the necessities of his case,
appeared to have pretty thoroughly studied the art of the oculist. Indeed it was a remark which every day impressed on me more forcibly,
that the State prisoner had studied no subject superficially, and that
his knowledge in all the useful arts and sciences was varied, extensive,
and very thorough in each branch.

Representations in regard to the need Mr. Davis stood in of different pabulum, both for his eyes and mind, had been previously made
by me to Major-General Miles, and had been confirmed, I rather believe, by Colonel Pineo,* Medical Inspector of the Department, who
had visited Mr. Davis in my company on the 12th of this month, having a long and interesting conversation with the prisoner—a fact which
should have been mentioned at an earlier date; but as the conversation
was one in which I took little part, the brief memorandum in my diary
escaped notice until revived by the fuller notes of this day's interview.
It was upon the day of Colonel Pineo's visit, also, that Mr. Davis mentioned having heard that my little daughter, moved by sympathy, had
volunteered as his housekeeper and superintended the sending of his
meals. Beautiful as woman's character always was, in its purity, grace,
delicacy, and sympathetic action, it was rarely, save in man's hours of
deepest affliction, that he realized how much his nature stood in need
of the support of his gentle counterpart. Then, picking up a volume
of prayer from the table, he said: "Doctor, my wife gave me this. Another, which she placed in my valise, I have since received. Pray present
this, with my love and grateful regards, to your little Anna, and say,
though I may never have an opportunity to thank her myself, my children will one day rise up 'to call her blessed.' "

And now to have done with this digression and return to my interview of June 24th.

While the State prisoner was yet speaking of the troubles of his sight,
Major-General Miles entered, with the pleasant announcement that
Mr. Davis was to be allowed to walk one hour each day upon the ramparts, and to have miscellaneous reading hereafter—books, newspapers, and such magazines as might be approved, after perusal at
headquarters—an improvement of condition, it must be needless to
say, very pleasing to the prisoner.

---

*Peter Pineo.

That afternoon, Mr. Davis took his first walk in the open air since
*say watching* entering Fortress Monroe; Major-General Miles <u>supporting</u> him on
one side, the Officer of the Day on the other, and followed by four
armed guards. Of this party I was not a member, much to my regret,
for the remarks of the prisoner on regaining so much of his liberty,
and looking upon scenes formerly so familiar, under happier circumstances, would beyond doubt have been of interest. I only noticed that
Mr. Davis was arrayed in the same garb he had worn when entering
his cell—indeed General Miles had possession of all his other wardrobe; and that while his carriage was proud and erect as ever, not losing a hair's breadth of his height from any stoop, his step had lost its
elasticity, his gait was feeble in the extreme, and he had frequently to
press his chest, panting in the pauses of exertion. The cortège prom-
enaded along the ramparts of the South front, Mr. Davis often stop-
ping and pointing out objects of interest, as if giving reminiscences of
the past and making inquiries of the present. He was so weak, however, that the hour allowed proved nearly twice too much for him, and
he had to be led back with only half his offered liberty enjoyed.

*June 25th.*—Visited prisoner with Captain Evans, 3d Pennsylvania
Artillery, Officer of the Day. Mr. Davis much better, and with spirits
greatly improved. The application to the back of his neck had immediately relieved the pain, and his sight was less wavering. He no
longer saw the cloud of black and amber motes rising and falling before his sight. The nervous and painful twitching of the eyelids had
also in great measure ceased. Of all diseases, he most feared photo-
phobia; having seen many cases of it, and heard it was the keenest agony of which the human nerves are susceptible. Injured as his sight
was, he knew such a disease must result in total blindness. "Not that
I expect many pleasant things to look out upon, Doctor, but that I need
my sight for my defence, which must also be the defence of the cause
I represented, and which my sufferings have been aimed to degrade."

Asked him how he had enjoyed his walk on the previous afternoon.
He said the sense of breathing air not drawn through iron bars was a
glorious blessing, only to be appreciated by prisoners—one of the
thousand common blessings which must be lost before we prize them.
The varieties of view and animation of the scene had stimulated and
reinvigorated his eyes; but his feebleness had been excessive—partly
arising, he thought, from a rush of novel emotions, partly from the
old recollections that came crowding back to him; and partly because,
looking towards the land of his people from the Southern front, it
seemed to his mind a vast charnel-house, with the black plumes of
political death nodding between it and the sun.

"And yet this should not be," continued Mr. Davis, "if your authorities at Washington be wise. The attempt of certain States to separate from the old confederation, in which their rights under the
fundamental law had been violated, having proved abortive, and they
being coerced back under the General Government by military force,
their rights under the Constitution at once return, and revive with their

submission, unless that instrument shall be deliberately and openly repudiated. Such was the absolute spirit of General Grant's negotiation upon which General Lee surrendered; and such both the spirit and letter of General Sherman's proposals to the General he was contending against" (General Johnson's name not mentioned). "It was also embodied in all the declarations of your Government and late President in all their public acts; and I think my people would have fought more desperately, and continued the war much longer, though hopelessly, had it not been for this expectation.

"But even apart from this—apart from all pledges of faith or obligations of constitutional law," Mr. Davis went on, "and looking on the matter only in the light of future expediency, let us see how the case stands. In the better days of the Roman empire, when its possessions increased, and conquered countries came in a few years to be integral, and even zealous members of the imperial system, it was the policy of conciliation, following that of military conquest, which achieved the desired results. Certain laws and restrictions of the imperial government were imposed—so much annual tribute, so many legions to our {?} military levies, and obedience to all such laws of the Central Government as may be issued for your {?} control. But within these lines, and with these points conceded, the empire strove in all minor and domestic matters to conform, in so far as might be possible, to the former habits, customs, and laws of the people absorbed, and the independent governments superseded. Even their peculiarities of morals, manners, and religious views were studied and respected, when not conflicting with the necessities of the empire; their leading men were justly treated, and no efforts were spared to make the new order of things sit lightly at first, and even pleasantly in a few years, on the necks of the subjugated provinces. Generosity is the true policy, both of nations and individuals. 'There is that maketh himself rich, yet hath nothing; there is that maketh himself poor, yet hath great riches.' While my people are held as conquered subjects, they must be to you a continued source of expense and danger—a country penned {pinned} together with bayonets. Let the past be expunged, if you please; we have nothing to blush for in it, and nothing to regret but failure. The necessities of the Northern treasury and public debt," Mr. Davis thought, "would, before long, compel us to do justice to this section."

Mr. Davis then spoke of the immense improvements in the art and practice of war which the recent struggle had developed; this in connection with the progress of work on the Rip Raps; {†} some iron- clads he had seen in the roadstead, and the fifteen-inch Rodman guns {X} which now stand *en barbette* on each bastion of the fort.

England's naval supremacy he considered lost by the invention of {(}iron-clads, {)} these converting the conditions of maritime warfare from a question of dexterity and *personnel* into one of machinery, and in machinery the Americans could have no superiors, while in all other qualities they were at least the equals of the British. The science of naval gunnery had also been revolutionized, the new

*† old work & slow progress. adopted before the war,— had much done to introduce it. (not so*

principle being to concentrate into a single crushing shot the former scattered forces of a broadside. The problem of the iron-clad was to attain the maximum of offensive power while exposing the least possible and most strongly armored objective points to the projectiles of the enemy; and in such plans of our iron-clads as he had lately seen, these desiderata seemed to have been very nearly attained. For crossing the ocean, however, and for cruising on peaceful stations, our vessels lay too low in the water, either for safety from storms, or the comfort and health of the crews and officers. If our present vessels had in them vast wells, which, when empty, would cause the hulls to float eight or ten feet above the water, and which, on being filled when going into action, would reduce them to their present level, he thought no grander instruments of belligerency could be imagined. Wooden bottoms, with armored sides and {(}armored turrets,{)} he could *not me)* not but think would prove the best. The enormous weight superimposed, coupled with the rollings of the sea, must soon chafe and wear away the rivets and plates of an iron bottom, no matter how carefully secured; while wooden hulls sat more easily on the water, and both avoided chafing and obtained greater speed by their capacity of yielding a little. Even the sea in its laws, concluded Mr. Davis with a smile, teaches the policy of conciliation—of concession; vessels making headway as their lines conform to the resistance {?} of the ocean, and have some power of yielding to the pressure of the billows. To attain the greatest speed, we should take for model the swiftest fish, and conform to that as much as circumstances would permit; and in this connection he referred approvingly to the cigar-shaped vessels of Mr. Winans, of Baltimore.*

In regard to the improvements in ordnance, he spoke at great length, displaying not merely a very observant knowledge of all the changes in modern artillery and projectiles, but also of the science of metallurgy as applied to the production of ordnance. He discussed the atomic theory, or relationship of particles, and the effects on iron fibre of different temperatures and treatments, as by hammering, rolling, and the various methods of cooling; detailing with a minuteness I could not hope to follow, numerous experiments in the construction and effect of ordnance while he was Secretary of War. The Swedish and Russian iron had been reputed best, but he thought experiment would prove *virginia* that the iron of {(}the Shenandoah Valley{)} and of Eastern Tennessee, when properly treated, would be at least as good, if not *purpose* superior, for this {|}climate.{X} In the Tredegar Iron-Works, an enormous amount of work had been done, and many improvements in puddling and casting introduced; but the continued and ever-increasing necessities of the war, as the blockade became more effective, made rapidity the one thing needful, and much of the work, more especially of late, had been rough and defective. {*no! best of iron guns.*}

---

*Ross Winans was a Confederate sympathizer who had developed a modern, cigar-shaped hull.

Rifled guns he had been at first inclined to favor, and for certain classes of service at long range, they must always remain the best. For tearing and destroying forts of masonry, the results at Pulaski and Sumter had demonstrated their value; but as earthworks would here- *strange misconception of my* after be employed wherever possible, their superiority in this respect *opinions The facts not so.* was of less importance. For naval engagements, at long range, they would also be better; but with iron-clad ships, all future engagements must be within a few hundred yards, and then the slow, crushing shot of the heavy smooth bore was the thing needed. For chasing a block-ade-runner or crippling a flying ship, the rifled gun; but for crushing in the sides or turret of an armored vessel, the heavy thirteen or fif-teen-inch shot from a smooth bore, propelled by slow-burning pow-der, would be most efficacious. Quick-burning powder strained the gun too much by its shock, hurled out the projectile before the powder be-hind it had been half developed, and also wasted not less than a third of the charge before the process of combustion had time to take place. He spoke of Captain Dahlgren* and his experiments in ordnance while he (Mr. Davis) had been Secretary of War, remarking that, rightly or wrongly, the Captain had been accused of appropriating as his own, *new to me* with very trivial alterations, if any, discoveries which were submitted to him for examination and report as chief of ordnance in the navy yard. Of the Rodman† he spoke approvingly, regarding its chilling *no meaning* process as the true one; but for perfection of elaborate workmanship and detail no guns he had ever seen were superior to some of those received through the blockade from England. It was a mistake, how-ever, to be too minute in war. War was a rough business, and rough tools would carry it through if there were only plenty of them, and in the hands of anything like a sufficiency of proper men.

From this time, the prisoner received books and newspapers freely, chiefly reading of newspapers, the *New York Herald,* and of books, *got such books as were in* histories—Mr. Bancroft‡ appearing his favorite American author. I *the Post Library One paper* recommended him to be very moderate at first in his open-air exer- *sent on some days no choice* cise, gauging the amount of exercise to his strength; and from this time *allowed* forward Mr. Davis went out every day for an hour's exercise, the weather and his health permitting.

---

*John A. Dahlgren, Union ordnance officer and later admiral.

†Brigadier General Thomas J. Rodman, Union ordnance officer, had in-vented a rifled artillery piece made of cast iron with a reinforced wrought-iron breech.

‡George Bancroft, American historian and Secretary of the Navy (1845-1846).

# •CHAPTER 11•

*Mr. Lincoln's Assassination.—Ex-President Pierce.—Torture of being Constantly Watched.—Mr. Davis on the Members of his Cabinet and the Opponents of his Administration.—Touching Tribute to the Memory of "Stonewall" Jackson.*

Sunday, *July 11th.*—Was sent for by Mr. Davis, and called in company with Captain R. O. Bickley, Officer of the Day.

Found prisoner very desponding, the failure of his sight troubling him, and his nights almost without sleep. His present treatment was killing him by inches, and he wished shorter work could be made of his torment. He had hoped long since for a trial, which should be public, and therefore with some semblance of fairness; but hope deferred was making his heart sick. The odious, malignant and absurd insinuation that he was connected in some manner with the great crime and folly of Mr. Lincoln's assassination, was his chief personal motive for so earnestly desiring an early opportunity of vindication. But apart from this, as he was evidently made the representative in whose person the action of the seceding States was to be argued and decided, he yet more strongly desired for this reason to be heard in behalf of the *ever* defeated, but to him {(}still{)} sacred cause. The defeat he accepted, as a man has to accept all necessities of accomplished fact; but to vindicate the theory and justice of his cause, showing by the authority of the Constitution and the Fathers of the Country, that his people had only asserted a right—had committed no crime; this was the last remaining labor which life could impose on him as a public duty. Mr. Davis then spoke of Ex-President Franklin Pierce in terms *of N.[ew] E.[ngland]* of warm admiration, as the public man who had studied constitutional law, and the relation of the States to highest profit, remarking, that if he were given any choice of counsel, Mr. Pierce would be one of those whose advice he would think most reliable. He also spoke of Mr. Charles Eames, of Washington, as a walking encyclopædia of constitutional law, very accurate and ready in his reference to precedents; adding that he had seen a report in the *Herald* that Messrs. Reverdy Johnson, of Maryland, and Charles O'Conor, of New York, had professed their readiness to assume his defence, when approached by some of his friends for that purpose, for which he felt grateful, both personally and for his people. His own fate was of no importance in this matter, save to the Government, on which history would devolve the responsibility for his treatment. Martyrdom, while {for} representing the deliberate action of his people, would be immortality; but for the sake of justice, not merely to his own people, but to the whole American people, whose future liberties were now at stake in his person, a fair and public trial was now the necessity of the situation.

"My people," he added, "attempted what your people denounced as a revolution. My people failed; but your people have suffered a revolution which must prove disastrous to their liberties unless promptly remedied by legal decision, in their efforts to resist the revolution which they charged my people with contemplating. State sovereignty, the corner-stone of the Constitution, has become a name. There is no longer power, or will, in any State, or number of States, that would dare refuse compliance with any tinkle of Mr. Seward's bell."*

Mr. Davis complained this sleeplessness was aggravated by the lamp kept burning in his room all night, so that he could be seen at all moments by the guard in the outer cell. If he happened to doze one feverish moment, the noise of relieving guard in the next room aroused him, and the lamp poured its full glare into his aching and throbbing eyes. There must be a change in this, or he would go crazy, or blind, or both.

"Doctor," he said, "had you ever the consciousness of being watched? Of having an eye fixed on you every moment, intently scrutinizing your most minute actions, and the variations of your countenance and posture? The consciousness that the Omniscient Eye rests upon us, in every situation, is the most consoling and beautiful belief of religion. But to have a human eye riveted on you in every moment of waking or sleeping, sitting, walking, or lying down, is a refinement of torture on anything the Camanches† or Spanish Inquisition ever dreamed. They, in their ignorance of cruel art, only struck at the body; and the nerves have a very limited capacity of pain. This is a maddening, incessant torture of the mind, increasing with every moment it is endured, and shaking the reason by its incessant recurrence of miserable pain. Letting a single drop of water fall on the head every sixty seconds does not hurt at first, but its victim dies of raving agony, it is alleged, if the infliction be continued. The torture of being incessantly watched is, to the mind, what the water-dropping is to the body, but more afflictive, as the mind is more susceptible of pain. The Eye of Omniscience looks upon us with tenderness and compassion; even if conscious of guilt, we have the comfort of knowing that Eye sees also our repentance. But the human eye forever fixed upon you is the eye of a spy, or enemy, gloating in the pain and humiliation which itself creates. I have {(} lived too long in the woods to be frightened by X

---

*William H. Seward, New York politician and secretary of state under Presidents Lincoln and Johnson.

†Comanche Indian tribe.

an owl {)?} and have seen death too often to dread any form of pain. But I confess, Doctor, this torture of being watched begins to prey on *mind—memory—thought* my {(} reason. {)} The lamp burning in my room all night would seem a torment devised by some one who had intimate knowledge of my habits, my custom having been through life never to sleep except in total darkness."

This conversation, so far as related to its medical aspect, I deemed it my duty to communicate that afternoon to Major-General Miles, who could not remove the lamp altogether, but directed that it should be screened at night, so that no direct and glaring beams should be thrown into the prisoner's eyes.

Soon after this interview, I received a third letter from Mrs. Davis, as follows:

SAVANNAH, GA.,
July 2, 1865.

DR. J. J. CRAVEN:

MY DEAR SIR,—I have written to you three times, and no answer has been returned; but I am not capable of the "stlli [sic] yet brave despair," which I know is required in my hopeless position. Thanks to God, that he has raised you up a "present help" in my husband's time of trouble, are daily rendered.

Am I intrusive in offering gratitude and earnest prayers for your welfare and that of your household, and for your manly disregard of everything but the suffering man before you? I know you have been kind, for the only concordance between any of the numberless harrowing statements which daily agonize me, is that you are always represented as kind to him—as ministering to his necessity. The last account tells me that your wife and little daughter are also kind enough to attend to his wants. With my gratitude and joy that even in such a dungeon, separated from all his earthly ties he is not alone, comes the sad memory that I can do nothing but write to say how I love them for their goodness; how I long to see their faces before my eyes are closed in death! I am not alone in offering to them loving thanks—our whole people join me in offering acknowledgments to them and to you. Many little children, besides my own poor little ones, have asked me if I had a likeness of your family, that they might form an idea of those whose kindness has become to them household words. Still no word of comforting response comes to me from you. I will not annoy you by importunities; but pray that we may meet at some future day, when such painful circumstances as now surround me may have been swept away by God's christianizing grace.

When "martial faith and courtesy" may again dictate the action of those who now hold my suffering husband "a prisoner of war," but treat him like a felon, a heart full of gratitude, overflowing in earnest, constant prayers for you, and for your dear wife, and little Annie, is all I have to offer; and these are ever present to

Yours most gratefully,
VARINA DAVIS.

*July 15th.*—Called on Mr. Davis, accompanied by Captain Grill,* 3d Pennsylvania Artillery, Officer of the Day. Found him extremely weak, and growing more alarmed about his sight, which was failing rapidly. The phenomenon had occurred to him of seeing all objects double, due chiefly to his nervous debility and the over-taxation of constant reading. Prescribed stimulants internally—weak brandy and water with his meals to aid digestion—and a stimulating wash.

Some remarks he had seen in one of the New York papers led Mr. Davis to speak of the difficulties which had surrounded his administration.

His Cabinet had been selected during the formation of the Provisional Government at Montgomery, when there were but seven States | *Made* in the Confederacy from which to select or accept Secretaries, and when all things were in dire confusion—even those of farthest sight in public affairs with but little prevision of what lay before them. Georgia, | *no* as the largest State represented in the Provisional Congress, claimed the portfolio of State and recommended Mr. Toombs†—a man of great natural force and capacity, but a destroyer, not a builder up; a man of restless nature, a born Jacobin, though with honest intentions. Alabama, as the second State, claimed the portfolio of War, and nominated Pope Walker‡ for the position—a gentleman of excellent intentions, but wholly without the requisite experience or capacities for so vast a trust. South Carolina placed Mr. Memminger§ in the Treasury, and while he respected the man, the utter failure of Confederate finance was the failure of the cause. Had Mr. Memminger | *such* acted promptly on the proposition of depositing cotton in Europe and holding it there for two years as a basis for their currency, their circulating medium might have maintained itself at par to the closing day of the struggle; and that in itself would have insured victory. Lou- | *statements* isiana sent Benjamin,★ the ablest and most faithful member of his advisory council; a man who realized that industry is the mistress of success, and who had no personal aspirations, no wishes that were not subordinate to the prosperity of the cause. In the early part of the war, Benjamin furnished a parallel to Mr. Seward, both believing and | *The* avowing that the impending crisis would not last longer than sixty or ninety days, though Benjamin relaxed no labor or preparation on that account. Texas had the Postal Department in the person of Mr. Rea- | *grain*

---

*Louis A. Grill.
†Robert A. Toombs.
‡Leroy Pope Walker.
§Christopher G. Memminger.
★Judah P. Benjamin.

*of truth* | gan,* who was a plain, strong man, of good common sense and a good heart, faithful to the cause with zealous fidelity, and faithful to the last, though endowed with no peculiar administrative abilities, and one of those who had not labored to precipitate secession, though accepting it heartily as a political necessity when it came. The Navy Department went to Florida, and was filled by Mr. Mallory,† who had large experience in the Naval Committee of the United States Senate. It was complained that there had been remissness in this department, no Confederate war vessel having been commenced until eight or nine months after the act of secession. In these complaints there was doubtless some truth; but after an event happened, prophesying was cheap. No one at that day could have foreseen the extent or prolongation of the struggle; and the belief was common, if not natural, that the necessities of Europe would compel foreign nations to raise the blockade, and finally bring the naval resources of England and France to the aid of his people.

Being interested by what Mr. Davis said of the failure of the Confederate currency as the failure of the cause, and of some scheme by which it might have been prevented, I expressed my curiosity and ventured to request some explanation, as there appeared to me no manner in which Confederate paper could have been sustained at par.

Mr. Davis replied that one rule of his life was, never to express regret for the inevitable: to let the dead bury its dead in regard to all political hopes that were not realized. Fire is not quenched with tow, nor the past to be remedied by lamentations. It would, however, have been possible, in his judgment, to have kept the currency of his people good for gold, or very nearly so, during the entire struggle; and had this been done, the contrast, if nothing else, would have reduced United States securities to zero, and so terminated the contest. The plan urged upon Mr. Memminger was as follows—a plan Mr. Davis privately approved, but had not time to study and take the responsibility of directing, until too late:—

At the time of secession there were not less than three million bales of cotton in the South—plantation bales, of 400 pounds weight each. These the Secretary of the Treasury recommended to buy from the planters, who were then willing, and even eager, to sell to the government, at ten cents per pound of Confederate currency. These three million bales were to be rushed off to Europe before the blockade was of any efficiency, and there held for one or two years, until the price *perverted* | reached not less than 70 or 80 cents per pound—and we all know it reached much higher during the war. This would have given a cash basis in Europe of not less than a thousand million dollars in gold, and *and* | all securities drawn against this balance in bank would maintain par value. Such a sum would have more than sufficed all the needs of the

*John H. Reagan.
†Stephen R. Mallory.

Confederacy during the war; would have sufficed, with economic management, for a war of twice the actual duration; and this evidence of Southern prosperity and stability could not but have acted powerfully on the minds, the securities and the avarice of the New England rulers of the North. He was far from reproaching Mr. Memminger. The situation was new. No one could have forseen the course of events. *hidden* When too late the wisdom of the proposed measure was realized, but *by a* the inevitable "too late" was interposed. The blockade had become too stringent, for one reason, and the planters had lost their pristine confidence in Confederate currency. When we might have put silver in *bushel of fiction* the purse, we did not put it there. When we had only silver on the tongue, our promises were forced to become excessive.

I asked how Mr. Memminger had obtained prominence in so aristocratic a State as South Carolina, the report being that he was a foundling born with little claim to either wealth or name. Mr. Davis said he knew nothing of the matter, and immediately turned away the conversation, appearing displeased.

When Mr. Benjamin was made Secretary of War, Mr. Davis continued—Mr. Walker having proved a failure—Congress was pleased to blame him for the successes of General Burnside at Roanoke Island, and so forth; events which no human activity or foresight, with the forces at his command, could have averted. Congress in some respect was slow to provide against reverses, but never lacking in promptness to find a scapegoat. From the first, there was a strong party in the South—or rather in the Southern Congress and political life—arrayed against his administration. They never deemed it wise to attack him personally or directly, for his people were devotedly and nobly faithful to the representative of their selection; but the plan was to assail any man or measure in whom or which Mr. Davis was supposed—often erroneously—to take special interest. He himself was much to blame for this, perhaps—his fidelity to friendship and the natural combativeness of his nature, prompting him to assume as personal to himself, any assaults directed against men or measures for whose appointment or origination he was in any degree responsible. This was a fault of his temperament, but each man must accept himself as he stands, and that man does well who makes out of himself the best possible.

Toombs, even when in the Cabinet, had been impracticable and *not so, When in the Cabi-* restless. Out of it he became an active malcontent, and was powerfully *net he gave no cause for* supported in every perverse and pernicious suggestion by Governor *distrust or complaint.* Brown, of Georgia.* Vice-President Stephens had lent the government no assistance, continually holding himself aloof from Richmond—perhaps on account of ill health; but certainly his health must have been very wretched indeed, if poorer than that of Mr. Davis, during many of his most trying and laborious months. Be the cause what

---

*Joseph E. Brown and Alexander H. Stephens, also of Georgia, were ardent states' righters who, at times, openly defied the Davis administration.

it might, however, the absence, if not apathy, of Mr. Stephens, had been an element of weakness, and led him to be regarded by the malcontents as a friend and pillar of their cause. In South Carolina, there was the Rhett* faction; never at home save when in the attitude of contradiction; men whose lives were expended in the negative, and who often recalled to his mind the contradictory gentleman described by Sydney Smith, who, when he had no one else to quarrel with, threw up his window at night for the purpose of contradicting the watchman who was shouting, "Two o'clock—all well." The {(} only open assailant {)} he had in Congress was Senator Foote,† of his own State—a man of no account or credit; an inveterate place-hunter and mere politician, who appeared laboring under a constitutional inability either to see anything correctly, or to report correctly what he had seen.

*not even as fair as that*

*not so but of Tenn*

Of Stonewall Jackson, Mr. Davis spoke with the utmost tenderness, and some touch of reverential feeling, bearing witness to his earnest and pathetic piety, his singleness of aim, his immense energy as an executive officer, and the loyalty of his nature, making obedience the first of all duties. {(} "He rose every morning at three," said Mr. Davis; "performed his devotions for half an hour, {)} and then went booming along at the head of his command, which came to be called 'Jackson's foot cavalry,' from the velocity of their movements. He had the faculty, or rather gift, of exciting and holding the love and confidence of his men to an unbounded degree, even though the character of his campaigning imposed on them more hardships than on any other troops in the service. Good soldiers care not for their individual sacrifices when adequate results can be shown; and these General Jackson never lacked. Hard fighting, hard marching, hard fare, the strictest discipline—all these men will bear, if visibly approaching the goal of their hopes. They want to get done with the war, back to their homes and families; and their instinct soon teaches them which commander is pursuing the right means to accomplish these results. Jackson was a singularly ungainly man on horseback, and had many peculiarities of temper, amounting to violent idiosyncrasies; but everything in his nature, though here and there uncouth, was noble. Even in the heat of action, and when most exposed, {(} he might be seen throwing up his hands in prayer. {)?} For glory he lived long enough," continued Mr. Davis with much emotion; "and if this result had to come, it was the Divine mercy that removed him. He fell like the eagle,

*not mine*

---

*Senator Robert B. Rhett, editor of the *Charleston Mercury* and a fire-eater, opposed the Davis administration's policies.

†Henry S. Foote was a longtime political enemy of Davis. He was suspected of treasonous activities against the Confederate government during the war. Davis's marginal comment was incorrect. Foote had been a United States senator from Mississippi and governor of that state before moving to California and then to Tennessee.

{(}his own feather{)?} on the shaft that was dripping with his life-blood. In his death the Confederacy lost an eye and arm, our only consolation being that the final summons could have reached no soldier more prepared to accept it joyfully. Jackson was not of a sanguine turn, always privately anticipating the worst, that the better might be more welcome."*

*If the writer ever conversed with me of Genl Jackson he must have heard quite the opposite of the above. It is most charitable to suppose that in this as in many other instances he has attributed to me the opinion of some one else, not knowing what I thought, and only careful to fill his book according to programme.*

---

*Halpine was a great admirer of Stonewall Jackson; Davis was not. Davis's dislike of Jackson stemmed from a misunderstanding in early 1862 between the two men. As with many other Davis clashes, personalities and vanity soon became involved with military issues. In January 1862 Gen. Jackson forwarded a petition by eleven officers who wished to abandon their winter quarters at Romney, Virginia. Although their commander, Gen. William W. Loring, approved their petition, Jackson, the overall commander, had rejected it, but sent it on to the War Department. After receiving the request along with other information, Secretary of War Judah P. Benjamin ordered Jackson to remove his headquarters from Romney to Winchester. Jackson, snubbed by this order, requested either that he be transferred back to the teaching faculty at the Virginia Military Institute or that he be permitted to resign from Confederate service. Neither was accepted, and Jackson, after obtaining a promise that he would never be overruled again, remained.

Although Davis was behind Benjamin's order, this fact was not known until much later. Even before the War Department had received the petition, Davis already had decided to order Jackson to move his headquarters to Winchester, which the president felt was less vulnerable to enemy forays than Romney. Davis, however, permitted Benjamin to shoulder the blame. Such internal evidence lends further credence to the authenticity of the marginalia. Only Davis, Benjamin, and a few other very close advisers knew Davis's true opinion of the pious captain.

Halpine, on the other hand, so admired Jackson that he visited the Confederate general's grave in Lexington in June 1864. While there Halpine "picked up a few blades of grass and sent them to his wife to be put in a locket. 'They are worth more than pure gold,' he told her." (Quoted in William Hanchett, "Reconstruction and the Rehabilitation of Jefferson Davis: Charles G. Halpine's *Prison Life*," *Journal of American History* 56 [September 1969]: 288.)

# •CHAPTER 12•

*Mr. Davis seriously Ill.—Restrictions on Correspondence with his Wife.— Clement C. Clay.—A Rampart Interview.—Religious Phase of Mr. Davis's Character.*

July *20th.*—Called on Mr. Davis, Captain Korte, 3d Pennsylvania Artillery, being Officer of the Day, and, of course, my companion. Was requested to call by Major-General Miles, who had received report that prisoner was seriously ill.

Found Mr. Davis in a very critical state; his nervous debility extreme; his mind more despondent than ever heretofore; his appetite gone; complexion livid, and pulse denoting deep prostration of all the physical energies. Was much alarmed, and realized with painful anxiety the responsibilities of my position. If he were to die in prison, and without trial, subject to such severities as had been inflicted on his attenuated frame, the world would form unjust conclusions, but conclusions with enough color to pass them into history. It seemed to me, let me frankly confess, due to the honor of America, and the future glory of our struggle for national existence, that this result should not happen.

Mr. Davis asked me could nothing be done to better his condition, or secure him the justice of a trial before death. The effort of his people to establish a country had failed, and they had no country now but America. It was {(}for the honor of America, not less than for his own, and {)?} for justice to his cause, that he pleaded.

Answered Mr. Davis that no effort of care or such skill as I possessed should be wanting for his benefit. Then commenced conversation on various topics, seeking to divert his mind from the afflictions preying on it.

Talking of the Confederate flag and the various flags under which the regiments of each State fought, I mentioned having once seen a curious practical realization of the flag of South Carolina—the palmetto-tree and rattlesnake.

The day after the success of Admiral Du Pont at Port Royal, and the landing of Sherman's expedition on Hilton Head, I had ridden out in company with General Horatio G. Wright to an abandoned cavalry camp of the expelled troops. There, twisted around the trunk of a palmetto-tree, and held in his place round it by ligatures of reeds, was a dead rattlesnake, the largest I had ever seen, some eight feet long, and probably nearly a hundred pounds weight. It had undoubtedly been

placed there in sport by some of the cavalry as an emblem of the flag
of their State.

"It was a good omen for you," said Mr. Davis, with a faint smile,
and then commenced talking of the snakes of the Southern coast. He
mentioned as curious that the deer, usually the most timid of animals,
or so popularly regarded, was the deadliest enemy of the rattlesnake.
Wherever and whenever finding one in the woods near the coast, or
on the grassy sand-heaps which the snake so loved, the deer commenced assailing it acrimoniously with its sharp and powerful though
dainty fore-hoofs. These it would job or dig into the rattlesnake's head,
half stunning it the first blow. Then the deer would graze a few moments—with a wary eye on the snake, however, repeating its stabs with
its sharp hoofs until its enemy expired. The negroes accounted for the    *X ?*
immunity of the deer in these encounters by the fact that its delicate
forelegs, being nearly all skin and bone, were the only parts exposed
within reach of the rattlesnake, and had too little blood or flesh in them
to convey the virus. It was not true that this snake could project himself the full length of his coil. He could only coil up half his length and
throw that forward. They are slow and of little danger to men or dogs,
unless suddenly trodden upon. No instance of their attacking a man,
unless attacked, was on record along the Southern coast. They like the
cool sea-breezes, and feed on rabbits and squirrels, which they have
great dexterity in catching. Mr. Davis had never heard of any specific
cure for their bite save when the part could be instantly amputated
before the poison spread. Powerful doses of whiskey were a remedy
in some cases—perhaps on the principle of the more powerful poison
expelling the weaker. He had known a case, when serving on the frontier, in which this remedy had proved worse than the disease. A very
worthy sergeant of the 1st Dragoons had been formerly of intemper-    *not mine*
ate habits, but had reformed and been perfectly abstemious for several
years. Some kind of a snake bit him—probably one whose bite was
not mortal, though painful—and heavy doses of whiskey were at once
prescribed. This re-aroused the slumbering devil, and less than six
months after the sergeant, degraded to the ranks, died of *mania a potu*
in the guard-house. Drunkenness is the great vice of soldiers, and
worked much misery with his people. The social glass, carried to excess, becomes a pair of spectacles through which men gaze into the
bottomless pit. Mr. Davis then referred jocosely {(}to the old form    *Had the writer known how*
of commissary requisitions for whiskey when he was in the army: "So    *silly his invention is he*
many barrels of whiskey to cure snake-bites."{)} This was because    *would not have attributed*
whiskey was forbidden in army stores, unless to be used for medicinal    *it to one who could not be*
purposes. He believed ten thousand soldiers had "seen snakes," as the    *supposed so ignorant of the*
phrase ran, through this agency, for the one who had been cured of a    *"old Army" & its possibili-*
snake-bite.    *ties.*

The mocassin-snake, [sic] which is also very poisonous—though not
so deadly on the southern coast-line as in the interior—seldom grows
to be over three feet in length, and is thicker and slower of motion
than the rattle-snake. The chicken or house-snake often grows to great

size, fully as large as the rattle-snake, but is not dangerously poisonous, though its fangs create an unpleasant pustule, death occasionally
resulting when they happen to pierce a vein. They are swift, feed on
birds and poultry of all kinds, and have greater power of convolution
and contortion than any other snakes, this being necessary to enable
them to climb trees in pursuit of their prey with the requisite quick-
ness. Children often attacked these snakes when finding them curled
up in the crevices of barns or abandoned houses, rarely failing to kill
them. The mocassin-snake [sic] is rather more omnivorous than the
others, feeding upon frogs, toads, birds, beetles, rabbits, or whatever
it can catch.

Mr. Davis said when he had last been out on the ramparts he had
met Mr. C. C. Clay, similarly walking under guard. Clay was looking
wretchedly, and seeing him made Mr. Davis realize more acutely his
own humiliating position. Men at sea in a ship never realize how for-
lorn and frail the vessel is they are on board, until their counterpart in
some closely passing vessel is brought under notice. Absorbed in exercise and the emotions of the scene, he had previously failed to realize his situation, with an officer at his side as custodian, and four
bayonets pacing behind him to secure that he should make no effort
to escape. The moment Mr. Clay passed, his own situation stood revealed; and nothing but his strong conviction that to remain in his cell
would be equivalent to suicide, could induce him to parade again in
the same manner. As he passed Mr. Clay, they exchanged a few words
*not correct* in French, nothing more than the compliments of the day and an inquiry for each other's health; but it seemed this had alarmed the officer, who did not understand the language, Mr. Clay not being
permitted to pass him again, but being marched off to another part of
the ramparts. Clay was naturally delicate, of an atrabilious type, and
his appearance denoted that he must be suffering severely.

Replied that I had been attending Mr. Clay, and saw nothing in his
state to occasion alarm. He had a tendency to asthma, but that was a
long-lived disease. Mr. Davis inquired how Clay was fed. Replied that
at first he had received soldiers' rations, but latterly, his condition demanding it, had been fed from the hospital. Mr. Davis expressed much
sympathy for his fellow-sufferer, begging me to do whatever I profes-
sionally could for his relief, and to hold up his hands. Let me here
remark that, despite a certain exterior cynicism of manner, no patient
has ever crossed my path, who, suffering so much himself, appeared
to feel so warmly and tenderly for others. Sickness, as a general rule,
is sadly selfish; its own pains and infirmities occupying too much of
its thoughts. With Mr. Davis, however, the rule did not work or rather
he was an exception calling attention to its general truth.

Prisoner complained bitterly of the restrictions imposed by General
Miles on his correspondence with his wife; certain subjects, and those
perhaps of most interest, being forbidden to both: The convicts in State
prisons were allowed this liberty unimpeded, or only subject to the
supervision of the Chaplain, whose scrutiny had a religious and kindly

character—that of a Father Confessor. His letters, on the contrary, had to be sent open to General Miles, and from him, he understood, similarly open to the Attorney-General.* What unbosoming of confidence—mutual griefs, mutual hopes, the interchange of tenderest sympathies—was possible, or would be delicate under such a system! He pictured idle young staff-officers here, or yet more pitiful clerks in the Law Department at Washington, grinning over any confession of pain, or terms of endearment, he might be tempted to use; and this thought embittered the pleasure such correspondence might otherwise have conferred. The relationship of husband and wife was the inner vestibule of the temple—the holy of holies—in poor human life; and who could expose its secrets, or lay his heart bare on his sleeve, for such daws to peck at? Even criminals condemned to death for heinous crimes, were allowed not only free correspondence with their wives, but interviews at which no jailor stood within earshot. What possible public danger could there be from allowing such letters to pass without scrutiny? Time will set all these petty tyrannies in their true light. He that first pleadeth his own cause seems justified; but his neighbor cometh and searcheth him. If the privilege were ever abused—if anything he wrote to his wife were published to the detriment of the government, or tending to disturb the peace, what easier than to say, "This privilege has been abused, and must cease?"

*July 21st.*—Visited prisoner with Captain Evans, 3d Pennsylvania Artillery, Officer of the Day. Mr. Davis better, but still in bed; the Bible and Prayer-Book his usual companions. Complained that his irritation of sight made reading painful; but there was consolation for greater sacrifice in what he read.

There was no affectation of devoutness or asceticism in my patient; but every opportunity I had of seeing him, convinced me more deeply of his sincere religious convictions. He was fond of referring to passages of Scripture, comparing text with text; dwelling on the divine beauty of the imagery, and the wonderful adaptation of the whole to every conceivable phase and stage of human life. Nothing that any man's individual experience, however strange, could bring home to him, but had been previously foretold and described, with its proper lesson or promise of hope, in the sacred volume. It was the only absolute wisdom, reaching all varieties of existence, because comprehending the whole; and, besides its inspired universal knowledge, all the learning of humanity was but foolishness. The Psalms were his favorite portion of the Word, and had always been. Evidence of their divine origin was inherent in their text. Only an intelligence that held the life-threads of the entire human family could have thus pealed forth in a single cry every wish, joy, fear, exultation, hope, passion, and sorrow of the human heart. There were moments, while speaking on religious subjects, in which Mr. Davis impressed me more than any

---

*James Speed.

professor of Christianity I had ever heard. There was a vital earnestness in his discourse; a clear, almost passionate grasp in his faith; and
the thought would frequently recur, that a belief capable of consoling
such sorrows as his, possessed and thereby evidenced, a reality—a
substance—which no sophistry of the infidel could discredit.

To this phase of the prisoner's character I have heretofore rather
avoided calling attention for several reasons, prominent of which,
though an unworthy one, was this: My knowledge that many, if not a
majority of my readers, would approach the character of Mr. Davis
with a preconception of dislike and distrust, and a consequent fear that
an earlier forcing on their attention of this phase of his character, before their opinion had been modified by such glimpses as are herein
given, might only challenge a base and false imputation of hypocrisy
against one than whom, in my judgment, no more devout exemplar
of Christian faith, and its value as a consolation, now lives, whatever
may have been his political crimes or errors.

And here, dropping the note-book a moment, let me say a few words
in my own character—a reflection continually brought to my notice
by each day's further acquaintance with Mr. Davis:

Is it not true that the chief mistakes and prejudices of public opinion come from our not understanding—not seeking to understand—
the true motives and characters of the men to whom we are opposed?
Blind and hot-headed partisanship, speaking in the haste of the press
and the heat of the rostrum, accepts without evidence whatever epithet of infamy can be applied to the object of its dislike; no stories of
guilt or folly that can degrade or render hateful the foeman we stand
arrayed against, can be too monstrous to find believers, at least while
the struggle lasts. But in a few years, as we recede from the convulsed
and frenzied period of the strife, we grow to be ashamed of the malignant delusions which have so grossly cheated our senses; and before
history takes up the pen to record her final judgment, the world will
be willing to concede that the man was not utterly bad—had, in fact,
great redeeming virtues—who was our most prominent foe; and that
no movement so vast, and eliciting such intense devotion on the part
of its partisans as the late Southern rebellion, could have grown up
into its gigantic proportions without containing many elements of truth
and good, which it may profit future ages to study attentively, though
the means taken for the assertion of its principles were false, criminal,
and only fraught with disaster.

To anticipate a little what must be the inevitable course of events,
to give the public such opportunity as was given the writer of judging
Jefferson Davis from a clearer standpoint, and to save the present generation of the North from the fatal error of continuing to regard and
treat as a common criminal the chief actor opposed to us in a struggle
the most gigantic the world has ever seen, and with which history will
ring for centuries to come—if these objects can be attained, the author
will not have toiled in vain. All the crimes that an evil ingenuity has
yet been able to impute to this man, are as new-fallen snow when

brought in contrast with the fabrications of the English and European press in regard to murderous and incestuous proclivities of the first Napoleon during the great wars in which that Captain involved the elder continent. But such is not now the judgment of him, either in England or in the world's history—nor will history consent to regard Mr. Davis in the odious, monstrous, or contemptible light which has been, for the last five years, the only one in which the necessities and passions of our recent struggle would permit him to be presented to our gaze.

# •CHAPTER 13•

*Southern Migration to Mexico.—Mr. Calhoun's Memory vindicated from one Charge.—Tribute to Albert Sidney Johnston.—Failure of Southern Iron-clads and Loss of the Mississippi.*

J*uly 24th*.—Called on Mr. Davis, accompanied by Captain Korte, 3d Pennsylvania Artillery, Officer of the Day. Found prisoner still very feeble, but said he could not resist the temptation to crawl out in such beautiful weather, even at the cost of the degrading guards who dogged his steps. Captain Korte absent during greater part of this interview, relieving guard in the casemates of Clay and other prisoners. Some officers of the day **{***not***}** often left me alone with prisoner for this purpose; others remained close to us as we conversed; but as Mr. Davis always spoke in a subdued manner, and my replies were given in the usual confidential tone of a doctor consulting a patient, the presence or absence of the Officer of the Day made little difference.

*used no such language. Never had a harsh feeling towards those who decided to expatriate themselves. On the other hand always sympathized with the brave soldiers of the Confederacy who when they could no longer serve this country shrunk from witnessing its misery and humiliation as the victim of a sectional despotism.*

*†The writer cannot understand a question which rests on state sovereignty and is older than those who sustained it in the late war—miscalled by him a "Rebellion."*

Mr. Davis spoke of the folly and something worse of those Southern leaders who had fled to Mexico. It was an act of cowardice—an evasion of duty only to be excelled by suicide. They had been instrumental in bringing the evils of military subjugation on the people, and should remain to share their burdens. The great masses of the people were rooted to the soil, and could not, and should not, fly. The first duty of the men who had been in command during the struggle was, to remain faithful fellow-sufferers with the rank and file.**{†}\*** By doing so they could yet exercise a moral and intellectual, if not political, weight against the schemers of rapine and oppression now swarming over the Southern country; while by deserting, they abandon helpless ignorance to the sway of powerful craft, and confessed judgment to whatever charges might be brought against them. The scheme of a political settlement in Mexico was preposterous in practice, though tempting to wounded pride. Settlements and colonies were governed, or governed themselves, by laws of material interest, considerations of profit and loss; and no settlers could be imagined less fitted for the requirements of a new colony than a body of embittered politicians, still sore and smarting from a conflict in which they had incurred defeat. Patience, indomitable industry and self-denial were the necessities of

---

\*At times later in his life Davis would be an ex-patriot. Unable himself to formulate an adequate response to reunion, it is not surprising that the Confederate president never condemned others who left the South for different soil.

every new settlement; and these—even were the colonists of a more suitable class—could scarcely be continued in Mexico, where languor, indolence and ease, are constituent portions of the climate.

Remarked to Mr. Davis that I had always regarded the filibustering expeditions of Lopez against Cuba, and Walker in Nicaragua,* as Southern projects for the acquirement of more territory and larger representation in Congress, to balance the increasing free States of the North and West. If his opinions against the feasibility of Southern men colonizing Mexico had been general with his people, how came the Lopez, and more especially the Walker expeditions, to find favor in his section, Walker proposing an American settlement so much nearer the equator? The desire for Cuba could be understood; its enormous slave population, wealth, and command of the Gulf, forming suffi-cient attractions.

Mr. Davis replied there had been a general desire in the South for Cuba, but none of any consequence for Central America. Neither ex-pedition, however, had been supported by any organized party of his people. The Walker foray in Nicaragua had its main origin in a quar-rel between two new New York commercial houses—those of Gov-ernor Morgan† and Cornelius Vanderbilt, as he understood—for the profits of the Transit Company across the Isthmus. The expedition against Cuba was favored by General Quitman, and had so much of direct Southern sanction as might be drawn from the General's rep-resentative position—which was deservedly of the highest—but no more. It was fostered on the statements and promises of Cuban plant-ers anxious for annexation, and promising a liberal cooperation of men and means the moment a landing was effected. These promises went off in smoke, as do all the promises of a tropical and luxurious people for active exertion; and so the matter ended.

In regard to his remarks about settlements in Mexico, it was not his intention—the reverse, in fact—to be understood as suggesting that his people could not, or will not colonize and reclaim the greater part or the whole of that country. His thought merely was, that a settlement of self-exiled politicians and soldiers, acting under the impulse of anger, and with no fixed purposes or habits of industry, and but little capital in money or materials, formed a poor basis for any colonization project of permanent

---

*Narcisco Lopez led a disastrous filibustering expedition against his native Cuba in 1851. Several Americans were among those captured and executed for their participation in Lopez's scheme. William Walker, the greatest American filibusterer, participated in expeditions against lower (Baja) Cali-fornia, Nicaragua, of which he was briefly president, and Honduras, where he was captured and executed in 1860.

†Halpine, who knew a great deal about politics and business in New York City, here probably confused Charles Morgan, who actively engaged in a commercial war with Cornelius Vanderbilt over the Nicaraguan Transit Co., and Edwin D. Morgan, who served as Republican governor of New York (1859-1862).

prosperity. His people needed more territory and would continue to need it, their line of expansion running towards Mexico; but this would have to come by natural processes of growth, perhaps assisted, when time was ripe, by some such political and military movements as added Texas to the country. Timely blossom gives timely fruit, and we can no more quicken the healthy growth of a nation by artificial aid than the growth of a child. If restraints be imposed on natural growth, violence may be useful to cast off such restraints, but beyond this can only serve to retard expansion.

Same afternoon, joined Mr. Davis, who was seated with Major-General Miles on the south front of the ramparts, the prisoner seeming to prefer this aspect of the compass.

General Miles remarked that the fortification known as the Rip Raps had already occupied much time, and must have cost the government vast sums of money.*

Mr. Davis replied, giving full statistics on the subject up to the period he had ceased to be Secretary of War, adding, that many years {(} ago it had approached completion, {?} but had slowly settled down until the second tier of embrasures reached the sea-level, owing to a spreading of the artificial rock-island on which it has been built. *all wrong* As it was so nearly finished, and might be useful in case of a foreign war, he supposed government would now complete its armament and maintain it as a permanent fort; but if the matter were to do over again, a couple of iron-clads would serve all its purposes better, at less than a tenth of its expense.

General Miles observed, interrogatively, that it was reported John C. Calhoun had made much money by speculations, or favoring the speculations of his friends, connected with this work.

In a moment Mr. Davis started to his feet, betraying much indignation by his excited manner and flushed cheek. It was a transfiguration of friendly emotion, the feeble and wasted invalid and prisoner suddenly forgetting his bonds, forgetting his debility, and ablaze with eloquent anger against this injustice to the memory of one whom he loved and reverenced. Mr. Calhoun, he said, lived a whole atmosphere above any sordid or dishonest thought—was of a nature to which even a mean act was impossible. It was said in every Northern *never used the base lie even for illustration.* paper that he (Mr. Davis) had carried with him five millions in gold when quitting Richmond—money pilfered from the treasury of the Confederate States—and there was just as much truth in that as in these imputations against Calhoun. One of the worst signs of the times is the looseness with which imputations of dishonesty are made and accepted against public men in eminent station. They who spit against the wind, spit in their own faces, and such charges come back to soil the men who make them. If an individual has any proof of dishonesty

---

*The Rip Raps (Fort Wool) is in the middle of Hampton Roads and is visible from Fort Monroe.

against a public man, he should bring his charges in due form and have an open trial; but when an entire people, or their great majority, greedily accept and believe any unsupported imputation of corruption against a distinguished statesman or other officer, it argues corruption in their own minds, and that they suspect it in others because conscious it would be their own course if endowed with power.

Mr. Davis then entered upon an explanation, too minute for me to follow, of the manner in which these charges against Mr. Calhoun arose from the malice of some speculators, between whose avarice and the public treasury Mr. Calhoun had interposed his pure and powerful influence. Calhoun was a statesman, a philosopher, in the true sense of that grossly abused term—an enthusiast of perfect liberty in representative and governmental action. Wrong, of course, in his conclusions, the opponents of his theory were free to judge him; but Mr. Davis believed the hands of George Washington not more free from the filthiness of bribes, than were those of the departed statesman who had been thus libelled.* Every public officer who crosses the schemes of rogues must prepare to pay this penalty. There was not a General in { I }either{ I } army of the recent war who was not accused by sutlers and camp-followers of having made fortunes from the exactions which their powers allowed them to impose. While the astronomer dwells in his tower watching the stars, bats may breed and slimy things crawl at will in the foundation-story of his edifice.

*not true, such charge could not be made except in the most ignorant malice. such was my answer.*

*not said by me.*

*not so in the C.S.A.*

*August 4th.*—Visited Mr. Davis with Captain Gusson,† 3d Pennsylvania Artillery, Officer of the Day. Found prisoner improving. Mentioned that I had spent the previous day on the wreck of the frigate *Congress,* sunk by the *Merrimac,*‡ describing minutely, at his request, the state of the vessel, and the process of elevating sunken vessels by building a bulkhead, etc., and the use of powerful pumps. Mr. Davis appeared much interested, saying the *Congress* had fought gallantly, and that it was in consequence of injuries to the prow of the *Merrimac* from her shot, and not owing to the attack of the *Monitor,* that the *Merrimac* had been compelled to retire. These injuries started a fatal leak, which the weight of armor rendered it impossible to cure; and this was the true cause of the vessel's final failure. Mr. Davis also spoke of the continued advances in engineering skill and mechanical

*Did not say so. The affair was exposed in our naval reports and showed in strong contrast, low craft and lofty chivalry.*

---

*This account refers to charges against John C. Calhoun accusing him of profiting from a fortifications contract while secretary of war. These allegations were investigated at the time, and Calhoun had been found innocent of all such allegations by a "grand inquest of the nation" conducted by the House of Representatives.

†The editor has been unable to identify any individual with the surname Gusson as a member of the Third Pennsylvania Artillery (152d Volunteers); see Samuel P. Bates, ed., *History of Pennsylvania Volunteers, 1861-1865,* vol. 4 (Harrisburg: B. Singerly, 1870) 698-771. This individual may be the same as the Capt. Grissin whom Halpine later mentions.

‡8 March 1862.

contrivance. When the *Royal George* capsized, she went to the bottom uninjured, and would have been in perfect order had such means for raising sunken vessels been then known. The British Government had made great exertions, and offered large rewards, he believed, to accomplish this result, but without success; and only such small articles, or piecemeal parts, had been regained as the divers could fasten ropes to, and cause to be hauled up. With the exception of the *Merrimac,* *not true* no armed vessel of the South had enjoyed a fortunate career, and hers was brief. They were either captured, like the *Atlanta,* while trying to run out to sea, or destroyed by our war vessels and gun-boats while still imperfect and unprepared for the combat. The capture of New X Orleans was a great calamity to his cause, but mainly {?} injurious from its sacrifice of the inchoate iron-clads of the Mississippi. With the mouth and headwaters of this vital river in our possession, no energy could have warded off the result beyond a certain time, if the North with its superior resources of manufacture and preponderance of population, should see fit to persist. Pemberton made a splendid defence of Vicksburg. He had been blamed for remaining there, but this was the last hope of saving the Mississippi and keeping open the beef, and other commissary supplies, of the trans-Mississippi department.

Had General Albert Sidney Johnston lived, Mr. Davis was of opinion, our success down the Mississippi would have been fatally checked at Corinth. This officer best realized his ideal of a perfect commander—large in view, discreet in council, silent as to his own plans, observant and penetrative of the enemy's, sudden and impetuous in action, but of a nerve and balance of judgment which no heat of danger or complexity of manœuvre could upset or bewilder. All that Napoleon said of Dessaix and Kleber,* save the slovenly habits of one of them, might be combined and truthfully said of Albert Sidney Johnston. Johnston had been opposed to locating the Confederate Capital *not true* at Richmond, alleging that it would involve fighting on the exterior of our circle, in lieu of the centre: and that as the struggle would finally be for whatever point was the capital, it was ill-advised to go so far north, thus shortening the enemy's line of transportation and supply. Whatever value this criticism may have had in a military point of view, added Mr. Davis, there were political necessities connected with Virginia which left no choice in the matter. It was a bold courting of the issue, clearly planting our standard in front of the enemy's line and across his path. Such reflections are of no use now, concluded Mr. Davis, and the Spaniards tell us when a sorrow is asleep not to waken it.

Talking of the financial future of the South, he believed negro labor requisite for the profitable working of the rice, sugar, and cotton crops. These staples peculiarly demanded the industry of this race. Ger-

---

*General Louis Desaix saved Napoleon's army at the Battle of Marengo (14 June 1800) and General Jean Baptiste Kleber commanded Napoleon's Egyptian army.

mans, or Irishmen, could grow tobacco with profit, and for a few years, perhaps, cultivate the other staples; but the climatic influences would overpower their constitutions, and the rice-fields, in particular, prove deadly to any laborers but the black.

To this I opposed my own experience on the Sea Islands of the Southern coast, where I had cognizance of the sanitary condition of an average of fifteen thousand soldiers, black and white, and of all nationalities, for nearly three years; and the result had been that negroes, to the "manor born," had suffered more than any others, white or black, with the exception of the troops from Maine. The work for all had been of the hardest and heaviest; guard-duty night and day along creeks, lagoons and swamps; incessant toil in the trenches and on the works; the severest portion of these labors having been performed on Morris Island, in the month of July. The Southern negro refugees— men, women, and children, living in villages on Port Royal, St. Helena, Edisto, Ladies, and other islands—suffered more from the fevers of the climate than our black troops from the North, and far more than our white troops, who were the healthiest in the whole armies of the Union, with the exception of those from the inland mountains of Maine, and perhaps New Hampshire.

Mr. Davis thought this very possible, but the mortality of the plantation negroes arose from the absence of restraint, and their inability to guide themselves. It was to the master's interest that they should be kept in health by regular hours, wholesome food, and proper periods of rest. The license of sudden freedom proved too much for their ignorant passions, and became perverted into debauchery. It was a feast or a famine with them, and such violent changes of habit never failed to work ruin. While slaves, they were confined to their quarters after certain hours of the night, and thus saved from malarial exposure; while in their new liberty they doubtless remained abroad until whatever hour they pleased. As to the health of the white troops, the excitement of war was in itself a prophylactic. But let the same men try regular labor in time of peace, and a different health-bill would be returned.

*Note: The Sea Islands have been long resorted to because of this salubrity in Summer. They are not the malarial region spoken of in connection with Rice, sugar & Cotton crops.*

# •CHAPTER 14•

*Mr. Davis on Negro Character.—The Assassination of President Lincoln.—How the Prisoner's Food was Served.—A Solemn and Interesting Statement.*

**A**ugust 14*th.*—Had been absent in Baltimore on official business some few days, during which Mr. Davis sent for me. Called with Captain Evans, Officer of the Day, and explained my absence. A pustule, somewhat malignant in character, was forming on prisoner's face, which was much inflamed and swollen. He reiterated belief that the casemate was full of malarial poison, caused by the rising and falling of the tide in the ditch outside (as previously explained), and wished the Washington people would take quicker means of dispatching him, if his death without trial was their object. That it was so he was led to suspect, for a trial must develop many things not pleasant to those in power. In particular it would place the responsibility for the non-exchange of prisoners where it belonged.

*And show who broke faith and violated the laws of war.*

Called the same evening. Prisoner in a high fever, the swelling of his face spreading to his back and head, with indications of latent erysipelas.* Mr. Davis wished he could have with him his faithful servant Robert, who, though a slave, had a moral nobility deserving honor. The negroes had excellent traits of character, but required, for their own sakes, guidance and control. They were docile, as a general rule, easily imbued with religious sentiment, quick in sympathies, and of warm family affection. Their passions, however, {(}were intense and uncontrollable.{)} Slavery had been blamed for their incontinence, but this was unjust. Were the free blacks any less libidinous? The Southern slaves were incomparably more chaste, or less unchaste, than people of the same race in the North. Slavery was a restraint upon promiscuous intercourse, and for commercial reasons, if for none higher. The negroes were improvident to a degree that must reduce them to destitution if not cared for. They had to be provided with fresh seeds for their little garden patches every year, no remonstrances sufficing to make them provide one season for the wants of the next. It was in their affections they were strong, and many of them had excellent traits. His man Robert was {*among*} the best and most faith-

*required the control of another*

---

*Erysipelas, or St. Anthony's fire, is an infectious, painful disease of the skin caused by a streptococcus and marked by a fever and sore redness. Before antibiotics it was sometimes fatal.

ful of his race, and had attended him through many serious illnesses.*
Was with his wife on board the *Clyde,* but might possibly have de-
serted the sinking ship by this time. Did not think he would, though
others with greater claims to keep them faithful were among his enemies.†

*August 16th.*—Called with Captain Gressin,‡ Aide-de-Camp of
General Miles, Officer of the Day. Prisoner suffering severely, but in
a less critical state, the erysipelas now showing itself in his nose and
forehead. Found that a carbuncle was forming on his left thigh, Mr.
Davis urging this as proof of a malarial atmosphere in his cell, reiter-
ating his wish that if the Government wanted to be rid of him without
trial, it might take some quicker process.

Prisoner said he had never held much hope for himself since entering Fortress Monroe, and was now losing it for his people. The action and tone in regard to the Richmond elections, gave evidence that
the policy of "woe to the conquered" would prevail. What a cruel farce
it was to permit an exercise of the elective franchise, with a proviso
that the electors must cast their ballots for men they despised or hated!
Either all pretence of continuing representative government should be
abandoned or free acceptance given to the men indorsed [*sic*] by the
people. To ask men who had fought, sacrificed, and lost their all for
a cause, to wheel suddenly, and vote into power men they despised as
renegades or cowards, was the sin of attempting to seethe the kid in
its mother's milk. Better for the South to remain disfranchised forever, than crawl back into office or recognition through such incred-
ible apostasy. Better remain prisoners, than be citizens on such terms.
In no district of Virginia could what we called a "loyalist," muster a
corporal's guard of men with similar sentiments. Why organize hypocrisy by attempting to force into elective positions men who were
not representatives of their alleged constituents—men who could only
excite the abhorrence or contempt of ninety-nine in every hundred of
the people? Either the South should be declared so many conquered
provinces under military rule, or given back the freedom of the ballot.
To offer bribes for wholesale falsehood, would be found poor policy;
and the men hereafter to create trouble in the South, would not be the
gallant and well-born gentlemen who fought loyally, and at every sacrifice of life and property for a cause they believed right, but that small
scum of poltroons and renegades who remained "neutral" through the
contest, only anxious to avoid danger for themselves, and jump over
to the side that won. The former class accepted defeat, and would
{(}loyally{)} preserve any obligations that might be imposed on *honestly*
them. The latter were worthless and pitiful intriguers, commanding

---

*Davis's good relations with the slaves on his plantation stand as a mon-
ument to his humane care and enlightened rule.

†See letter of Mrs. Davis further on, in regard to this worthy servant [Hal-
pine's note].

‡Capt. Charles E. Grisson, U.S. Volunteers.

no popular confidence, chastened by no memories of the struggle; and now that no personal risk could be incurred, would seek to attain popularity—the popularity of demagogues—by re-fanning into flame the passions and prejudices of the ignorant and vulgar. They will be clamorous for Southern rights, now that Southern rights are dead, and out-Herod Herod in their professed devotion to the Southern cause.*

*August 20th.*—Called with Captain Evans, Officer of the Day. Mr. Davis suffering great prostration, a cloud of erysipelas covering his whole face and throat. The carbuncle much inflamed. Spirits exceedingly dejected, evinced by anxiety for his wife and children. That he should die without opportunity of rebutting in public trial the imputed stigma of having had share in the conspiracy to assassinate Mr. Lincoln, was referred to frequently and painfully. That history would do him justice, and the criminal absurdity of the charge be its own refutation, he had cheerful confidence while in health; but in his feebleness and despondency, with knowledge how powerful they were who wished to affix this stain, his alarm, lest it might become a reproach to his children, grew an increasing shadow.

*Had no personal knowledge of Mr. L. Accepted the statements as to his good heart. Could not approve his course.*

Of Mr. Lincoln he then spoke, not in affected terms of regard or admiration, but paying a simple and sincere tribute to his goodness of character, honesty of purpose, and Christian desire to be faithful to his duties according to such light as was given him. Also to his official purity and freedom from avarice. The Southern press labored in the early part of the war to render Mr. Lincoln abhorred and contemptible; but such efforts were against his judgment, and met such opposition as his multiplied cares and labors would permit. Behind Mr. Lincoln, during his first term, stood an infinitely more objectionable and less scrupulous successor (Mr. Hamlin);† and the blow that struck down the President of the United States would place that successor in power. When Mr. Lincoln was reinaugurated, the cause of his people

*not my opinion*

was hopeless, or very nearly so—the struggle only justifiable in continuance by its better attitude for obtaining terms; and from no ruler

X the United States could {?} have, might terms so {?} generous have been expected.‡ Mr. Lincoln was kind of heart, naturally longing for the glory and repose of a second term to be spent in peace. Mr. Johnson, § being from the South, dare not offer such liberal treatment; his motives would be impugned. In every embittered national strug-

---

*This paragraph is a most accurate description of Davis's view of Reconstruction. However, like the entire book, it was not written to convey Davis's opinions but rather Halpine's. The *Prison Life* was designed to be a piece of Democratic party political propaganda. The fact that Halpine's opinions were, at times, similar to Davis's was not by design but by accident.

†Vice-President Hannibal Hamlin of Maine.

‡Davis was willing to negotiate peace on his own terms at any time during the war. This peace, of course, would have recognized the successful severance of the Union.

§President Andrew Johnson of Tennessee.

gle, proposals to assassinate the rival representatives were common, emanating from different classes of men, with different motives: from spies of the enemy, wishing to obtain evidence how such proposals would be received; from fanatics, religious or patriotic, believing the act would prove acceptable to Heaven; from lunatics, driven mad by sufferings connected with the struggle; and from boastful and often cowardly desperadoes, seeking gold and notoriety by attempting, or promising to attempt, the crime. At the time it occurred, Mr. Lincoln's death, even by natural causes, would have been a serious injury to the prospects of the South; but the manner of his taking-off, frenzying the Northern mind, was the last crowning calamity of a {(}despairing and defeated, though{)} righteous cause.

*His own view perhaps.)*

*August 21st.*—Called with Captain Corlis,\* on the staff of General Miles, Officer of the Day. Prostration increased, and the erysipelas spreading. Deemed it my duty to send a communication to Major-General Miles, reporting that I found the State prisoner, Davis, suffering severely from erysipelas in the face and head, accompanied by the usual prostration attending that disease. Also that he had a small carbuncle on his left thigh, his condition denoting a low state of the vital forces.

*August 23d.*—Called with Captain Evans, 3d Pennsylvania Artillery, Officer of the Day. Prisoner a little improved, febrile symptoms subsiding. Had no appetite for ordinary food, but found the coolness and moisture of fruits agreeable. Said he had concluded not to lose any more spoons for me, but would retain the one that morning sent with his breakfast. Unless things took a change, he would not require it long.

[This was an allusion to the desire some of the guards had to secure trophies of anything Mr. Davis had touched. They had carried away his brier-wood pipe, and from time to time taken five of the spoons sent over with his meals from my quarters. The meals were sent over by a bright little mulatto boy named Joe, who handed them to the sergeant of the guard outside the casemate, who passed them through the window to the lieutenant of the guard in the outer cell, by whom they were handed to the prisoner through the grated doors of the inside room, the keys of which were held by the Officer of the Day. No knife and fork being allowed the prisoner, "lest he should commit suicide," his food had to be cut up before being sent over—a needless precaution, it always seemed to me, and more likely to produce than prevent the act, by continually keeping the idea that it was expected before the prisoner's mind. It was in returning the trays from Mr. Davis to my quarters that the spoons were taken—an annoyance obviated by his retaining one for use. This only changed the form of trophy, however; napkins that he had used being the next class of prizes seized and sent home to sweethearts by loyal warders at the gates.]

Mr. Davis expressed some anxiety as to his present illness. He was not one of those who, when in trouble, wished to die. Great invalids

---

\*Stephen P. Corliss.

seldom had this wish, save when protracted sufferings had weakened the brain. Suicides were commonly of the robuster class—men who had never been brought close to death nor thought much about it seriously. A good old Bishop once remarked, that "dying was the last thing a man should think about," and the mixture of wisdom and quaint humor in the phrase had impressed Mr. Davis. Even to Christians, with the hope of an immortal future for the soul, the idea of physical annihilation—of parting forever from the tenement of flesh in which we have had so many joys and sorrows—was one full of awe, if not terror. What it must be to the unbeliever, who entertained absolute and total annihilation as his prospect, he could not conceive. Never again to hear of wife or children—to take the great leap into black vacuity, with no hope of meeting in a brighter and happier life the loved ones left behind, the loved ones gone before!

He had more reasons than other men, and now more than ever, to wish for some prolongation of life, as also to welcome death. His intolerable sufferings and wretched state argued for the grave as a place of rest. His duties to the cause he had represented, and his family, made him long to be continued on the footstool, in whatever pain or misery, at least until by the ordeal of a trial he could convince the world he was not the monster his enemies would make him appear, and that no wilful departures from the humanities of war had stained the escutcheon of his people. Errors, like all other men, he had committed; but stretched now on a bed from which he might never rise, and looking with the eyes of faith, which no walls could bar, up to the throne of Divine mercy, it was his comfort that no such crimes as men laid to his charge reproached him in the whispers of his conscience.

"They charge me with crime, Doctor, but God knows my innocence. I indorsed [sic] no measure that was not justified by the laws of war. Failure is all forms of guilt in one to men who occupied my position. Should I die, repeat this for the sake of my people, my dear wife, and poor darling children. Tell the world I only loved America, and that in following my State I was only carrying out doctrines received from reverenced lips in my early youth, and adopted by my judgment as the convictions of riper years."

Mr. Davis spoke with intense earnestness—the solemnity of a dying man, though not then, in my judgment, in any immediate danger. His words, as quoted, were taken down on my return to quarters, and are here given for what each reader may think them worth. They certainly impressed me as sincere, and as if—whether true or not, judged by the standard of law—the speaker uttered them in the good faith of a religious man, who thought death might very possibly be near, if not imminent and certain.

# •CHAPTER 15•

*Southern Non-Belligerents.—The Ant-Lion and its Habits.—Mr. Davis on the Future of the Southern Blacks.*

$A$ugust *24th.*—Visited Mr. Davis with Captain Titlow, Officer of the Day. Found him slightly better in body and mind. Expressed hope that no sensational reports of his illness had appeared in the newspapers to alarm his wife more than necessary. His hope was faint, however. The swarm of newspaper correspondents, more than quadrupled by the war, no longer finding food for their pens in camps or on battle-fields, had to seize every item of the slightest interest and swell it into importance by exaggeration, in order to retain their employment. Spoke of the {*inferior morals &*} superior literary and {*literary and*} inventive powers of our correspondents during the war. To contrast the dry official report of some affair of outposts or the skirmish line, in which half a dozen men on either side had been killed or wounded, with the wonderfully enlarged and intensely colored mirage of the same appearing some few days subsequently in the Northern press, formed an amusing and amazing study, giving one a higher ideal of man's imaginative power. The Southern press, on the contrary, was short of printers, short of paper, and all other requisites for exciting journalism, insomuch that latterly only the meagerest skeletons of events could appear; and even official documents, and debates of the highest consequence, had to be briefly epitomized.

Mr. Davis said the press of the South had enjoyed more liberty and given more trouble to its government than that of the North. Properly conducted, its power was an important adjunct to the machinery of war; but engineering {?} it was a complex study, calling for special *X* education in its professor. The only men still remaining vindictively belligerent and anxious to perpetuate trouble in the South—so far as he knew, and as their words could reach—would be found in the small-fry of little country editors, and certain classes of civilians who had *not mine* been exempted from military service by special legislation, the purchase of substitutes, or the procurement of details. It was the non-belligerents of actual conflict who had always been and would remain most ferociously belligerent in speech and writing. Not having borne arms in the struggle, they might claim rewards for their loyalty or neutrality in Federal patronage, or offices to be filled by popular vote; and such claims would likely be allowed by our people to the exclusion of those fearless and honorable men, who—having fought, failed, and accepted defeat—were now only anxious to erase all painful souvenirs and legacies of the unfortunate and unavailing strife.

Observing me brush away with my foot some crumbs scattered near his bedside, Mr. Davis asked me to desist; they were for a mouse he was domesticating—the only living thing he had now power to benefit. The drawback to this companionship was, that the crumbs called forth a swarm of red ants as well as the mouse; and he suggested, with a smile, that a few ant-lions should be caught and brought in from the *pshaw* beach. Placed in a cigar-box, with some fine sand and a lump of sugar, or a few dead locusts, to attract the ants, they would soon rid him of his insect visitors, and afford him, though on a small scale, the nearest approach to sport he could now have.

Finding my curiosity excited, Mr. Davis then described the ant-lion *not mine* with much minuteness and pleasant humor, saying it was next to the bee as an interesting study in natural history. It is about the size of a small, elongated pea, three legs on each size, a forceps proportionably immense arming its head, and between these nippers a sharp stiletto, which can be drawn in or thrown out at pleasure. It is found all along the Southern coast, and would seem to have a difficult problem in supporting life. It is painfully slow of movement, always walking backward and dragging its heavy forceps along the ground behind it; while the ants, on which it chiefly preys, are extremely active. Nature, however, has compensated by subtlety what the ant-lion lacks in spring. It digs a funnel-shaped hole in the fine sand of the Southern coast, circular at the top, of an inch diameter and an inch in depth. At the bottom it secretes itself in the sand, only its forceps protruding. These pitfalls are located about an inch or so from the stems of shrubs or tufts of grass—the ants flocking to these latter, because finding in them a species of grass-louse called the ant-cow, which the ant milks by suction as its favorite food, the cows not resisting lest worse befall them, and not appearing injured by the process. While the ants are thus hastening to their food, some one of them will approach the brink of the ant-lion's pitfall, and instantly the fine sand of the edge gives way, precipitating the unwary traveller to the bottom. Here he is seized by the forceps, and firmly held, while the stiletto is driven through his body. His juices are soon sucked dry by the secreted monster of the cave, and then with one jerk of the forceps, the carcass is flung up and out two or three inches beyond the edge of the funnel—a distance as much as if a man were thrown one hundred and fifty times his length. Should the ant, when first tumbling, escape the grasp of the forceps, and seek to clamber out of the trap, the ant-lion foils the attempt by jerking little jets of sand on the body and across the path of his flying victim, who is soon stunned, bewildered, and losing his foot-grasp on the slippery sides, falls back a helpless prey to his destroyer. Mr. Da-*never there* vis, when on the coast of Georgia, many years ago, had often spent hours in watching them, and their whole performance could be witnessed by placing one in a cigar-box half filled with fine sand, and dropping in some sugar or a dead locust to attract the ants. The ant-lion would not be in the box half a day, before commencing to earn his livelihood by digging out his trap. So great was the habit of subtlety in this insect, that when moving from place to place, it always burrowed along just a little beneath the surface of the sand; and he had heard, if compelled to cross a stone, log, or other obstruction, that it seized a chip or leaf with its forceps, thereby covering its body, as it slowly and painfully toiled backward. This, however, he could not verify from personal observation.

Every conversation of this kind with Mr. Davis recalled the saying of some eminent writer whose name has escaped me, that "it is a noble thing to know how to take a country walk," or words containing that idea, but more concisely and vividly expressed. Educated by the microscope and habits of observation, we become afraid of treading on some of God's beautiful little things at every step.

*August 25th.*—Called upon Mr. Davis, accompanied by Captain Gresson* of the staff of Major-General Miles, Officer of the Day. The Captain gave me an order from General Miles, allowing State-prisoner Davis to have a knife and fork with his meals hereafter. Mr. Davis was pleased, but said he had learned many new uses to which a spoon could be put when no other implement was accessible. In particular, it was the best peach-peeler ever invented, and he illustrated as he spoke on a fruit that lay on his table. Denying him a knife and *not so accounted for to me* fork {(}lest he should commit suicide,{)} he said, was designed *or by me* to represent him to the world as an atrocious criminal, {(}so harrowed by remorse that the oblivion of death would be welcome.{)} His early shackles had partly the same object, but still more to degrade *If he knew of such pretext,* his cause. *I did not.*

Prisoner's health very delicate, but the erysipelas subsiding. Asked could he soon resume his walks in the open air? The change of {(}scene being a great delight,{)} and the exercise improving his *air needful* sleep.

He referred to an account he had been reading of an attack on a negro named Davenport, in Connecticut, for marrying or living with a white woman. Also, to the New York riots, in which mobs rose suddenly upon the blacks, hanging them to lamp-posts and roasting them at slow fires. The papers bore evidence, from all sections, of increasing hostility between the races, and this was but part of the penalty the poor negro had to pay for freedom. The more political equality was given or approached, the greater must become the social antagonism of the races. In the South, under slavery, there was no such feeling, because there could be no rivalry. Children of the white master were often suckled by negroes, and sported during infancy with black playmates. Old enough to engage in manlier exercise, it was under black huntsmen the young whites took their first lessons in field-sports. They fished, shot, and hunted together, eating the same bread, drink-

---

*Charles E. Grisson.

ing from the same cup, sleeping under the same tree with their negro guide. In public conveyances there was no social exclusion of the blacks, nor any dislike engendered by competition between white and negro labor. In the bed-chamber of the planter's daughter it was common for a negro girl to sleep, as half attendant half companion; and while there might be, as in all countries and amongst all races, individual instances of cruel treatment, he was well satisfied that between no master and laboring classes on earth had so kindly and regardful a feeling subsisted. To suppose otherwise required a violation of the known laws of human nature. Early associations of service, affection and support were powerful. To these self-interest joined. The horse we hire for a day may be fed or not fed, groomed or not groomed, when returned to the livery-stable. The horse owned by us, and for which we have paid a thousand or fifteen hundred dollars, is an object both of pride and solicitude. His grooming, stabling, and feeding are cared for. If sick he is doctored, and cured if possible. When at work, it is the owner's interest that he shall not be overtaxed.

The attainment of political equality by the negro will revolutionize all this. It will be as if our horses were given right of intruding into our parlors; or brought directly into competition with human labor, no longer aiding it but as rivals. Put large gangs of white laborers, belonging to different nationalities, at work beside each other, and feuds will probably break out. Endeavor to supplant a thousand Irishmen working on a levee or canal by a thousand Germans ready to accept lower wages, or *vice versa*, and military power will be required to keep the peace. Emancipation does this upon a gigantic scale and in the most aggravated form. It throws the whole black race into direct and aggressive competition with the laboring classes of the whites; and the ignorance of the blacks, presuming on their freedom, will embitter every difference. The principle of compensation prevails everywhere through nature, and the negroes will have to pay, in harsher social restrictions and treatment, for the attempt to invest them with political equality. To endow them with the ballot by Act of Congress was impossible, until the trunk of the Constitution, already stripped of many branches once full of shade and pleasant singing-birds, was torn up by the roots. Each State had the privilege of deciding the qualifications of its own citizens; and some of the States most clamorous for universal negro suffrage in the South, where such a measure would send unlettered blacks to both Houses of Congress, and pass the State Legislature and judiciary altogether into their hands, themselves refused the ballot to the negro, though not numerous enough in any district to decide the majority of a pound-keeper.

Took issue with Mr. Davis on the labor question. What necessity for competition in a country so vast, and only partially developed, as the South? The relations of the races would adjust themselves, under the laws of supply and demand, and the whites still owned their old plantations and other property, which was their capital; and to this the labor of the blacks would have to bow. White labor could not long remain, nor to any great extent, in competition with black. It had accumulative energies, guided by intelligence, which must soon lift it into the employing class; while the blacks, if so incapable of thrift as he seemed to think, must remain hewers of wood and drawers of water for ever. The antagonisms of so violent a revolution in the labor-system of the South were natural, but must soon fade out. There never had been any desire North to give the negroes social equality; but our pride, not less than sense of justice, demanded that there should be no political bar to their improving their own condition to equal that of the whites, if they possessed the capacity for such elevation. As to the outrages upon the blacks in New York, they were the work of a few abandoned and maddened wretches—men certainly not representing nor belonging to the party in control of our national destinies. It was a riot to resist the draft, and the inoffensive blacks became objects of vengeance, from the democratic cry that the war making the draft necessary was a "war for the nigger." The case in Connecticut was a protest in violent and illegal form of certain turbulent whites against the intermarrying of the races. It was lawless, of course, and one of the rioters had lost his life at the hands of the black, who was held justifiable. Nevertheless, the sentiment that prompted the attack—one of the opposition to such deteriorating interminglements—was all but universal, and offered sufficient guarantee that the dominant race would never suffer material injury to its blood or character from the political equality of the negroes.

Mr. Davis said no argument could make us agree, for we occupied different planes of observation. There could be no problem of the negro at the North, for they were too few to be of consequence; and each census showed their number diminishing. It was in the Cotton States, where they equalled, and in many districts largely outnumbered the whites, that the adjustment of relationship would prove impossible under such ideas as now threatened to prevail in the Federal Government. As for himself and his people, they were now only passengers in the ship of State—no longer of the crew, nor with places on the quarter-deck; and must take, he supposed, whatever decision of the question the powers that had lifted themselves above the Constitution might see fit to impose.

# •CHAPTER 16•

*Mr. Davis on Fenianism.—Highly Important.—His Views of Reconstruction.*

August *26th.*—Called upon Mr. Davis, accompanied by Captain Evans, 3d Pennsylvania Artillery, Officer of the Day. Health slightly improved, and spirits decidedly more cheerful. Mr. Davis said his imprisonment had one advantage, giving him time to re-read Bancroft's History of the United States, and read Macaulay's History of England—the latter something he had long wished, but could not find time for. The system of settlement and confiscations under Cromwell, in Ireland, was precisely what his people were now threatened with. The cry then was, "To * * * * or Connaught!"* whither an attempt was made to drive and herd together the whole people. Whole estates, and even counties, were confiscated by orders in council, on no other plea than that the proprietors were either of the Irish race, or, being born on Irish soil, had Irish sympathies or habits. This history now threatened to repeat itself in the United States, the cry only varying to read, "To * * * * or Mexico!" and the locality changed from Ireland to the South. There was no excuse for it here; there had been *no justification* {(}some{)} in Ireland. Between the conquering forces of Cromwell and the Irish there were essential differences of race, religion, habits, laws, and hopes. There had been war for centuries, and no promise of future tranquillity on less rigorous terms. Were the races the same, though controlled by different ideas; their religion, habits, and laws almost identical, and with only a single internecine war to interrupt the harmony of their joint occupation of the continent—there was the further parallel that both countries suffered for loyalty to what each regarded as the rightful government; Ireland, for devotion to {*their local government, acknowledged by*} the Royal Family of the Stuarts; and the South, for its fidelity to the principles defined by the Constitution of 1787.

The present Fenian movement for Ireland was a {(}farce to make *not mine* angels weep.{)} The last attempt was in 1848, when the population of Ireland was more than a million larger—the movement originating at home, and all Europe in a convulsive and volcanic condition. His-

---

*Halpine feared that Republican rule in the South could lead to horrors similar to those experienced in his native Ireland under Oliver Cromwell. Chapter 16 provides the clearest statement of Halpine's ideas on Reconstruction and is the core of the book.

tory gave no example of an oppressed race that had accepted exile, returning with success to liberate their native land. The aristocratic refugees of the French Revolution, indeed, got back to their country, but only under the swords of a combination in which England, Austria, Russia, Prussia, and the German States were enlisted, with their whole military resources. It was a mere catch-penny clamor of designing demagogues in its cis-Atlantic aspect; nor could he see that in Ireland there was organization, or even a vigorous purpose to accomplish the object proposed. ⟬X⟭ England's control of the sea was absolute, at least so near home, against any ⟬(⟭less combination than the navies of France and America. ⟬)⟭ To land men or arms in any sufficient quantity in Ireland, would require some desperate sea-fights by navy with navy, and a transport fleet, costing for vessels and their equipment not less than some hundred millions. The men engaged in this matter must be ⟬(⟭either fools or rogues. ⟬)⟭ He had no special cause to love England, nor dislike; but such impracticable and ⟬(⟭pigmy threatenings⟬)⟭ of her empire would be ludicrous if not too sad. Against the rocks of her coast, storm-clouds of a thousandfold the Fenian power had dashed with clamor of waves and mist of spray, but next morning the sun shone bright again, the air was calm, and only in a shore strewn with wrecks could evidence be found of any past commotion.

*not mine*

*not so*   *X*

*not mine*

*note. May have said that without a flag and a navy failure must result, and this being so evident, I must in the absence of all knowledge suppose the Fenians had the apurance [sic] of support by some maritime power.* *as what?*

Asking Mr. Davis what were his views in regard to the reconstruction of the Union, he spoke pretty nearly verbatim as follows; this report not being condensed as with other conversations, but taken down in full from memory, immediately on my return to quarters:*

"We could not otherwise define reconstruction, than as a renewal to and by all the States, of all the rights, privileges, duties, immunities, and obligations prescribed and recognized by the Constitution, or original compact of Union. There were several possible alternatives to this plan of reconstruction:

"1st. Consolidation: the swallowing up of all State governments by the General Government, making the whole country one State, only divided into provinces for easier administration, but connected as one entity ⟬ | ⟭ of ⟬in | ⟭ policy and power.

"2d. Territorialism: the control of the Southern States by a Congress and Executive representing only the Northern States—that is, colonial vassalage and government by authority of greater force.

"3d. By open subversion and usurpation to establish a despotism over North and South, while yet preserving a certain Republican form.

"In replying to one who served through the war for no other purpose, as you avow, than to defend and maintain the Union as defined by the Constitution," continued Mr. Davis, "there can be no necessity for considering any other policy than that of re-establishing the rela-

---

*It was to obtain this account that Craven returned to interview Davis in prison.

tions of all the States and their citizens to each other and the United States Government.

"Every man's experience must teach him that quarrels between friends are best healed when they are healed most promptly. The alienation which was at first a pain, becomes by time habitual, and the mantle of charity being withdrawn, the faults of each become more and more distinct to the other, and thus the bitterest hates naturally spring from the ashes of the closest friendship.

"It is therefore probably to be regretted that so much delay has occurred in the work of reconstruction, because of the enhancement thereby of the difficulties in the way of speedy and cordial reconciliation. This opinion is qualified as 'probable,' because of my want of recent intercourse with the people. A short time before the close of the war, the idea *?* was infused into <u>my</u> **{?}** people,* as you are well aware, that if they would cease resistance, the Union would be restored, and all their rights of person and property respected, save the property held in slaves, which would be a question for the courts. I have no doubt that a majority—a very large majority—of the Southern people accepted this proposed settlement with singleness of purpose; and would, if confidingly and generously treated, have been now industriously engaged in repairing their wrecked fortunes, without any thought of again resisting or obstructing the General Government in its ordinary functions.

"How far the public wealth would by this course have been increased, the public expenditures lessened, may be measured by many hundred millions of dollars. If it be true that much has been lost, morally and materially, by delay, it would seem that true policy indicates the promptest action in what is termed Reconstruction. The North says we have done evil, and when bidding us 'cease to do evil' should *changed* not prevent us 'learning to do well.' This can only be done by removing all impediments to the exercise of State functions and the re-enjoyment of such civil and political rights as are left us in the Union.

"Each House of Congress is judge of the election and qualification of its own members. The Constitution has settled the question of rep- *voice* resentation. A constituency may lose its **{(}**rights**{)}** for a time by selecting ineligible persons to be its representatives; but the right of representation is not impaired thereby, and the mistake or abuse may be remedied by a new election. Test-oaths are evil continually, *X The omission a reference* and only evil. They restrain those honorable men who require no fet- *to those Senators & Reps.* ters, while men of a different class will either take them perjuriously *from the North who used to* or with a 'mental reservation.' All history has proved them ineffectual *take the oath to support the* and something worse.† **{X X X X}** *Constu. with a mental res-* "Our forefathers emigrated to a wilderness, and waged the war of *ervation not to observe the* the Revolution, to have and to hold a government founded on the

*clause for the rendition of*
*fugitive slaves & the laws*
*made in pursuance of it.*

---

*See 16.

†There can be no excuse for this misquote since this came not from a conversation but from a written statement especially, but surreptitiously, obtained from Davis for this work (see 93).

consent of the governed. They consulted and compromised with each other to establish a voluntary Union. If that idea is to be followed, confidence, generosity, fraternity, and not test oaths, disabilities, and armies quartered in the interior, must be relied upon to restore the Union and make it re-effective for the ends for which it was formed.

"Reconstruction," continued Mr. Davis, "cannot properly involve or be made to depend on those social problems which have arisen from the sudden disruption of the relations existing between the white and the black races in the Southern States. These problems belong to the several States, and must have treatment according to the different circumstances of each. No general rule can properly be made applicable to all, and it will prove unfortunate if the subject is controlled by distant and but poorly-informed, if not prejudiced authority. The self-interest of individuals and communities, together with the demand for labor so far exceeding the supply, may safely be left to protect the laborer.

"The public actions of the Southern State Conventions furnishes [sic] conclusive evidence of the desire of the Southern people to resume their position in the Union; and it must strike all observers with surprise, that while those who strove so desperately to leave the Union, are now so earnestly endeavoring to reassume their places in it, it is the very men who sent fire and sword to destroy them, or compel them to return, who now bar the door and deny them readmission to that very condition to which it was throughout the war proclaimed to be their first and last duty to return. Solitary reflection," concluded Mr. Davis, "has given me no key to the mysterious origin of this change in Northern opinion, which I find evidenced in every newspaper that reaches me; and perhaps my own sad state has tinged with its gloom the vista of the future, if, thus alienated, disjointed, adrift, the country should be visited with such trials of foreign war, either with France or England, or both, as are now so often suggested in the public journals of America, and their extracts from the European press."

{*} This conversation impressed me much, and has been recorded with peculiar care, Mr. Davis delivering it with great deliberation and earnestness, as though the subject were one upon which he had been reflecting. It is as nearly as possible reproduced in his own words, without abridgment, and may, perhaps, be of some suggestive value—perhaps of none. Let the wise of the land determine.

* It was not a conversation, but a written reply made to an officer who furnished me pencil & paper for the purpose at a date long subsequent to the departure of Dr. Craven. Inaccuracies in reports of conversations have an excuse not to be found for the "abridgement" or alteration of a manuscript of opinions regarded as in the text.

# •CHAPTER 17•

September 1st.—Was called at daylight by Captain Titlow, Officer of the Day, to see State-prisoner Davis, who appeared rapidly sinking, and was believed in a critical condition. The carbuncle on his thigh was much inflamed, his pulse indicating extreme prostration of the vital forces. The erysipelas which had subsided now reappeared, and the febrile excitement ran very high. Prescribed such remedies, constitutional and topical, as were indicated; but always had much trouble to persuade him to use the stimulants so urgently needed by his condition. Let me here say, however, that in docility and a strict adherence to whatever regimen was prescribed, Mr. Davis was the model patient of my practice. He seemed to regard the doctor as captain of the patient's health, and obeyed every direction, however irksome, disagreeable, or painful, with military exactness.

Mr. Davis renewed his complaints of the vitiated atmosphere of the casemate, declaring it to be noxious and pestilential from the causes before noticed. Mould gathered upon his shoes, showing the dampness of the place; and no animal life could prosper in an atmosphere that generated these hyphomycetous fungi. From the rising and falling of the tides in the loose foundations of the casemate, mephitic fungi emanated, the spores of which, floating in the air, were thrown off in such quantities, and with such incessant repetitions of reproduction, as to thoroughly pervade the atmosphere, entering the lungs and blood with every breath, and redeveloping their poisonous qualities in the citadel of life. Peculiar classes of these fungi were characteristics of the atmosphere in which cholera and other forms of plague were most rankly generated, as had been established by the Rev. Mr. Osborne, in a long and interesting series of experimental researches with the achromatic microscope during the cholera visitation of 1854 in England.* Men in robust health might defy these miasmatic influences; but to him, so physically reduced, the atmosphere that generated mould found no vital force sufficient to resist its poisonous inhalation.

---

*Rev. Lord Sidney Godolphin Osborne (1808-1889) wrote numerous works on the conditions of the agricultural poor, including public sanitation.

Assured Mr. Davis that his opinion on the matter had for some time been my own, and that on several occasions I had called the attention of Major-General Miles to the subject. Satisfied that the danger was now serious if he were longer continued in such an atmosphere, I would make an official report on the subject to the General Commanding, recommending a change of quarters.

Referring to the consolation he derived from the Bible, Mr. Davis spoke of its power to present beautiful and comforting pictures, full of promise and instruction, apposite to every situation of joy or calamity in life, but never so well appreciated as in our moments of deepest despondency and sorrow. No picture had impressed him more than that of Abraham preparing to sacrifice Isaac, his son—the son of promise. The grim fidelity of the narrative only heightened its irresistible pathos. The sad journey to Mount Moriah of Abraham with his two young men and Isaac, the father only knowing the terrible burden of the duty imposed on him by angelic order. The halt when they came in sight of the hill of sacrifice. Abraham's brief, sad order to his two attendants; "Abide ye here with the ass, and I and the lad will go up yonder and worship." The silent procession to the place of sacrifice, Isaac with the wood upon his shoulders, the father striding along in dumb despair, with the knife in one hand and the torch in the other. Isaac's child-like inquiry, "Behold the fire and the wood, but where is the lamb for a burnt-offering?" and Abraham's reply of faith, Jehovah jireh—"My son, God will provide it." Last scene of all, the son of promise bound on the faggots his young shoulders had so joyously borne; the miserable father bending over the lad he loved, the joy of his old age, grasping the knife that was to slay him. Then comes the Divine interference, in the voice of the angel once again. The promise of faith, Jehovah jireh, is redeemed, and behind the father, as he turns, beholds a ram entangled in a thicket by his horns. In many an hour of bitter calamity the words Jehovah jireh had been his only consolation. When troubles that seemed hopeless of extrication encompassed him on every side, the words Jehovah jireh were full of whispering consolation to his spirit. His mind had framed the picture in gold, and it was but one of a thousand.

Another beautiful picture Mr. Davis spoke of as suspended in the gallery through which his thoughts, in their despondent moments, loved to trace. Dark night over Jerusalem. A little group, a Master and faithful followers, emerging from the gates. As they descend into the valley, their mantles are drawn more closely round their hurrying and silent figures, for the night-wind is chill and damp. Where the little brook Kedron runs, we see them picking their way across the stones; and now they move silently up the Mount of Olives into the Garden of Gethsemane. That night, before quitting Jerusalem, they had sat at supper—a Supper since commemorated in all Christian lands; and as they sat and did eat, the Master foretold that one of these followers should betray Him. And now they have arrived at the garden; and the Master, calling three of His most beloved disciples, leads them apart from the others, and breathes into their ears as they move along in the double shadows of night and the olive grove, that "His soul is sorrowful even unto death." When sufficiently removed from the larger group, and as they approach a darker cluster of olives, the Master says to the three, "Tarry ye here and watch." In the great agony that is upon Him, He longs to be alone. Already the burden of the sins of mankind, whom He so loves that He is about to die for them, grows too weighty for his tenement of flesh. About a stone's cast from the lesser group, the Master falls upon the ground, and prays with thick sobs into the pitying darkness, that if it be possible, this hour may pass from Him—the human in His nature crying out under its intolerable burden, "Take away this cup from me; for with thee, O Father, all things are possible." But again the Divine will becomes paramount; faith reasserts her ascendancy; and bowing His head upon His hands, the Master sobs, "Nevertheless, not my will, but thine be done." And here, as with Abraham on the hill of Jehovah jireh, an angel appears to strengthen and comfort the obedient heart. Mr. Davis said he could bear to witness the agonizing scene of the garden, but wished to blot from his memory the unfaithfulness of the watchers.*

Mr. Davis again spoke of the wretchedness of being constantly watched—of feeling that a human eye, inquisitive and pitiless, was fixed upon all his movements night and day. This was one of the torments imposed on the Marquis de Lafayette in the dungeons of Magdeburgh and Olmutz. Indeed, the parallel between their prison lives, if not in some other respects, was remarkable. Lafayette was denied the use of knife, or fork, lest he should commit self-destruction. He was confined in a casemate, or dungeon, of the two most powerful fortresses of Prussia first, and then Austria. While in Magdeburgh, he found a friend in the humane physician, who repeatedly reported that the prisoner could not live unless allowed to breathe purer air than that of his cell; and on this recommendation—the Governor at first answering that he "was not ill enough yet"—the illustrious prisoner was at length allowed to take the air—sometimes on foot, at other times in a carriage, but always accompanied by an officer with drawn sword and two armed guards.

Mr. Davis then narrated, with great spirit and minuteness, the efforts made by Count Lally-Tolendal, assisted by Dr. Eric Bollmann, of Hanover, and Mr. Huger, of South Carolina, to effect Lafayette's liberation.† Mr. Huger was a young gentleman of Huguenot extraction; and Lafayette, upon landing near Georgetown, South Carolina, accompanied by Baron De Kalb, had first been a guest of Major Huger, the father of his rescuer. Dr. Bollmann's visit to Vienna, where he remained six months, lulling suspicion by pretending to study or practise medicine; his there meeting with young Huger, and the manner

---

*Halpine cites two biblical passages that deal with sacrifice and a scapegoat: Abraham and Isaac, and Jesus in the garden of Gethsemane.
†Drs. Justus E. Bollman and Francis K. Huger aided Lafayette.

in which these two cautious, though daring, men mutually discovered to each other their similarity of object; the code of signals which they gradually established with the prisoner, and his final rescue for some brief hours from captivity by their exertions, together with his re-arrest and the capture and terrible punishment inflicted on his res-cuers—all these points Mr. Davis recited with a vividness which made each feature in the successive scenes pass before the mental eye as though in the unrolling of a panorama. Huger and Bollmann were heavily ironed round the neck, and chained to the floors of separate dungeons, in utter darkness. Once every half hour the Austrian Of-ficer of the Day entered, flashed a dark lantern into their faces to iden-tify them and see that they still lived, and then carefully examined every link of the chains binding their necks to the floor and shackling their feet and wrists. This treatment lasted, night and day, for six months, the prisoners being almost skeletons when finally obtaining their re-lease, which was secured by the representations of General Washing-ton, the powerful advocacy of Mr. Fox and the Liberals in the British Parliament, and the humane sympathy of the Count Metrouskie, who wielded a powerful influence in the Austrian court.* Lafayette, how-ever, even in his second imprisonment, was never shackled; and though treated with the utmost cruelty, no indignities were offered to his per-son, save that he was robbed of his watch and some other trinkets on being recommitted, reduced to a single suit of clothes, and stripped of every little comfort that had been previously allowed him, save such occasional betterments of food—his regulation diet being bread and water—as were certified by his medical attendant to be necessary for the support of life.

It may be here remarked, that the power of memory possessed by Mr. Davis appeared almost miraculous—a single perusal of any pas-sage that interested either his assent or denial enabling him to repeat it almost verbatim, when eulogizing its logic or combating what he considered its errors. This wonderful gift of memorizing, and appar-ent universality of knowledge, were remarked by every Officer of the Day as well as myself, Mr. Davis having kindly relations with all, and conversation suited to each visitor. As instances of this—at which I was not present myself, but heard related from the officers immedi-ately after their occurrence—let me mention two conversations.†

An Officer of the Day, very fond of dogs, and believing himself well posted in all varieties of that animal, once entered the prisoner's cell,

---

*Charles James Fox (1749-1806), British politician and supporter of both the American and French revolutions; Count A. F. Mittrowsky.

†Davis did have a remarkable memory, but he feared the conditions he had to endure in prison might impair it. He wrote his wife, "The saddest ef-fect which has been produced in me is in impaired memory, accustomed to rely on it with confidence it is painfully embarassing [sic] to me, especially as to names and dates." (Davis to Mrs. Davis, 20 October 1865, Jefferson Davis Collection).

followed by a bull-terrier or some other breed of belligerent canine. Mr. Davis at once commenced examining and criticising the dog's points with all the minuteness of a master, thence gliding into a general review of the whole race of pointers, setters, and retrievers; terriers; bull-dogs, German poodles, greyhounds, blood-hounds, and so forth; the result of his conversation being best given in the words of the dog-fancying officer: "Well, I thought I knew something about dogs, but hang me if I won't get appointed Officer of the Day as often as I can, and go to school with Jeff Davis." On another occasion "some lewd fellows of the baser sort" in the garrison had been fighting a main of cocks; the Lieutenant of the Guard in the outer room being the proud possessor of the victorious chanticleer. It thus came to pass that the conquering bird, with dripping plumage, was brought under the prisoner's notice, and again the same scene as with the dog-fancier was repeated in regard to game-cocks and fighting-birds of all varieties— *Cuba possibly* Mr. Davis describing the popularity of the sport in Mexico, {?} *Not true either as to habit* and adding, that when a boy in Mississippi, {(}he had seen only *or prohibition* too much of it, until found out and forbidden by his parents. {)}

On quitting Mr. Davis this day, and in compliance with the order of Major-General Miles, I transmitted to headquarters the following report:

Office of the Chief Medical Officer,
FORT MONROE, VA.,
September 1, 1865.

BREVET MAJOR-GENERAL N. A. MILES,
*Commanding Military District,*
*Fort Monroe, Va.*

GENERAL:—I have the honor to report prisoner Davis still suffering from the effects of a carbuncle. The erysipelas of the face had entirely subsided, but yesterday reappeared. His health is evidently rapidly declining.

I remain, General, very respectfully,

Your obedient servant,
JOHN J. CRAVEN,
Bv't Lieut.-Col. U. S. Vol's, and C. M. O.,
Military District, Fort Monroe, Va.

*September 2d.*—Visited prisoner early, accompanied by Captain Sanderson,* 3d Pennsylvania Artillery, Officer of the Day. Condition of Mr. Davis may be seen in the two following reports, the first being the ordinary one addressed to Major-General Miles, accompanied by a verbal recommendation (often previously made), for a change of quarters. The second, a fuller report, covering the same point, in official form, intended to be transmitted by General Miles to the authorities at Washington. The routine report merely ran:

---

*Joseph W. Sanderson.

"I have the honor to report prisoner Davis's condition not perceivably different from that of yesterday: very feeble; no appetite."

The second report, of same date, intended for transmission to the War Department, ran as follows:

> Office of the Chief Medical Officer,
> FORT MONROE, VA.,
> September 2, 1865.

BREVET MAJOR-GENERAL N. A. MILES,
*Commanding Military District,*
*Fort Monroe, Va.*

GENERAL:—I have the honor to report that I was called to see prisoner Davis on the 24th day of May last. I found him very feeble; prematurely old; all the evidence of an iron will, but extremely reduced in physical structure. As he continued to fail, changes were suggested in his prison life; and kindly granted; his food was changed from prison food to a liberal diet; the guards **{(}** and light **{)}** were removed from his room; he was permitted **{(}** to walk in the open air **{)}** and to have miscellaneous reading. Indeed, **{(}** everything **{)}** was done for him to render him comfortable as a prisoner.

*it was not?*

*how & when surprising in view of his statement that Genl. Miles prevented him from sending any thing which could be denominated a luxury, and reportedly inquired whether my health wd not bear a return to prison regimen.*

Within the last week, I have noticed a great change in the prisoner. He has become despondent and dull, a very unnatural condition for him. He is evidently breaking down. Save a small patch of erysipelas upon his face, and a carbuncle upon one of his limbs, no pointed disease, but general prostration.

I am of opinion that it may be in a measure attributed to the dampness of his room, for I have noticed lately a great change in the atmosphere of the casemates, and would respectfully recommend that he be removed from the room he now occupies to some other apartment. I have no other suggestions to make as to his treatment. He has the best of food and stimulants.

*?*

I remain, General, very respectfully,
> Your obedient servant,
> JOHN J. CRAVEN,
> Bv't Lieut.-Col. and Surg. U. S. Vol's and C. M. O.,
> Military District, Fort Monroe, Va.

*How unlike the statements made to me of Miles obstruction to all his efforts for my relief*

On this occasion, Mr. Davis referred to some remark of Miss Anna Dickenson, hostile to himself, which he had seen in the papers, also recalling that he had heard of the lady's honoring Fort Monroe with her presence some six weeks before—he supposed to derive her inspiration from an actual view of his casemate; or possibly to catch a secret view of him through the admiring favor of Gen. Miles or some smitten officer.* He had noticed that Miss Dickenson had figured

---

*Anna E. Dickinson, a highly successful lyceum lecturer, was known for her dislike of President Johnson and her advocacy of rights for blacks and women.

largely upon the lecturing stage, and had undeniable talent, but the talent rather of a Mænad or Pythoness than most of the mild virgins who worshipped Vesta and kept the fires of faith and charity forever burning on her pure altars. Woman's appearance in the political arena was a deplorable departure from the golden path which nature had marked out for her. The male animal was endowed with more than sufficient belligerency for all purposes of healthy agitation; and woman's part in the social economy, as she had been made beautiful and gentle, should be to soothe asperities, rather than deepen and make more rough the cross-tracks plowed in the road of life by the diverging passions and opinions of men. It was a revolutionary age; transpositions and novelty were the fancies of the day, and woman on the political rostrum was only an outcropping of the disorganized and disorganizing ideas now in control of the popular mind. The clamor of certain classes of women for admission to the professions and employments heretofore engrossed by men, was another phase of the same malady. They demanded to be made self-supporting, forgetful that their most tender charm and safest armor lay in helplessness. Woman's office embraced all the sweetest and holiest duties of suffering humanity. Her true altar is the happy fireside, not the forum with its foul breath and distracting clamors. Physically unable to defend themselves from injury or insult, their weakness is a claim which the man must be utterly base who disregards. The highest test of civilization is the deference paid to women. They are like the beautiful vines of the South, winding around the rugged forest-trees and clothing them with beauty; but let them attempt living apart from this support and they will soon trail along the ground in muddy and trampled impurity. While woman depends on man for everything, man's love accepts, and his generosity can never do enough to discharge the delicious and sacred obligations; but let woman enter into the ruder employments of life as man's rival, and she passes herself as a slave under those inexorable laws of trade which are without sex or sentiment. Perhaps in one branch of medicine there might appear a fitness in her claim to matriculation; but even in that branch, circumstances of sudden difficulty and danger were of every-day occurrence, requiring the steadier nerves, cooler judgment, and quicker action of a medical man to deal with. If asked for his sublimest ideal of what women should be in time of war, he would point to the dear women of his people as he had seen them during the recent struggle. The Spartan mother sent forth her boy bidding him return with honor—either carrying his shield, or on it. The women of the South sent forth their sons, directing them to return with victory; to return with wounds disabling them from further service, or never to return at all. All they had was flung into the contest—beauty, grace, passion, ornament; the exquisite frivolities so dear to the sex were cast aside; their songs, if they had any heart to sing, were patriotic; their trinkets were flung into the public crucible; the carpets from their floors were portioned out as blankets to the suffering soldiers of their cause; women bred to every refinement of luxury wore home-spuns made by their own hands; when materials for an army-balloon were wanted, the richest silk dresses were sent in, and there was only competition to secure their acceptance. As nurses of the sick, as encouragers and providers for the combatants, as angels of charity and mercy adopting as their own all children made orphans in defence of their homes, as patient and beautiful household deities, accepting every sacrifice with unconcern, and lightening the burdens of war by every art, blandishment, and labor proper to their sphere,—the dear women of his people deserved to take rank with the highest heroines of the grandest days of the greatest countries. Talking further upon woman, Mr. Davis stated his belief that when women prove unfaithful to their marriage vows, it will in almost every instance be found the husband's fault. Men throw their wives, or allow them to be thrown, into the companionship of male associates whom they know to be dissolute; neglect them, while the illicit lover pays every attention, and then grow angry at the result of their own criminal folly. It is either this, or that the man has chosen, without sufficient inquiry, a woman whose unfitness for the relations of wife might have been readily ascertained. No woman {*fit to be a wife*} will err if treated properly by a husband worthy of the name; but she is the weaker vessel and must be protected.

# •CHAPTER 18•

*Mr. Davis on Sensation News.—The Condition of the Negro.—Gen. Butler at Drury's Bluff.—Bishop Lynch and the Sisters of Charity.—A Story after the manner of President Lincoln.*

**S**eptember 3d.—Called upon prisoner, accompanied by Captain Evans, 3d Pennsylvania Artillery, Officer of the Day. Had passed a comfortable night, the erysipelas again receding, and the carbuncle commencing to slough out. Reported to General Miles: "Prisoner Davis slightly better this morning." Still complained of the unwholesome atmosphere of his casemate, pointing to some crumbs of bread which he had thrown to the mouse only a day or two before, now covered with mould. Made no reply to this, not knowing what would be the action of the authorities on my recommendation, though hoping, and, indeed, fully trusting that it would be favorable.

Mr. Davis referred to some financial frauds in Wall Street, then exciting much attention in the Northern press, remarking that these insanities or epidemics of financial and other kinds of crime appeared by some unknown law to follow every period of great political excitement. Perhaps the average of crime was at all time the same in every given population—as many eminent statisticians had maintained—the apparent increase of viciousness only arising from the fact that during the greater excitement, whatever that might be, we could spare no attention to minor matters, and now they struck us with a sense of novelty. The Northern press had been working with treble power and at fever-heat for some years, and would require another year to calm back into ordinary journalism. Sensationalism was the necessity at present, and offences which would have been dismissed with a paragraph in the police reports four or five years ago, were now magnified into columns or a page of startling capitals. The cruelty of dragging in family history and the names of relatives Mr. Davis dwelt upon, speaking with great sympathy of a venerable father whose grey hairs, heretofore without a blemish, were now sprinkled by the reports in Northern papers with the mire into which his son had fallen. With the criminal, and all his conscious aiders and abettors, the law and public opinion were entitled to deal; but when journalism passed beyond this limit, and dragged before the gaze of unpitying millions the lacerated and innocent domestic victims of a son's or husband's crime, the act was so inhuman that to term it brutal would be to wrong the dumb creation. True, in tracing out and developing a crime, we had often to enter upon the otherwise sacred privacy of domestic relations; and if anything therein found could materially forward the ends of justice, the lesser right would have to be sacrificed to the greater. But the practice of dragging before the public the whole history of a criminal in his non-criminal relations—his wife and wife's family, his father and father's family, their manner of life, circle of friends, and so forth— deserved reprobation. It is the innocent and pure—and always in the exact measure of their purity and innocence—who most suffer from such offences as the one he was noticing. To the guilty man himself, unless hardened beyond reach of conscience, or dread of shame, the explosion which consigns him to prison must be a positive relief. The agony of anxiety is over; pride has suffered its benumbing shock, and the pain of its former protest is paralysed. In the solitude of his cell he is at peace, or in the companionship of the convict-yard there are none to mock his degradation. Mr. Davis spoke with great feeling on this matter, mentioning several cases which had come to his knowledge, and in particular the default of an army officer while he was Secretary of War. It had been a most painful case, for, up to the moment *?* of the exploitation, he had been on terms of intimacy with the defaulter's family. *?*

Speaking of army defaults, Mr. Davis remarked that our Government seemed to have trouble with the officers appointed to take care of the negroes. The better plan would be to remit their care and future to the several States. None could manage the black for his own good and the public interest so well as those who had been reared with them and knew their peculiarities. Once free, the necessities of labor and the laws of supply and demand would interfere to secure justice to the black laboring class, even were there any disposition to deny it, which he did not believe. Mr. Davis said, judging from the inevitable logic of the case and reports reaching him during the war, that the class of civilians who rushed South in the wake of our armies, professing intense philanthropy for the negro as their object, were about the most unsafe class to whom the destinies of any ignorant and helpless people, out of whom money were to be made, could have been entrusted. Men, the most pure and upright in previous life, when suddenly given control of wealth for distribution to the ignorant and helpless, in too many cases, if not the majority, will gravitate, by force of protracted temptation, into corruption. He instanced the dealings of the Department of the Interior with the Indians—a hideous history, for which the country should blush, though not a little of the peculations and extortions practised by our Indian Agents against the various tribes, had been placed on record. Mr. Davis then spoke of the various Indian nations with whom he had been thrown in contact during his earlier life when serving in the army, giving the habits and leading characteristics of each, but with a rapidity and fluency of Indian names which (the subject being new to me) I could not follow. The general spirit of his remarks was kind to the Red Man, lamenting his wrongs, and the inevitable obliteration of his race as a sacrifice under the Juggernaut of civilization.

Recurring to the management of the negroes by professed philanthropic civilians of the North, Mr. Davis said that all the best men of
both sections were in the armies, and that these civilian camp-followers partook in their nature of the buzzards who were the camp-followers of the air. He said they reminded him of an anecdote told in
Mississippi relative to a professed religionist of very avaricious temper, which ran as follows:

Driving to church one Sunday, the pious old gentleman saw a sheep
foundered in a quagmire on one side of the road, and called John, his
coachman, to halt and extricate the animal—he might be of value. John
halted, entered the quagmire, endeavored to pull out the sheep; but
found that fright, cold, damp, and exposure had so sickened the poor
brute that its wool came out in fistfuls whenever pulled. With this do-
lorous news John returned to the carriage.

"Indeed, John. Is it good wool—valuable?"

"Fust class. Right smart good, Massa. Couldn't be better."

"It's a pity to lose the wool, John. You'd better go see; is it loose
everywhere? Perhaps his sickness only makes it loose in parts."

John returned to the sheep, pulled all the wool, collected it in his
arms, and returned to the carriage.

"It be's all done gone off, Massa. Every hair on him was just a fallin'
when I picked 'um up."

"Well, throw it in here, John," replied the master, lifting up the cur-
tain of his wagon. "Throw it in here, and now drive to church as fast
as you can; I'm afraid we shall be late."

"But de poor sheep, massa," pleaded the sable driver. "Shan't dis
chile go fotch him?"

"Oh, never mind him," returned the philanthropist, measuring the
wool with his eye. "Even if you dragged him out, he could never recover, and his flesh would be good for nothing to the butchers."

So the sheep, stripped of his only covering, was left to die in the
swamp, concluded Mr. Davis; and such will be the fate of the poor
negroes entrusted to the philanthropic but avaricious Pharisees who
now profess to hold them in special care.

I remarked that this story reminded me of Mr. Lincoln's happy way
of arguing his own position, while not appearing to argue at all.

Mr. Davis said he had heard many of Mr. Lincoln's stories, or stories attributed to him, but knew not how much to believe. When a
man once got a reputation of this sort, he was given credit for all the
curious stories afloat; nor could he conceive how a man so oppressed
with care as Mr. Lincoln, could have had any relish for such pleas-
antries. Recurring to the subject of the philanthropic guardians of the
negro, he asked me, if ever released from duty in Fort Monroe—which
he as selfishly hoped would not be until he also was released, either
by order of man or the summons of death—to visit New England and
count for myself how many doughty talkers for the negro, before the
war, had worn sword on thigh or carried musket in hand during its
continuance? For the agitators of the South, as they were called, this

could be said: that they had veritably staked life, property, and honor in support of their ideas.

Of the negro race Mr. Davis spoke most kindly, saying that the irregularities into which they had been betrayed, arose from misinformation spread amongst them by these civilian philanthropists.* They were taught that the General Government was about transferring to them in fee the estates of the Southern whites, thus enabling them to live in opulence and idleness (as they hoped) through all future time. Whatever might be the designs of the future, this had not yet been done; and hence the disappointment of the negroes, who began to regard freedom as a much less blessing than they at first supposed. They took their idea of freedom from what they had seen of their masters, and imagined that to be free—pure and simple—implied as a concomitant all the comforts and luxuries which they had seen their masters enjoying under the old system of labor. He was sorry for the poor negroes with his whole heart. The future might possibly better their condition—in the next generation, not in this; but to him, the freed slaves seemed like cage-bred birds enjoying their first hour of liberty, but certain to pay a terrible penalty for it when night and winter came, and they knew neither where to find food or shelter.

*not so. my opinion was & is that the next generation will be still worse off.*

Mr. Davis said that we—himself and the writer—had once, from my account, been opposite each other in battle. It was on May the 16th, 1864, at the engagement which we called Drury's Bluff,† but not properly so, the battle having its central point at the house of the Rev. Mr. Friend, and both its wings resting on Proctor's Creek. There were several lines of defence between that battle-ground and the works at Drury's Bluff. Beauregard had been fooling Butler for some days by skirmishing and falling back, in order to draw Butler on. Davis was present on the foggy morning of the decisive day—the day which rendered Butler permanently powerless for further evil, and hoped that morning to capture our entire army. This would have been done if General Whiting (I think) had obeyed orders.‡ His orders were to flank Butler, while the battle was going on in front, and cut him off from his base and works at Bermuda Hundred. This might easily have been done, but the orders miscarried in some manner, and General Butler,

*no.*

*most wrong in regard to Genl Whiting but in every detail greatly at variance with my recollections*

---

*Regarding the freedmen, Davis wrote his wife, "The negro is unquestionably to be at last a victim because when brought into conflict, the inferior race must be overborne, but if it is possible to defer the conflict, & to preserve a part of the common relations heretofore existing between the races, when in long life common interest united them, the object is worthy of our effort. To be successful the policy must be as far removed from the conservatism that rejects everything new, as from the idealism which would retain nothing which is old" (Davis to Mrs. Davis, 21 November 1865, Jefferson Davis Collection).

†Drewry's Bluff.

‡General William H. C. Whiting was rumored to have been either drunk or drugged during this battle.

with the 10th and 18th Corps, forming his force, escaped—though Mr. Davis heard we had hardly enough shovels in our army to bury the dead. General Terry,* with the 10th Corps, had been allowed to carry their exterior line of rifle-pits. Then, Beauregard massed his forces, charged out of his works, cut the 18th Corps to pieces, and very badly crippled the 10th.

I replied that I remembered all the incidents of the day very well, hav-

*not true*

ing been nearly captured by some of {(}his cavalry bushwhack-ers{)?} while endeavoring to take care of my wounded near Chester Station, on the railroad from Richmond to Petersburg. Nothing but let-ting them count the nails in the hind-shoes of my horse had saved me. Returned about half an hour after that, and brought off my wounded without difficulty. Then related to Mr. Davis the incident of General Walker, of Beauregard's staff, which forms the introduction to this vol-ume. {*not published as related to me by Dr. C.*}

*Did not say so to me but heard something like it nomine mutata*

From this point the conversation diverged to the treatment of our wounded by the Confederate surgeons. {(}I said{)} that com-plaint had been made, and with justice, as I could personally certify in some cases, that unnecessary amputations had been performed on

*utter fabrication, no such conditions of the medical staff of the C.S.A. ever ex-isted. I remember to have told him of a statement made to me in relation to an amputation performed on Col. Mott by a Federal Surgeon under circum-stances indicating a pur-pose to kill him, also of a report communicated to me as coming from a Federal Surgeon that one of their Genls. in the seven days re-treat of McClellan had de-stroyed the surgical means necessary for their own wounded left to our care; when we were known to be deficient in hospital stores. I also spoke to him of their bad faith in capturing our surgeons, while we observed the agreement to leave such officers free from arrest. This mistatement [sic] is specially noticed because it is in a case where his mem-*

wounded Union soldiers falling into the hands of Confederate sur-geons. Mr. Davis said this was undeniable; but not more so with our men than with the boys of his own people. They had been obliged to accept as surgeons in the Southern army many lads who had only half finished their education in Northern colleges. Besides, their facilities for transporting and taking care of the sick were greatly deficient; nor had they had proper hospital stores, nor appliances for cure, in any such abundance as with us. To bunglers in the art of surgery, or men too hurried for scientific treatment, amputation is always a readier remedy than the slow process of splints, removing daily dressings; and all he would claim on behalf of his surgeons was, that they had treated all the wounded, Confederate or Union, with impartiality; and that if too many amputations had been performed on the one, they had like-wise been performed on the other. He then referred to the courtesy of the medical profession towards each other, as exhibited when sur-geons had been taken prisoners. They were always treated on his side, and so far as he knew upon our side, with the respect due to scientific non-combatants, whose business was the healing, not the wounding, art. It was by these little humanities war endeavored to soften the nat-ural brutalities of its nature to the educated mind.

Mentioned to Mr. Davis that I had once had a very interesting day's service exchanging some three or four hundred Confederates for about an equal number of our own wounded boys. Brigadier-General James F. Hall had been our officer of exchange, and Surgeon Bontecue† my associate. We steamed up Charleston Harbor in the hospital-ship *Cos-*

---

*Alfred H. Terry.
†Dr. Reed B. Bontecou.

*mopolitan,* and were met by Bishop Lynch\* on a vessel carrying our wounded. The Bishop had been extremely kind, receiving the blessings of our boys, who spoke in warm terms of his Christian humanity. So far as I could judge from that specimen, our wounded had not anything to complain of in their treatment—at least nothing which the necessities of their situation rendered avoidable. To this Mr. Davis replied in warm eulogy of Bishop Lynch, as also of the Sisters of Charity, not one of whom he could ever pass without raising his hat—an act of involuntary reverence. They had indeed been the silent angels of the war, carrying comfort and religious faith to every couch of suffering. Of what they had done, history might make no mention; but it would remain for ever engraven upon the hearts of the tens of thousands they had helped and comforted. Emblems of purity and mercy, no lives in the whole world could be more beautiful than theirs. Their hymns were an undertone or diapason of sacred melody through all the crash of arms and the harrowing chorus of groans. If it had been possible in his estimation to elevate the respect for woman, the conduct of the Sisters of Charity would have done so. Meeting Bishop Lynch casually one day, he asked him in the usual commonplace how the world went with him. Never should he forget—for it was but an echo from his own soul—the tone in which the Bishop replied, "This war, Mr. Davis; this war. I am heart-sick, heart-sick, heart-sick!"†

*ory could not be expected to fail so signally. The motive to conceal my opinions is the same as that which appears elsewhere. In the field it is often necessary to amputate a limb which in other circumstances might be saved. This much I may incidentally have mentioned as a familiar fact, and also a well remembered source of regret.*

*unfounded, untrue, and out of charactrer.*

---

\*Patrick N. Lynch, Roman Catholic bishop of Charleston.

†Davis had mixed feelings about the Catholic clergy. As a youth he had toyed with the idea of becoming a Catholic himself. In prison he received an autographed photograph from the pope and a scapular from the Sisters of Charity in Charleston. After he learned that his daughter was studying in a convent school in Montreal, he told his wife, "When I was a child the kindness of the Friars so won upon my affection that the impression has never been effaced, but has been rather extended from them to their whole church." Yet, in another letter, he also told her, "My early impressions and continuing affection for the Priests of 'Saint Thomas' [the Catholic school he attended in Kentucky] led me to clothe all their brethren in a moral robe as white as the toga of my early friends. In Havana I first learned how great was the mistake & elsewhere and subsequently was forced to believe that the vows which had seemed so well to fit the Roman Priest for the ministry of God, were in some places and with some, perhaps, in all places,—'cheap as the custom-house oaths' " (Davis to Mrs. Davis, 20 October, 30 December 1865, Jefferson Davis Collection).

# •CHAPTER 19•

*Treason.—State and National.—The Fish-Hawk and Bald-Eagle.—Mr. Davis on Senator Benton, Ex-President Buchanan, and President Andrew Johnson.—Preparations to remove Mr. Davis to Carroll Hall.*

September 6th.—Called upon Mr. Davis once or twice, I remember, between the interval of my last date and this, but have lost notes. Called to-day, accompanied by Captain Titlow, 3d Pennsylvania Artillery, Officer of the Day, and found prisoner in a more comfortable state of mind and body than he had enjoyed for some days. Healthy granulations forming in the carbuncle.

Mr. Davis said the clamor about "treason" in our Northern newspapers was only an evidence how little our editors were qualified by education for their positions. None seemed to remember that treason to a State was possible, no less than to the United States; and between the horns of this dilemma there could be little choice. In the North, where the doctrine of State sovereignty was little preached or practiced, this difficulty might not seem so great; but in the South a man had presented the unpleasant alternatives of being guilty of treason to his State when it went out of the Union, by remaining, what was called "loyal" to the Federal Government, or being guilty of treason to the {(} General Government {)} by remaining faithful to his State. These terms appeared to have little significance at the North, but were full of potency in the South, and had to be regarded in every political calculation.

*not so. The Constu. of U.S. defines treason, not a word about genl. govt.*

Mr. Davis said he had been much interested all the morning watching from the grated embrasure, near which his bed lay, the free flight of fish-hawks, so plentiful during the summer in Hampton Roads, and some of which still lingered. The bird was a sacred guest, visiting the coast on particular days in every season, and carrying with its appearance the glad tidings to so many fishermen that the shoals of shad, alewives—mossbunkers he believed we called them in the North—and blue-fish, were upon the coast. The fish-hawk or osprey was associated with the bald-headed eagle in such intimate relations, that to describe the habits of the one, necessitated some description of the habits of the other.

The osprey or fish-hawk visited the coast in early spring, on the same day that the fish he had named made their appearance. It built its nest in some dead tree standing near a barn or house, long experience having assured it that it ran no danger from man. Its food was upon the deep; and from the farm it dwelt upon, the osprey took nothing but the support of a single decaying tree. Here it huddled together in the forks nearest the ground, a couple of cart-loads of twigs and branches to form its nest—sticks varying in thickness from a man's little finger to that of a cart-rung. On these were laid coatings of meadow-grass, and finally the feathers from its own breast, and so the nest was made and in it the eggs deposited. From this perch the fish-hawk mother kept a wary eye upon the waters, its male being close at hand, either to bring it food or protect the eggs or young during its absence. At the first ripple, betokening a shoal of fish in the distance, away sailed the male or female parent, poising over the surface of the waters on balanced wing until the fish—who had seen its shadow coming and struck for the bottom—should reappear. Then it folded its wings and dropped down like a bullet, reëmerging presently with a shad, or blue-fish, or alewife, varying in weight from half a pound to four pounds, clutched firmly in its talons—the head of the fish being always directly under its own head, which was not idle in picking out the eyes. Thus it sailed along the water for half a dozen yards until the grasp of its talons was made more secure; then suddenly rose on perpendicular wing in the air and struck off for its nest near the barn-yard.

But there is another bird on the coast, added Mr. Davis, for whom these fishing operations have much interest. It is the bald eagle, who builds on some crag, if there be any crag within vision of the sea; and if not, in the tallest tree that he can find, and farthest from the haunts of men. As he sees the fish-hawk sail forth, the eagle rivets his far-piercing eyes on the bird's motions. Then, as the osprey rises with his prey, the eagle shakes out the broad vans of his wings, looks at them to see that every feather is in place, and sullenly swoops upward into the air with the assurance of a conqueror. There is a wild scream from the osprey as it endeavors to rise higher, not satisfied as yet but some other fish-hawk with its prize may be the eagle's quarry. A few moments more and the hunt is certain; the fish-hawk drops its prey, and flies out to sea with redoubled screams, while the grave eagle rapidly descends with unblinking eyelids upon the prize that has been dropped for his morning or noon repast, often seizing it before it strikes the ground or water, and proceeds to make a meal. "This is the history of these birds," concluded Mr. Davis, "and I have watched them with the *fiction* most lively interest, though the circumscribed view from my inclosure gave me no means of observing more than the exploits of the gulls and fish-hawks in the capture of their prey."

This rule of prey and being preyed on, added Mr. Davis, appeared universal through nature. Up to the regal footstool of man, no beast, or bird, or fish, could be pointed out which did not prey on some minor creation of the animal or vegetable world, and was not preyed on in turn. Even with man, the stronger by nature preyed upon and absorbed the weaker; and this, though a harsh philosophy, was the sum and result of worldly experience. The terms virtue and vice were comparative, not absolute. The man of natural virtue might have no virtue at all. It is the man who restrains his passions when they are strongest, who is entitled to wear the crown. Mr. Davis then quoted, though rarely quoting poetry, the well known lines from Burns:—

Who knows the heart—it's he alone,
     Decidedly can try us;
He knows each chord—its various tone;
     Each spring, its various bias;
Then at the balance let's be mute,
     We never can adjust it—
What's done we partly may compute,
     But know not what resisted.*

A remark, that I hoped to see him soon resuming his walks on the ramparts, and reading less continually in a recumbent posture, called *Inaccurate* out several anecdotes from Mr. Davis relative to Senator Benton† of Missouri, who was, he said, an incessant student, never quitting his room except in necessity, but taking all the exercise he thought needful with dumb-bells and calisthenic exercises of his own choice. Senator Benton had one peculiarity very amusing to those who knew him, his desire to contradict and make a case against such of his associates as were about speaking on some point peculiarly within their own province of practical observation or education. Thus, if a Senator from California gave notice that on such a day he would introduce a resolution relative to gold-mining, or the Senator from Massachusetts gave similar notice relative to the fisheries, Mr. Benton would immediately bury himself in his library and commence coaching up, or "cramming," as it was called in college, for the forthcoming debate. He would read all varieties of books on the subject, arm himself with the most minute and comprehensive statistics, and thus intellectually equipped, take the field against whatever view the Senator who had given notice of the motion might advance. The result would be that a few home-thrusts from the lance of practical experience would bar all the delicate theories of Mr. Benton's authorities to shreds; but these debates were useful as giving the Senate a sketch of the two sides which every question has—that of theory and fact.

As Mr. Davis was speaking of the Senate, asked him his opinion of President Johnson, to which for some moments he made no reply, apparently hesitating whether to speak on the subject or not. At length he said that of President Johnson he knew no more than the papers told every one; but that of Mr. Johnson, when in the Senate, he would as freely speak as of any other member. There were, of course, differences between them, more especially just previous to the retirement of the Southern representatives from Congress. The position of Mr. Johnson with his associates of the South had never been pleasant, not from any fault or superciliousness on their side, but solely due to

---

*"Address to the Unco Guild."
†Thomas Hart Benton.

the intense, almost morbidly sensitive, pride of Mr. Johnson.* Sitting
with associates, many of whom he knew pretended to aristocracy, Mr.
Johnson seemed to set up before his own mind, and keep ever present
with him, his democratic or plebeian origin as a bar to warm social
relations. This pride—for it was the pride of having no pride—his associates long struggled to overcome, but without success. They respected Mr. Johnson's abilities, integrity, and greatly original force of
character; but nothing could make him be, or seem to wish to feel at
home in their society. Some casual word dropped in debate, though
uttered without a thought of his existence, would seem to wound him
to the quick, and again he would shrink back into the self-imposed
isolation of his earlier and humbler life, as if to gain strength from
touching his mother earth. In a word, while other members of the
Senate were Democrats in theory or as their political faith, Mr. Johnson was a Democrat of pride, conviction, and self-assertion—a man
of the people, who not only desired no higher grade of classification,
but could not be forced into its acceptance or retention when friendly
efforts were made to that end.† He was an immense worker and student, but always in the practicalities of life; little in the graces of literature. His habits were marked by temperance, industry, courage, and
unswerving perseverance; also, by inveterate prejudices or preconcep-
tions on certain points, and these no arguments could shake. His faith
in the judgment of the people was unlimited, and to their decision he
was always ready to submit. One of the people by birth, he remained
so by conviction, continually recurring to his origin, though he was by
no means the only Senator of the South in like circumstances. Mr. Davis mentioned Aaron V. Brown, of Mississippi, who had been Post-     ?
master-General under President Buchanan and several others, who
were of like Democratic education with Mr. Johnson, but who seemed
to forget, and in regard to whom it was forgotten by their associates,
that they had ever held less social rank than that to which their talents
and industry had raised them. Of Mr. Johnson's character justice was
an eminent feature, though not uncoupled—as true justice rarely fails

---

*Davis and Johnson nearly came to blows when the former, speaking in
Congress on General Zachary Taylor's successes at the Battles of Palo Alto
and Resaca de la Palma (8-9 May 1846), asked if "a blacksmith or a tailor
could have secured the same results?" Johnson, a tailor by trade, took um-
brage at the remark and denounced Davis as a member of "the illegitimate,
swaggering, bastard, scrub aristocracy." Davis apologized to Johnson, explaining that he chose these two occupations as examples of the types of individuals who sometimes comment upon military affairs with no real
knowledge. In Congress Davis declared, "Once for all, then, I would say, that
if I know myself, I am incapable of wantonly wounding the feelings or of
making invidious reflections upon the origin or occupation of any man." James
T. McIntosh, ed., *The Papers of Jefferson Davis* (Baton Rouge: Louisiana State
University Press, 1974) 2:627-28.

†These words of praise were used by Halpine in letters to Johnson solic-
iting appointments for Halpine's friends.

to be—with kindliness and generosity. He was eminently faithful to his word, and possessed a courage which took the form of angry resistance if urged to do, or not do, anything which might clash with his convictions of duty. He was indifferent to money and careless of praise or censure when satisfied of the necessity of any line of action. But for *?* his decided attitude against secession, he would probably have been given the place of Mr. Stephens on the Presidential ticket of the Confederacy. Mr. Stephens, indeed, held the same attitude up to the last moment; but on the secession of his State, had two alternatives of State *ignorant fabrication?* or Federal "treason," as it was called, presented, and chose the latter.

Mr. Davis remarked that Mr. Buchanan more fulfilled the European ideal of a Chief-of-State in his social relations than any American since Washington. He was dignified, polished, reticent, and suave; fond of lady-gossip and the atmosphere of intrigue; a stickler for the ceremony of power. His misfortune was, as regarded his reputation North, that he could not forget in a month, and at the dictation of a party only representing the majority of one section, all those principles which had been imbibed in his youth and formed the guiding-stars of his career through over fifty years of public service. Of Mr. Cushing,* of Mas-*Still inaccurate* sachusetts, Mr. Davis spoke in terms of praise, eulogizing his general talents, and more especially his soundness as an exponent of Constitutional law. He also referred to Mr. George M. Dallas as his model for the externals of a diplomatic representative, quoting something he had once known Mr. Cobden,† of England, to say or write; in substance, that Dallas reminded him of some stately courtier-portrait in an old picture-gallery, suddenly clothing itself with flesh and stepping down from the wall to again pace with living men, while preserving all the passionless immobility of its pictorial experience.

After quitting prisoner, proceeded, by invitation of General Miles, and in company with that officer, to make an inspection of the fort, for the purpose of selecting more healthful quarters for the State prisoner. Decided that rooms in second story of the south end of Carroll Hall would best suit—a building long used as officers' quarters, near the main sally-port, and in which nearly every officer of the old army was for some months quartered after quitting West Point, and before being assigned to general duty elsewhere. It is a tradition in and around Old Point Comfort, that both Grant and Sherman occupied in their day the very chambers selected for the second incarceration of Mr. Davis. As with the casemate, there were to be two rooms used for the prisoner's confinement. In the outer one a lieutenant and two soldiers were constantly stationed on guard, having a view of the interior chamber through a grated door. Opposite this door was a fireplace. To its right, when facing the door, a window heavily grated, and with a sentinel continually on duty before it, pacing up and down the pi-

---

*Caleb Cushing.
†Richard Cobden.

azza. Opposite the window a door leading into the corridor, but permanently fastened with heavy iron clamps, and in this door a sliding-panel in which the face of a sentinel was continually framed by night and day, ready to report to his officer the first sign of any attempt on the prisoner's part to shuffle off this mortal coil by any act of self-violence. It was of this face, with its unblinking eyes, that Mr. Davis *New to me?* so bitterly complained in after days; but this is anticipating. The prisoner, as was said of Lafayette, is perhaps "not sick enough yet," and has to suffer some further weeks of exposure in his present casemate.

The rooms being selected, General Miles gave orders to the En- *?* gineer Department for their speedy conversion from quarters to a prison, the piazza being prolonged and raised by a flight of stairs, *?* so that access to the ramparts could be had by Mr. Davis without a descent to the ground-tier, which invariably caused a crowd to collect, with its usual unpleasant attendants of staring and whispering com- *?* mentaries.

*September 7th.*—Called on Mr. Davis, accompanied by Captain Corlis,* aide-de-camp to General Miles, Officer of the Day. Found the health of prisoner not differing from the preceding day, and so reported to the General commanding in the bulletin required of me at this time.

Told Mr. Davis, thinking it would cheer him and help to soothe his nervousness, that I had reason to hope he would soon be removed to more comfortable quarters. Was sorry for this afterwards, as the protracted and unforseen delays in his removal only made him more painfully fretful {?} in regard to the poisonous atmosphere of his *He always commanded my* present casemate. Had only a brief interview with Mr. Davis, there *calm resolution &c &c* being much sickness in the fort then, and many demands upon my time. Mentioned that I thought in a few days of paying Richmond a visit; General Alfred H. Terry, my old commander in the 10th Army Corps, having now his headquarters at that place. I had spent many days in front of the city as Chief Medical Officer of the 10th Corps, and Acting Medical Director of the Army of the James; had once caught a glimpse of the promised land from the Pisgah of a battery on the south-east, and about four miles removed, but had not then been permitted to enter. Mr. Davis pleasantly replied that if Richmond were my land of promise, the Caleb and Joshua visiting it would carry back but slender bunches of grapes. His people had suffered terrible privations, but with the severities and necessities of war removed, he hoped they would now be better supplied.

---

*Stephen P. Corliss.

# •CHAPTER 20•

*Visit to Richmond.—General Lee.—Mr. Davis on Horseback Exercise.*
*—Macaulay's Pictorial Power.*

**S**eptember 11*th.*—Called on Mr. Davis, accompanied by Capt. Bickly,*
3d Pennsylvania Artillery, Officer of the Day. Found him convalescent
in all respects, able to walk on the ramparts and in good spirits, considering his situation. Told him, as he was well, I was about starting that
day for Richmond, to be gone about a week, and would be happy to carry
any social messages he might wish to send any friends in that city. Mr.
Davis asked me to call upon his former pastor, the Rev. Dr. Minnegerode,† Rector of St. Paul's; also upon other friends, giving me their names,
who would be glad to receive me. He requested me to make his afflictions
in prison appear as light as possible, for they had sufficient troubles of
their own without borrowing more from his misfortunes. He also said
Richmond had been a very beautiful city in the days gone by; but what
with years of military operations and the fire, he feared its appearance
must now be sadly altered. "Oh, the anxious moments I have spent in
that city!" exclaimed Mr. Davis. "Cares that none can understand who
have not been called to fill the first positions of responsibility in revolutionary times. What hopes and fears, tried by enemies without and mur-
murers or mutineers within—though of the latter there were
comparatively few. Taking all they suffered into view, my dear people
stood firm and upheld my hands with a devotion and unanimity for which
I can never be too grateful. God bless them, one and all, and grant them
the sustaining influence of His grace!"

Mr. Davis spoke the last sentence with great fervor, his thin hands
clasped, and tears brimming up in his eyes, though not allowed to run
over. It was in such moments that his face, though not handsome,
judged by any mere artistic standard, became very striking and noble
in the delicate expression of its intellectual power and fervor.

Mr. Davis became solicitous for removal from his casemate, and wished
to know when his new quarters in Carroll Hall would be ready? Would
he be likely to be transferred there before my return? Told him I hoped
to find him there on coming back, but could give no definite assurance—
the engineers having to make some alterations in the rooms, and possibly
some authorizing order being required from Washington.

---

*Robert W. Bickley.
†Charles A. Minnegerode.

To question of Mr. Davis, replied that Mr. Clay was far from well, extremely nervous, a prey to dyspepsia and want of sleep, but not in any immediate danger. Clay was my complaining patient, but Mr. Mitchel* was a model of patience and good-humor, though terribly afflicted at times with asthmatic difficulties. Mr. Davis answered with a smile, that Mitchel was used to it—had been in this or a worse strait before; but allowance must be made for himself {?} and Clay, who were only serving their apprenticeship to Baron Trenck's profession.† Took leave of prisoner, assuring him I would call on the friends he indicated in Richmond, deliver his messages of affectionate remembrance, and bring back all the social news.

*Why make allowance if as he always said he was surprised at my patience?*

*September 22d.*—Called on Mr. Davis for the first time since returning from Richmond, accompanied by Captain Titlow, 3d Pennsylvania Artillery, Officer of the Day. Found he had been inquiring for me several days, in consequence of suffering erysipelas to his face. Reported his condition to Major-General Miles, respectfully asking permission to call in Colonel Pineo, Medical Inspector of the Department, for consultation.

Mr. Davis inquired about friends in Richmond, asking, with a smile, was he still remembered there, or whether it had been found {(}convenient{)} to erase his name from the tablets of memory? Assured him that his friends appeared most solicitous for his welfare, especially the ladies, who had overwhelmed my wife with attentions during our brief visit, as the only means of expressing their gratitude for any alleviations of his situation which my duty{)} as his medical attendant had imposed. Told him the destruction from the fire had been great, but in less than two years the city would have retrieved a prosperity not only equalling, but surpassing any it had yet known. Overlooking Richmond from the top of Gamble Hill, the clamor of trowels and hammers everywhere resounded beneath me, and it seemed like an enormous beehive, so incessant was the industry. Mentioned that General Terry, my old commander, had kindly placed {(}the carriage of Mr. Davis{)} at my disposal during the visit; and that I had visited with much interest, and not without sympathy, the beautiful ground of Hollywood Cemetery, where General J. E. B. Stuart and so many other distinguished officers of the late Southern army now lie in graves, not nameless indeed, but as yet with no enduring monuments. Also spoke of having seen Mr. Lyons, Judge Ould, the Grants, and many other friends of his during my stay at the Ballard House.‡

*necessary under martial law*

*They knew of her kindness*

*?*

---

*John Mitchel, editor of the *Richmond Enquirer* and the *Richmond Examiner,* had been released from Fort Monroe in October 1865.

†Baron Friedrich von der Trenck (German adventurer, 1726-1794) wrote a popular autobiography of his varied military service and many imprisonments.

‡James Lyons, Judge Robert Ould, and the James Grant family who lived next door to the Confederate White House.

Mr. Davis laughed about his carriage, and said that since some "Yankee" had to ride in it, he would prefer my doing so to another. During the war they had no time to build monuments to the illustrious dead—scarcely time enough or means enough to take care of the wounded living. If their cause had been successful, the gratitude of {(}a new nation{)} would have built splendid mausoleums and trophies to those who had lost their lives in founding it; but with the failure of the cause, this study of piety and gratitude must now devolve on private associations of patriotic gratitude. General Jackson ("Stonewall") appeared to have some lively presentiment of death shortly before its occurrence, and had asked that his only monument might be a battle-flag hoisted over his grave until such time as the cause for which he fought was crowned with victory and secure from aggression. Speaking of a message of condolence and cheer the Rev. D. Minnegerode had sent him, Mr. Davis spoke in warm terms of the learning, zeal, eloquence, fidelity, and Christian courage of that gentleman. General Lee had occupied a pew in the same church, and unless when absent unavoidably in the public service, was one of the most regular and devout attendants. General Lee was, undoubtedly, one of the greatest soldiers of the age, if not the very greatest of this or any other country; but had he drawn sword on the Federal side, must have been remitted to obscurity, under our system, in the first six months of the war. Nothing, however, shook the confidence of military men, competent to form a just opinion, in his superior qualifications for high command, and his career had nobly vindicated the calm estimate of professional judgment.

*[margin note:]* not my expression

*[margin note:]* new to me & not believed to be true

*[margin note:]* ?

Mr. Davis inquired anxiously what signs there were, if any, of his removal to the new quarters I had mentioned before my Richmond visit? He was more than ever satisfied of the unhealthiness of his casemate, and the nights were now growing so chill, that one might as well be condemned to sleep in a stone coffin—a little better, for when the coffin comes the body has no feeling.

*September 23d.*—Called with Lieutenant A. H. Bowman,* 3d Pennsylvania Artillery, Officer of the Day. Found the condition of Mr. Davis not materially changed, and so reported to General Miles.

Prisoner renewed his questions about the proposed change in his place of confinement, begging me, if I knew anything, even the worst, that he was to be kept as now until death put an end to his sufferings, not to conceal it from him any longer; that suspense was more injurious to him than could be the most painful certainty. Assured him that I had no further information. A place had been selected for his incarceration in Carroll Hall, the requisite changes in the rooms made, and I heard no reason for his non-transfer. If I did so, he should be informed immediately.

Recurring to my Richmond visit, Mr. Davis made many minute inquiries relative to former friends, the apparent condition of the tradespeople in regard to prosperity, the social relations, if any were al-

---

*Alphonsus H. Bowman.

lowed, {?} between the occupying army and the inhabitants. He said X
his people, having done all their duty in war, had now the two duties of
{(} forgetting the past {?} preparing to accept the future. One of X
their great troubles in agricultural districts must be the difficulty of getting draft animals—horses, mules, and oxen having been so nearly swept
away by the war. With nothing to regret in the past but its failure, the
failure and its consequences should be accepted in good faith, and without a murmur. The future is always under the control of resolute men;
and with industry and the influx of Northern {?} and European cap- X
ital, which must soon be tempted by the preabundant natural resources
in the South, there could be no reason why national {?} prosperity X
should not be fully reestablished within half a dozen years—that is, if the
Federal Government pursued a wise and generous course, allaying irri-
tations, and diverting the minds of the people from their unsuccessful
sacrifices, by pointing out and encouraging the splendid rewards of industry.

*Say rather ceases to meddle and oppress*

Mr. Davis renewed my attention to the steady deterioration of his
health, which he regarded as chiefly due to the unfitness of his cell for a
human habitation. His head had a continual humming in it, like the
whizzing of a wound watch when its main-spring is suddenly broken.
Little black motes slowly ascended and descended between his sight and
whatever page he was reading, or object inspecting; and his memory like-
wise gave distinct indications of losing its elasticity. The carbuncle, however, was quite well, having left a deep-red cicatrice where it had been,
precisely like the healed wound of a Minie bullet. Mr. Davis had not much
flesh to lose on entering the fort; but believed he must have lost what
little of it could be spared while still preserving life. Was glad to see from
the papers that General Lee had accepted the presidency of Washington
College, in Virginia. Happy would be the pupils who would grow up under the tutelage, and with the noble exemplar before them of his pure
life, Christian faith, stainless integrity, and varied acquirements. The
crying sign of our present educational system is a neglect of the moral ?
nature, while overloading the intellectual with premature food, which it
must be strained in digesting.

*September 24th.*—Called on Mr. Davis, accompanied by Captain Bickley, 3d Pennsylvania Artillery, Officer of the Day. Prisoner much better.
The symptoms of a return of erysipelas gone. Had enjoyed his walk on
the ramparts, and had seen a young lady on horseback who saluted him
prettily as she passed. Did not know when raising his hat that he was
bowing to his young hostess, but was informed she was my daughter.
Remarked that she rode gracefully, sending her his compliments, and then
commented on the little attention paid to horseback—the most healthful
and delicious form of exercise—in the Northern States, and more especially amongst the ladies, who from their sedentary habits would derive
most benefit from its practice. When ladies unaccustomed to the saddle
did begin horseback, they had something like a mania for fast cantering,
or even galloping, it being not only a pride but wonder to them at the
termination of each ride that they were still in their seats. This was un-
graceful, which should be a sufficient bar to its continuance; it was also

a strain both on the rider and beast. A short burst now and then along good parts of the road was very well occasionally, to warm the horse and *fast walk* quicken the rider's blood; but a gentle trot or rack was the true gait for all who wished to derive health from this exercise—more especially ladies; and yet the canter or gallop was their favorite pace. The Texan, Mexican, and Indian riders were among the best he had ever seen; the *what does he mean, if any-* men of these countries—for the women never ride, except on journeys *thing it must be error* of necessity, horseback as a pleasure or for health—being several grades beyond their advance of civilization. Mr. Davis then spoke of Indians dismounting and remounting while their ponies were in full gallop, swinging their bodies down and picking up stones, etc.; but added there were none of these feats which he had not seen some of our dragoons do better *? not mine* and more certainly when once taught by the Indians. As a general rule, his people were better horsemen than those of the North. This was due partly to some remnant of cavalier origin in their education and sentiments, but still more to the distance between plantations, the want of good roads, and their devotion to agricultural pursuits. Their cavalry had been superior to ours in the commencement of the war for these reasons, but their stock of horses gave out sooner, and towards the close of the struggle it became difficult to mount a Confederate regiment, except by *not mine* capturing a regiment of their enemies. General R. Stuart* had been styled the Prince Regent of the South; but the name, as in many other cases, had not been to his advantage. He was a rarely gallant and noble gentleman, well supporting by his character the tradition that royal blood flowed in his veins. Subsisting his command gave him great difficulty—the cavalry having to be scattered for winter quarters in the Shenandoah valley, and other places more remote, where forage was plentiful, thus relaxing its discipline and bringing it already somewhat jaded into the field on the return of spring.

Mr. Davis then spoke of Macaulay's History of England with a freedom and unreservedness of admiration such as he rarely expressed. The portrait painting it contained was more vivid and subtle than anything on this side of Plutarch, and gave the surrounding circumstances to serve as a frame with broader scope and more liveliness of panoramic effect. The sketches of Clarendon, Shrewsbury, Marlborough, etc., etc., were not lifeless simulachre [*sic*], but instinct with the turbulence and intrigues both of the social and political atmospheres *The writer probably con-* in which they moved. No events of his actual life seemed more real *founded Allison & Mc-* than the life into which he was transferred by the absorbing power of *Cauley & Clarendon* Macaulay's genius. The portrait of Marlborough, Mr. Davis thought *between whose sketches I* the great masterpiece of the work, though drawn with a pencil not suf- *had about that time been* ficiently tempered by allowance for the unsettled, revolutionary, and *making comparative reflec-* conspiratorial times in which the scenes were laid. *tions.*

---

*James Ewell Brown (Jeb) Stuart.

# •CHAPTER 21•

October 5th.—Visited Mr. Davis once or twice in the interval between this date and my last; but the memoranda of such calls cannot be found. Remember, however, that the fort was visited during the interval by Colonel Louis H. Pelouze, U.S.A., of the War Department—an able, kind, and gallant young officer, whom I had previously known as Assistant Adjutant-General of the Sherman expedition at Port Royal. Colonel Pelouze called for a report of the health of the prisoner, with my opinion as to the advisability or necessity of a change in his place of confinement; visited the new quarters in Carroll Hall, and directed General Miles—being thereto empowered by his instruction—to remove Mr. Davis from the casemate to his new and more pleasant abode.

Called this day (October 5) with Captain Korte, 3d Pennsylvania Artillery, Officer of the Day, and found Mr. Davis already looking much brighter, exclaiming as I entered, "The world does move, after all." The panel in the side-door opening on the corridor, in which a sentry's face was framed, gave him some annoyance, and he referred again to Lafayette in connection with the torture of a human eye constantly riveted on his movements. If his wish were to commit suicide, such a precaution would prove wholly unavailing. It looked rather as if the wish were to drive him to its commission. He then referred to some eminent French general, who, while a prisoner in England, procured and studied anatomical diagrams for the purpose of learning how life could be most certainly and painlessly lost, or with least disfigurement. He discovered that precise part of the breast in which the heart, unprotected by any rib, lay nearest the surface. Sticking a small pin through this spot in the diagram, he next applied the diagram to his breast, and marked, by a puncture, the exact place in which even the slight wound of a pin-prod would be fatal. Some time after, being transferred to France, and reincarcerated for a conspiracy against the life of the Emperor, he was found dead in his cell—the pin sticking in his heart, and the diagram, which he had never parted with, lying at his feet. This was an instance of how absurd it was to attempt preventing suicide by watchfulness. Even before being allowed knife or fork, there was no moment in which Mr. Davis could not have thrown

*Again he makes me speak of a suspicion to me unknown.*

down his burden of life, if wicked enough to have wished so rushing into the presence of his Creator.

Mr. Davis said his transfer to Carroll Hall had brought back many curious reminiscences of his past life. In the very building he now occupied, he had once, as Secretary of War, extended the prerogative of clemency to an officer, since eminently distinguished on the Federal side, who was before (or sentenced by) a court-martial under grave charges as an officer, though not affecting his honor as a man. The coincidences of life are very striking; of which he gave several curious examples, specially mentioning the simultaneous deaths of John Adams and Thomas Jefferson on the 4th of July, 1826, the half century anniversary of the Declaration of Independence, which had been so largely their joint work. Jefferson's only wish when failing was to live to that morning, on waking up to which his first exclamation was: "It is then Independence Day; Lord, now lettest thou thy servant depart in peace, for mine eyes have seen Thy salvation;" while the last words of Adams, his illustrious coadjutor, were: "It is a great and a good day—Jefferson yet survives." To many similarly strange coincidences Mr. Davis called my attention; but only those are preserved, though I vaguely remember his reciting some curious facts about the anniversaries of his birthday.

Mentioned to him that I had received an order from General Miles, through Captain Church,* that morning, directing "the meals for prisoner Davis to be furnished him punctually at $8\frac{1}{2}$ A.M., and 3 and 8 o'clock P.M., until further orders." These hours, I knew, did not suit his wishes or appetite, but of course must be accepted. He never ate more than two meals a day, and desired them more equably distributed.

Mr. Davis asked me some questions about the little young, big-headed, black boy, rechristened "Joe," though his true name was Thomas Bailey, who now carried over and delivered his meals. The boy was from the vicinity of Richmond, and had been for some time, with other members of his family, a refugee within our lines. It seemed natural to him to be so served, and the food came kindlier than from the hands of a soldier, though indeed, upon the whole, he had been most kindly and considerately treated by officers and men. {)} Between the fighting men on both sides there was a generous and appreciative spirit; it was the rancorous non-belligerents of the different sections—they who had skulked the test of manhood—who would now prove most difficult to be appeased. What they lacked of honorable record during the progress of the struggle, they would endeavor to make up by ferocious zeal after the victory had been decided. The principle of compensation prevailed everywhere through nature; and for the immense theoretical boon of freedom, with its consequent incalculable destruction of property, he feared his poor friends of "Joe's" race would have to suffer fearfully in material privations and an increased hostility of race.

*marginal note:* not true I never was in the building

*marginal note:* until removed to it as a prisoner.

*marginal note:* never said so.

*marginal note:* The Dr. should not in remembrance of the brutality with which he knew I was treated during the earlier part of my imprisonment have made his statement so broad, nor at a later period could he have supposed that I did not make exceptions to the general acknowledgement.

---

*Will E. Church.

Something—I cannot tell what, but probably the constituents of his breakfast, for he was very fond of fish—led Mr. Davis to speak of the manner in which our fresh-water fish are disseminated; and his views, though possibly old, were new to me and of much interest. We are often astonished by finding various breeds of fish appear in some accidental cavity of the ground which was filled with water; also, water-lilies and other aquatic plants, though the new pond has no visible connection with any old pond supplied with such production. Mr. Davis explains this by supposing that the quawk, poke, bittern, and the various fresh-water ducks, play in the economy of nature's pisciculture a part similar to that played by bees and butterflies in the world of flowers. Bathing and feeding in some older pond frequented by fish, their feathers become impregnated with the fecundated spawn, the seed of the water-lilies, and so forth, and these are transferred to the new pond on their first visit. The supposition of spawn being sucked up into the clouds and descending in rain was not worthy of regard, though so generally accepted. If nothing else, the cold atmosphere at the height of the clouds would kill whatever animal life the spawn contained. The analogy of flower-life was entirely in favor of his explanation.

*October 13th.*—Called with Capt. Theodore Price, 3d Pennsylvania Artillery, serving on the staff of Major-General Miles, Officer of the Day. Mr. Davis in good health, but complained of being treated as though he were a wild beast on exhibition, not a prisoner of state awaiting trial. Ladies and other friends of ⁅(⁆persons in authority at the fort, ⁅)⁆ were let loose on the ramparts about the hour of his walk, to stare at him as though he were the caged monster of some travelling menagerie. He had endeavored to rebuke this during his last walk, when he saw a group of ladies waiting for his appearance, by turning short round and reëntering his cell. Dear and valuable as was the liberty of an hour's exercise in the open air, there were prices at which he could not consent to purchase it, and this was of the number. His general treatment Mr. Davis acknowledged to be good, though there were in it many annoyances of detail—such as the sentry's eye always fastened on his movements, and the supervision of his correspondence with his wife—unworthy of any country aspiring to magnanimity or greatness.

The following letter will be read with interest as giving a most graphic view of what the prisoner's wife and family had to endure from his quitting them on board the *Clyde*, in Hampton Roads, down to the day of its date; certain parts, ⁅(⁆reflecting upon individuals by name, ⁅)⁆ I have taken the liberty to strike out, but the remainder of the letter is as written:

*I said Genl. Miles knew of no other. Dr. C. & his wife witnessed the event he described & he spoke of it to me with indignation*

†*What of the orders to the officers, the Surgeon inclusive, to abstain from the courtesies usual among gentlemen when they entered my room, and the regulations in regard to passing in my meals which frequently involved their being kept in the guest room until entirely cold &c &c*

*see p. 333* [122 in this edition]

MILL VIEW (NEAR AUGUSTA, GA.),
October 10, 1865.

COLONEL JOHN J. CRAVEN,
*Chief Medical Officer, Fort Monroe, Va.*

MY DEAR COLONEL,—

Though you remain irrevocably dumb I am sure you hear me, and in addressing you I feel as if writing to one of my oldest and most reliable friends. Every letter from my husband comes freighted with good wishes for you, and thanks for all your kindness to him in his hours of anguish and solitude. Can you doubt that my prayers for you, and appreciation of your goodness, have been even greater than his, for I could do nothing but pray? Mr. Davis sent me a carte de visite of your dear Anna, whose sweet face my baby knows and has been taught to kiss as her father's friend. The baby sends her a little fan, and a few white flowers, made in Augusta. I hope she may like them. Mr. Davis writes me that she has gone to the Moravian school, near Easton,* where, I trust, our niece may have the pleasure of seeing her.

I am rendered very anxious by the obstinacy of the erysipelas with my suffering husband. He complains—in answer to entreaties for an account of his condition without concealment—of a loss of sleep. I dread paralysis for him, his nerves have been so highly strung for years without relief. If you can, dear Doctor Craven, do entreat, and perhaps you may prevail upon the authorities to let him sleep without a light. He is too feeble to escape, and could not bear a light in his room when in strong health. The sequel of these attacks has always been an attack of amaurosis, and in one of them he lost his eye. It first came on with an attack of acute neuralgia; but it is useless for me to begin to tell you of his constitution. You must have seen pretty well its peculiarities, in the long and kind watches you have kept with him.

I had hoped to relieve his mind by a full letter of personal narrative, but that letter he has not received. * * * * *

When he was taken from me on the ship, the provost-guard and some women detectives came on board, and after the women searched our persons, the men searched our baggage.

Either they or the soldiers standing around took everything they fancied, and some things so large that I did not see how their conduct could escape the eye of the guard, and of the officer who superintended the search. They then told my servants that they could go ashore, if they did not desire to go to Savannah. The husband of my negro nurse forced her to go, and the white girl left from an unwillingness to be exposed to a Southern climate. I entreated to be permitted to debark at Charleston, as my sister, Miss Howell, still continued to be ill, and I feared to return on the ship with a drunken purser, who had previously required Colonel Pritchard's authority to keep him in order; and going back, Mrs. Clay, my sister, and myself, would be the only women on the ship—but this was refused. Acting as my own chambermaid and nurse, and the nurse also of my sister† and Mrs. Clay, who were both ill, we started for Savannah. We had a fearful gale, in which the upper decks once or twice dipped water, and no one could walk; but as I felt as wretched as could be, I did not fear a future state.

God protected us from the fury of the elements; but the soldiers now began to open and rob our trunks again. The crew, however, gave us some protection, and one of the officers in the engine-room gave up his cabin and

*X These stars of omission do not represent the name of some one reflected on as stated by Dr. C. but a request that he would give me the information contained in the letter. it was another mode of furnishing me with the "personal narrative." To publish it was base enough, even had it been accurately done.*

---

*Moravian Seminary, Bethlehem, Pennsylvania.
†Margaret Howell.

locked everything we had left up in it. The Lieutenant of the 14th Maine, Mr. Grant,* though a plain man, had the heart of a gentleman, and took care of us with the greatest assiduity. Some of the soldiers and crew helped me to nurse, and saved me many an hour of wakefulness and fatigue. My little daughter Maggie was quite like an old woman; she took her sister early every morning—for the nights were so rough I could not sleep, because it was necessary to hold the infant to avoid bruising it—and with the assistance of our faithful servant Robert, who held her still while she held her sister, she nursed her long enough for me to rest. Little Jeff and I did the housekeeping; it was a fair division of labor, and not unpleasant, as it displayed the good hearts of my children.

At the harbor of Charleston the sick began to improve. We procured ice and milk, and the day's rest, which the ship at anchor gave them, improved them much.

Arrived at Savannah, we trudged up to the hotel quite in emigrant fashion, Margaret with the baby and Robert with the baggage; I, with Billy and Jeff and Maggie in quite an old-fashioned manner, keeping all straight and acting as parcel-carrier, for we could not procure any carriage, and must walk until we reached the Pulaski House, where, after a day and night, we procured comfortable rooms. The innkeeper was a kind man, and felt for my unfortunate condition. He, therefore, did everything in his power to make us comfortable. A funny incident happened the day I arrived there.

A black waiter, upon answering my bell, and being told to call my man-servant Robert, replied very impertinently that "if he should see Robert he would give the order, but did not expect to see him." When Robert heard it, he waited till all the black servants had assembled at dinner, and then remarked that he should hate to believe there was a colored man so low as to insult a distressed woman; but if so, though a peaceable man, he should whip the first who did so. The guilty man began to excuse himself, whereupon Robert said: "Oh, it was you, was it? Well, you do look mean enough for that or anything else." From that time all the greatest assiduity could do was done for me, first from *esprit de corps*, and then from kind feeling.

The people of Savannah treated me with the greatest tenderness. Had I been a sister long absent and just returned to their home, I could have received no more tender welcome. Houses were thrown open to me, anything and everything was mine. My children had not much more than a change of clothing after all the parties who had us in charge had done lightening our baggage, so they gave the baby dresses, and the other little ones enough to change until I could buy or make more.

Unfortunately for me, General * * * * *, who, I hear, was "not to the manor born," was in command of the district at the time.† I asked per-

---

*Second Lieutenant Joseph W. Grant.

†Varina here is referring to General Henry W. Birge, whom she called "Hog Birge." She wrote to William Preston Johnston in Montreal (3 October 1865) that "Hog Birge" had told her that if she left Savannah, she "should never be

mission to see him, and as I was so unwell that I could not speak above my breath with a cold, and suffered from fever constantly—the result of exposure on the ship—I wrote to beg that he would come to see me, for his aide had told me the night before that I could not be permitted to leave Savannah, and having been robbed of nearly all my means, I could not afford to stay at the hotel; and, besides, as soon as I reached the hotel, detectives were placed to watch both me and my visitors, so I did not feel at liberty, thus accompanied, to go to private houses.

General * * * *'s aide, whose animus was probably irreproachable, but whose orthography was very bad, was directed to tell me that, except under very extraordinary circumstances, he did not go out of his office, and "all such" (which I afterwards found to mean myself) "as desired to see him would call at his office." To which I answered, that I thought illness and my circumstances constituted an extraordinary case; but that I was sorry to have asked anything which he "felt called upon so curtly to refuse," and requested to be informed what hour would please him on the following day, and I would do myself the honor to call upon him. Whereupon the same unfortunate, well-meaning, ill-spelling young gentleman wrote to me that "all such ("}as desired might draw nigh{"} from nine until three."

I went, accompanied by General Mercer of Savannah.* Need I say that General * * * * did himself justice, and verified my preconceived opinion of him in our interview, in which he told me he "guessed I could not telegraph to Washington, write to the heads of Departments there, or to anybody, except through the regular channel approved;" and I could not write to my friends, "except through the Provost-Marshal's office;" and that I was permitted to pay my expenses, but must remain within the limits of Savannah.

With many thanks for this large liberty accorded so graciously, I bowed myself out, first having declined to get soldiers' rations by application for them to this government.

In this condition I remained for many weeks, until, fortunately for me, General Birge relieved him; who had it not in his power, however, to remove the restrictions any further than to take the detectives away, of whom I heard, but did not see. But General Birge permitted me to write unrestrictedly to whom I pleased, and appeared anxious, in the true spirit of a gentleman, to offer all the courtesies he consistently could.

My baby caught the whooping-cough, and was ill almost unto death for some days with the fever which precedes the cough; and then she slowly declined. I did what I could to give her fresh air; but the heat was so intense, the insects so annoying, and two rooms such close quarters, that she and I suffered much more than I hope you or yours will ever know by experience.

My most acute agony rose from the publication and republication in the

---

allowed to come back . . . the wretched porker" (Jefferson Davis Papers, Manuscripts Section, Special Collections Division, Tulane University Library, New Orleans, Louisiana).
*Hugh W. Mercer.

Savannah *Republican* of the shackling scene in Mr. Davis's casemate, which, to think of, stops my heart's vibration. It was piteous to hear the little children pray at their grace, "That the Lord would give father something which he could eat, and keep him strong, and bring him back to us with his good senses, to his little children, for Christ's sake;" and nearly every day during the hardest, bitterest of his imprisonment, our little child Maggie had to quit the table to dry her tears after this grace, which was of her own composition.

I believe, Doctor, I should have lost my senses if these severities had been persevered in, for I could neither eat nor sleep for a week; but opiates, and the information of the change effected by your advice, relieved me; and I have thanked God nightly for your brave humanity. It is easier to fight with a revolver than to repeat unpleasant truths to a hostile and untrammelled power in the full indulgence of its cruel instincts. All honor to the brave men who fearlessly did so.                                        X

Though I ate, slept, and lived in my room, rarely or never going out in the day, and only walking out late at night, with Robert for protection, I could not keep my little ones so closely confined. Little Jeff and Billy went out on the street to play, and there Jeff was constantly told that he was rich; that his father had "stolen eight millions," etc. Billy was taught to sing, "We'll hang Jeff Davis on a sour apple-tree," by giving him a reward when he did so; and he made such good friends with the soldiers that the poor child seemed to forget a great deal of his regard for his father. The little thing finally told me one day, "You thinks I'se somebody; so is you; so is father; but you is not; so is not any of us, but me. I am a Yankee every time." The rough soldiers, doubtless, meant to be kind, but such things wound me to the quick. They took him and made him snatch apples off the stalls, if Robert lost sight of him for a moment.

Finally, two women from Maine contemplated whipping him, because they found out that he was his father's son; but "a man more wise did them surprise," and took him off just in time to avoid a very painful scene to them as well as to me. These things went on in the street—I refer only to the street-teachings—though these women were, with one other, dishonorable exceptions to the ladies in the house, until Captain * * * was ordered to Savannah on duty. He brought with him a person who I heard was his wife. As I never went into the parlor I did not see her, but my little son Jeff went accidentally into the room one day and interrupted a conversation she was indulging herself in with one of the negro waiters, in which she was laying down "the proper policy to be pursued towards Mr. Davis."

The servant, having been brought up by a lady, felt very uncomfortable, and said, "Madam, there is his son." She called little Jeff up to her and told him his father was "a rogue, a liar, an assassin, and that means a murderer, boy; and I hope he may be tied to a stake and burned a little bit at a time with light-wood knots. God forbid you should grow up a comfort to your mother. Remember, you can never be a gentleman while this country lasts. Your father will soon be hanged, but that death is too quick."

The negro retired mortified, and sent my nurse to call little Jeff; and so, with his little face purple with mortification, and wet with tears from his streaming eyes, he came up to me, leaving the pious and patriotic lady to find another audience as congenial to her tastes as the first had been.

X

I commended Jeff's gentlemanly conduct in making no reply; cautioned him against ever persecuting, or distressing a woman, or a friend, if it took that shape; made application for permission the next day to go away to Augusta; was refused and then prepared the children to go where they would not see such indignantly patriotic and prophetic females. Nothing, however, but the dread of intruding into a secret and sacred grief prevented my writing poor Capt. * * * a sympathetic note, to condole with him upon the dispensation of Providence under which, in the person of his wife, he groaned.

Hourly scenes of violence were going on in the street, and not reported, between the whites and blacks, and I felt that the children's lives were not safe. During General * * *'s* *regime,* a negro sentinel levelled his gun at my little daughter to shoot her for calling him "uncle." I could mourn with hope if my children lived, but what was to become of me if I was deprived of them? So I sent them off with many prayers and tears, but confidant [*sic*] of the wisdom of the decision. On the ship I understood a man was very abusive in their hearing of Mr. Davis, when my faithful servant Robert inquired with great interest, "Then you tell me I am your equal? You put me alongside of you in everything?" The man said "Certainly." "Then," said Robert, "take this from your equal," and knocked him down. The captain was appealed to, and upon a hearing of the case, justified Robert, and required an apology of the levelled leveller.

Little Jeff is now at the endowed grammar-school, near Montreal, in charge of a Mrs. Morris, who has the care of ten little boys of good family, some of them Southern boys, and is happy, so he writes me. Mrs. Morris superintends his clothes and person, and teaches him his lessons. She was chosen by the faculty of the college for her high character. Maggie is at the Covenant of the Sacred Heart, in the same place, where Gen. William Preston's little girls are, and very kind they are to her. A nun is always present with the small girls, who are separated from the large girls. Little Billy is his grandmother's one pet and idol, always with her, and in pretty good health. I have sent their dear father a picture of Maggie's school, and a little scribbled letter from his big boy to me.

As soon as the dear children were gone, I hoped with my little weak baby (you see I am very honest with you) to make my escape out of the country to them; but when, upon coming to Augusta—which General Steadman† gave me leave to do immediately upon his accession to command, through the very kind intercession of General Brannen,‡ who succeeded General Birge—I was informed by a gentleman who said he had been told so authoritatively, that "if I ever quitted the country under any possible object, I would—no matter what befell Mr. Davis—never be allowed to return." I abandoned the intention. As might makes right in my case, and as my sister's health had failed rapidly in the South, and

---

*Birge's.

†General James B. Steedman had succeeded General Birge as the military commander of the Savannah area.

‡John M. Brannan.

as she is a girl of rare judgment and good feeling, I sent her with my nephew to New York *en route* for Canada to take care of my devoted mother, who is now too old and delicate to be left alone.

My two nephews joined me here about a month ago and desired to take me home with them; but finding that the length of my tether only permitted me to browse "in Georgia," they stayed two days and were then forced to go home to their families. My baby has grown fat and rosy as the "Glory of France:" a rose which Mr. Davis recollects near the gate of our home. Under the kind treatment I have received, the fine country air (five miles from Augusta) and the privacy, I have also grown very much better; can sleep and eat, and begin to feel alive again with the frosty air, and loving words, and letters which meet me here as in Savannah.

Mr. Geo. Scheley is my host, and never had a child in her father's home a warmer welcome. I am at no expense, and entirely gladly welcome. The little baby eats hominy and drinks fresh milk; grows in grace and weight; talks a little, and being more gentle than little Jeff's friend, Mrs. * * * *, is a great pet with all. The difficulty is to accept all the invitations I get, or to refuse them rather—-the whole Southern country teeming with homes, the doors of which open wide to receive me; and people are so loving, talk with such streaming eyes and broken voices of him who is so precious to them and to me, that I cannot realize I do not know them intimately. Mr. Davis should dismiss all fears for me. Money is urged upon me—everything. I only suffer for him. I do not meet a young man who fails to put himself at my disposal to go anywhere for me. I cannot pay a doctor's bill, or buy of an apothecary. "All these things are added unto me."

If I have written you too long a letter, my dear sir, it is because I have not collected my facts, but sought "quid scribam, non quem ad modum." Please give your good wife as much gratitude as she will receive from me; and I cannot permit you to measure it for yourself. My children shall rise up and call her blessed. May God show her and hers that mercy which you have been the means of bringing to my poor husband, and you will be blessed indeed. This is the constant prayer of your grateful friend,

VARINA DAVIS.

# •CHAPTER 22•

*A New Regiment on Guard.—Ordered not to Communicate with Mr. Davis, save on "Strictly Professional Matters."—The Correspondence about Prisoner's Overcoat.*

October *20th.*—Called on Mr. Davis, accompanied by Captain Titlow, 3d Pennsylvania Artillery, Officer of the Day. His health appeared satisfactory, and his change of quarters had already been of evident benefit.

Some remarks in the papers led him to say, that nothing could be more unjust than to accuse the South of having wished the destruction of the Constitutional Union of the States. It was not amongst his people that the Constitution had been continually denounced as a "bond with death and covenant with hell." To them the government had invariably been described as the "most beneficent and just government upon the face of the earth;" and it was only when **{***with declared purposes hostile to the federative system of the Union***}** what they regarded as a sectional Presidential ticket had been elected, and their rights of liberty and property threatened, that they rose to vindicate the reserved rights **{***of the People by the interposition***}** of State sovereignty, under **{***under***}** a constitution which they believed to have been subverted. **{***being no longer reliable as a shield***}**

Speaking of Mr. Bancroft, whose history of the United States he much read and admired, frequently marking passages of it with his finger-nail, as a pencil was denied him, Mr. Davis said it was appalling to contemplate the extra labors which must be imposed on future historians by the increased activity of the press in these latter days, and the looseness with which their **{***their***}** reports were made. It will require the labors of several lives to make the mere sifting of materials from the columns of the press, unless the historian shall boldly go to work by discarding all such authorities, and confining his scrutiny to the official reports on either side. **{***either* both sides}** He was glad to see that the various provisional State governments of the South were accepting the reconstruction policy of President Johnson, practically and in good faith. Universal amnesty—though he did not ask it for himself—with restoration of property and civil rights to all willing to **{(}**take the oath of allegiance,**{)}** would speedily restore to the whole country so much of harmony and homogeneity as was now possible, and so much needed by its political and financial interests. No apprehensions need be felt from any war with England or France, unless the South should be permanently alienated by despair of tolerant

*Ignorance. the state allegiance follows its compact.*

terms. Even then, as an American with no other country left him, he
would be for unanimous support of the country against its European
enemies, but the same sentiments, might not be likely to prevail
amongst the masses of his people. They had in their blood the faults
{?} of a Southern sky, "sudden and quick in quarrel, jealous of    X
honor." The question of negro soldiers was not a new one in this war.
Such class of soldiers had twice before been enlisted in the history of
the country, but not {(}trusted upon active service{)} on either    X
occasion; and when he had been in the War Department, a proposition had been urged by several eminent officers of the regular army
for garrisoning the defences of the Southern coast with regiments of    *not true*
blacks, on the ground that they could resist the exposures of the climate better.

*October 25th.*—Called upon Mr. Davis, accompanied by Captain
Korte, 3d Pennsylvania Artillery, Officer of the Day. Mr. Davis had
been for some time complaining that his light suit of grey tweed was    *p. 364* [133 in this edi-
too thin for the increasing cold of the days on the ramparts of the for-    tion]
tress, and finding that his measure was with a tailor in Washington,
I requested a friend of mine to call there and order a good heavy black
pilot-cloth overcoat for the prisoner, and that the bill should be sent
to me. Also, ordered from a store in New York some heavy flannels    *?*
to make Mr. Davis comfortable for the winter. These acts, to me appearing innocent, and even laudable, caused great trouble, as may be
seen by the following correspondence, finally leading to a peremptory
order which almost altogether broke off the previously free relations
I had exercised with Mr. Davis. This, however, will more properly appear further on, when the various letters on the subject are inserted
under their proper date.

*October 29th.*—Called, accompanied by Captain R. W. Bickley, 3d
Pennsylvania Artillery, Officer of the Day, who announced that his
regiment was under orders to quit the fort on the last day of the month,
preparatory to being mustered out of the service. Mr. Davis replied
with much feeling, expressing his regret that a regiment whose offi-    *?*
cers had shown him so much genuine kindness within the limits of
their duty, and whom he had come to regard more as friends than cus-
todians, should be about quitting him—though he had no doubt of
being treated with equal consideration by the officers of the incoming
regiment, the 5th United States Artillery, with many of whose officers
he had been acquainted before the war. To a prisoner new faces were    *? incorrect*
never pleasant, unless the old faces had become intolerable from cruelty, which had been the reverse of this in his case. No matter what
his fate might be in the future, he could never forget the 3d Pennsyl-    *As usual, not exact.*
vania Artillery.

Mr. Davis also referred to the kindness of Captain Grisson, of the
staff of General Miles, in regard to a little matter which, though trivial
in itself, had given him much annoyance. It arose in this manner: he
had requested a barber to be sent to him, as his hair was growing too
long. Captain Grisson brought a hair-dresser, but on the termination

of the operation said it was the order of General Miles that the lopped hair should be carried over to headquarters. To this Mr. Davis objected, first from having a horror of having such trophies or "relics" paraded around the country, and secondly because he wished to send it to Mrs. Davis; this latter probably an excuse to avoid the former disagreeable alternative. Captain Grisson replied that his orders were peremptory, but if Mr. Davis would fold the hair up in a newspaper, and leave it on a designated shelf in the casemate, the Captain would step over to headquarters, report the prisoner's objections, and ask for further orders. This was done, and Captain Grisson soon returned with the glad tidings that the desire to obtain possession of these "interesting relics" had been abandoned. Mr. Davis also spoke with great interest of a volume called the Schonburgh Cotta Family, which had been sent for his perusal by a lady in Richmond. It had been brought, I believe, {?} by the Rev. Mr. Minnegerode, when that gentleman called at Fort Monroe on the day of my return from Richmond to administer the Sacrament to his former parishioner.

*October 31st.*—Called with Captain Titlow, Officer of the Day, the last officer of the 3d Pennsylvania Artillery, who had charge of the prisoner. Mr. Davis renewed his friendly and grateful messages to the officers of the regiment, specifying several by name, and desiring to be remembered by them. As it stormed, there had been a fire built in the grate, and Mr. Davis spoke of its cheering effect both on body, eye, and mind; the stove being both injurious and unpleasant, as it concealed the best part of the fire, which was its rich, homelike, and enlivening appearance. It had always appeared natural to him that savage nations, in the absence of revealed religion, should adopt fire as their god. It was the nearest approach in the material world to the invisible spirit of life. Negroes and Indians, even in summer-time, would build a fire and squat down around it, forgetting all the demands of labor and amusement. Indeed, one of the earliest instincts of humanity, whether civilized or savage, was to collect around a bonfire in our childhood.

The change to Carroll Hall had been of the greatest benefit to the prisoner's health, the air being purer as it was loftier, his own room more cheerful, and only {†} subject to the drawback that he had human eyes from three directions continually fixed upon him through the grated door entering his room, the window opening on the piazza at his left, and the door opposite the window, with an open panel in it, opposite which stood a sentry.

*November 1st.*—Called with Brevet-Captain Valentine H. Stone, 5th U.S. Artillery, First Officer of the Day, from the new regiment garrisoning the fort. Mr. Davis appeared out of sorts—not body-sick, but heart-sick, {?} as he said himself. He appeared to scrutinize Captain Stone with great care, asking him all about his term of service, his early education, etc., as if anxious to find out everything ascertainable about the new men into whose hands he had fallen—an operation repeated with each new Officer of the Day who called to see him. In-

*Inexcusable, as he had promised to send it*

*not true*
*I refused to give up the hair, but said it should remain on the mantel piece so as to give Genl. Miles the opportunity for further action he might choose to take and Capt. Grisson never renewed the subject. Genl. Miles now decries having given the order Why then did Dr. C. become alarmed when he heard of the event and ask me to keep the hair for the present promising to send it at a future time.*

*† The tramp of sentinels on three sides of the room was a far greater infliction than their eyes, and Dr. C. was so well aware of this that he offered matting to deaden the sound, and criticised [sic] the failure to accept his offer.*

deed this habit of analysis appeared universal with the prisoner. It seemed as if he put into a crucible each fresh development of humanity that crossed his path, testing it therein for as long as the interview lasted, and then carefully inspecting the ingot which was left as the result. That ingot, whether appearing to him pure gold or baser metal, never lost its character to his mind from any subsequent acquaintance. He never changed his opinion of a man, or so rarely as merely to prove the rule by its exception; and this was one of the faults alleged against him as a leader by his opponents. It may have been pride that would not abandon a judgment once formed; or, more probably, that Mr. Davis had been taught by his experience of the world, how rarely we improve the correctness of such estimates by subsequent alterations. In our first judgment, it is the nearly infallible voice of instinct, unbiassed by any other causes, which delivers the verdict; while in closer acquaintance afterwards, the acts of the hypocrite, or the familiarity which so blunts and deadens our perceptions, may interfere to lead us astray.

Mr. Davis said it was scandalous that government should allow General Miles to review his letters to his wife. They had to pass through the hands of Attorney-General Speed, who should be a quite competent judge of offensive matter, or what was deemed offensive. General Miles had returned to him several pages of a letter written to Mrs. Davis, containing only a description of his new prison in answer to her inquiries, the General declaring such description to be objectionable, perhaps suspecting that if told where he was confined, Mrs. Davis would storm the fort and rescue him *vi et armis*. This was both absurd and cruel—one of those acts of petty tyranny which was without excuse, because without any sufficient object. In regard to attempts at escape, General Miles might give himself no uneasiness. Mr. Davis desired a trial both for himself and cause, and if all the doors and gates of the fort were thrown open he would not leave. If anywhere in the South the Confederate cause yet lived, the thing would be difficult, but as that cause was now wrapped in the shroud of a military defeat, the only duty left to him—his only remaining object—was to vindicate the action of his people, and his own action as their representative by a fair and public trial.*

---

*Davis did welcome a fair and public trial, which he believed would establish the rightness of the Southern constitutional position. He told his wife, "The newspapers have recently represented that I am to be tried to test the doctrine on which I acted, & against it establish the authority of the general government. The question involved has been the basis of political divisions in the United States since the second year of the administration of the elder Adams, it was earnestly and fully discussed in colonial times, and reach [sic] back through European history to the reign of King Solomon's Son. Many men have died for it, but their condemnation was not accepted as a decision concluding the question." (Davis to Mrs. Davis, 26 November 1865, Jefferson Davis Collection.)

*November 10th.*—This day, in consequence of reports in some of the papers that an overcoat had been ordered for Mr. Davis from Mr. S. W. Owen, his former tailor, doing business at Washington, and a further report that I had been the medium for ordering it, the following letter was sent to me:

> HEADQUARTERS,
> MILITARY DISTRICT OF FORT MONROE,
> FORT MONROE, VA.,
> NOVEMBER 18, 1865.

SIR:—

The Major-General commanding directs me to inquire of you if any orders have been given by you, or through you, for an overcoat for Jefferson Davis?

Such a report has appeared in the papers.

Very respectfully,

    A. V. HITCHCOCK,*
      Captain and Provost-Marshal.

To which, on the same date, I returned the following answer:

> OFFICE OF POST SURGEON,
> FORT MONROE, VA.,
> NOVEMBER 10, 1865. [*sic*]

CAPTAIN:—

I have received the communication dated November 10th, Headquarters Military District, Fort Monroe, in which the Major-General commanding, directs you to inquire if any orders have been given by me, or through me, for an overcoat for Jefferson Davis.

In reply, I would respectfully state that I did order a thick overcoat, woollen drawers, and under-shirts for Jefferson Davis. I found as the cold weather approached he needed thick garments, the prisoner being feeble in health, and the winds of the coast cold and piercing.

I have the honor to be,

    Very respectfully,
      Your obedient servant,
        JOHN J. CRAVEN,
          B'vt Lieut.-Col., Surg. U.S.V.
Capt. A. O. HITCHCOCK, A.D.C.

That any objection to my action in the matter should have been made, was about the last thing I should have expected—the prisoner's health being under my charge, and warm clothing for cold weather being obviously one of the first necessities to a patient in so feeble a

---

*Daniel Hitchcock was the aide-de-camp and acting provost marshall under Gen. Miles. Most likely a typographical error changes the initials to A. O. Hitchcock after this first reference.

condition. Let me add, that Mr. Davis had never asked for the warm  X
clothing I deemed requisite, and that sending for it, and insisting upon
its acceptance, had been with me a purely professional act. In the valise belonging to Mr. Davis, which was kept at the headquarters of
General Miles, no heavy clothing could be found, merely containing
a few articles of apparel chiefly designed for the warm climate of the
South. General Miles, however, took a different view of my action, to
judge from the following letter:

HEADQUARTERS, MILITARY DISTRICT,
FORT MONROE, VA.,
NOVEMBER 18, 1865.

COLONEL:—

The Major-General commanding directs that, in future, you give no orders for Jefferson Davis, without first communicating with these Head
Districts.

Also, that in future, your conversations with him will be confined strictly
to professional matters, and that you comply with the instructions regarding the meals to be furnished to prisoners Davis and Clay, and have
them delivered more promptly. Also, report the price paid for Mr. Davis's overcoat, and by whom paid.

A. O. HITCHCOCK,
Capt. and A.D.C.
B'vt Lieut.-Col. J. J. CRAVEN,
Post Surgeon.

This order I then regarded as cruel and unnecessary, nor has subsequent reflection changed my opinion. The meals for Mr. Davis I had
sent at hours to suit his former habits and present desires—two meals
a day at such time as he felt most appetite. I was now ordered to send
his meals three times a day, and at hours which did not meet his wishes,
and were very inconvenient to my family, his meals being invariably
sent over at the same hour I had mine. The order to abstain from anything but professional conversation was a yet greater medical hard-
ship, as to a man in the nervous condition of Mr. Davis, a friend with  X
whom he feels free to converse is a valuable relief from the moodiness
of silent reflection. The orders, however, I felt bound to accept and
carry out in good faith; and hence, from this point, my memoir must
unavoidably lose much of its interest. The next step in this difficulty
will be seen in my annexed letter, dated the day following the receipt
of my last communication from General Miles:

CAPT. A. O. HITCHCOCK, A.D.C.:

CAPTAIN:—

I have the honor to acknowledge the receipt of your communication dated
Headquarters, Military District, Fort Monroe, Va., Nov. 18, 1865; and
in answer to your inquiry concerning the cost of the coat ordered by me
for Mr. Davis, I would say:

That I do not know the cost of the coat; I have not yet received the bill. As soon as received, I will forward it to the Major-General commanding. I do not know that any person paid for the coat, having directed that the bill should be sent to me when ordering it.

> I remain, Captain, very respectfully,
> JOHN J. CRAVEN,
> Bv't Lieut.-Col. and Post Surg. and Chief Medical Officer,
> Military District, Fort Monroe, Va.

The next day—on the 20th, though dated the 17th—I received from Mr. Owen the subnote in reply, as will be seen, to a letter of inquiry addressed to him some nine or ten days previously:

DR. J. J. CRAVEN, U.S.A.,
Chief Medical Director,
Fortress Monroe, Va.:

DEAR SIR,—

In reply to your favor of the 14th inst., I would say the price of the coat sent you was $125; and as regards the question you ask about who paid for the coat, parties called at the store and desired to pay for it. Not knowing your wish on that subject, the money was left here until such time as I should hear from you about payment for it.

> Yours respectfully,
> (Signed) S. W. OWEN,
> PER RUSSELL.

To conclude this correspondence, the two following letters will explain themselves:

> Headquarters, Mil. Dist.,
> Fort Monroe, Va.,
> December 14, 1865.

Bv't Lt.-Col. J. J. CRAVEN,
Surgeon U.S.V.:

SIR:—

The General commanding directs me to ask if the overcoat furnished the prisoner Davis has been paid for.

> I am, very respectfully,
> Your obedient servant,
> JOHN S. MCEWAN,
> Capt, A. D. C., and A. A. A. G.

Fort Monroe, Va.,
December 15, 1865.

Capt. JOHN S. MCEWAN,
A. D. C., and A. A. A. G.:

SIR:—

I have the honor to acknowledge the receipt of your communication, bearing date December 14th, 1865, stating that the Major-General commanding directs you to ask if the overcoat furnished Jefferson Davis has been paid for. In reply, I would respectfully state that parties, without my approval, knowledge, or consent, called upon S. W. Owen, the tailor, interfered and interested themselves in the coat, leaving on deposit the price for the same. Seeing the coat was unlike the one I had ordered (a plain, black, pilot overcoat), I interested myself no further in the matter, leaving Owen, the tailor, to receive or refuse the money as he saw fit. He has received no money from me, neither did I authorize him to receive the pay for the overcoat from another.

I am, sir, very respectfully,
Your obedient servant,
JOHN J. CRAVEN,
Brevet Lieut.-Col., Surg. U. S. V., and Post Surgeon.

# •CHAPTER 23•

*General Summary in Conclusion.—The Character of Mr. Davis.—Let us be Merciful!*

And now my diary of a most interesting patient ceases, for under the orders dated November 18th, contained in the close of the preceding chapter, I could hold no conversation with him except on "strictly professional matters," up to the date of my being relieved from duty at the fort, which took place near the end of December 1865, and these

*X* would be of no interest to the public, even were I at liberty to reveal them. Mr. Davis occasionally suffered in health during the last month of my remaining his medical attendant, but the history of his trifling ailments *per se*, and unrelieved by any conversation, would not form either a pleasant or amusing record. With the officers of the 5th U.S. Artillery, as with his previous friends of the 3d Pennsylvania, he continued to have most agreeable relations—Major Charles P. Muhlenburgh, Captain S. A. Day,* and many others, displaying both generosity and consideration in their treatment of the distinguished captive. Indeed, it was a remark which must have been forced on every observer, both during the war and since, that it is amongst the nonbelligerents of the North—the men, one would think, with least cause to hate or oppress our recent Southern enemies—that we must look for those who appear actuated by the most vindictive feelings.

*? whose* It was not my intention to have published this narrative until after the trial of the prisoner; but on submitting the matter to friends, whose judgment I relied upon, it was decided that there was no material in these pages which could bias or improperly interfere with public opinion, or the due course of justice. It must be remembered that during the past year Mr. Davis has lain a silent prisoner in one of our strongest forts, unable to reply by so much as a word to the myriad assaults which have been made both on his private character and public course. This is absolutely the first statement in his favor—if so it can be regarded—which the Northern press has yet given to the world; and the case against that prisoner must indeed be weak which cannot bear allowing a single voice to be raised in his defence, while seven-eighths of the Northern journals have been industriously engaged in manu-

---

*Seldon A. Day; his sister, Mary Day Burchenal, wrote about her memories of the Davises' life at Fort Monroe in "A Yankee Girl Meets Jefferson Davis," published in *Holland's, the Magazine of the South* in 1931.

facturing public sentiment to his injury. I know my notes are very imperfect—that I have lost much which would have been valuable to history; but such brief memoirs as I made were not originally intended X for publication, but for my own pleasure or instruction, and that of my family; and it has been my conscientious effort to report him as he was, neither inventing any new sentiments to put in his mouth, or suppressing any material views on public questions which appeared in my note-book. In many of the important political conversations, let me add, the words are as nearly as possible the exact language used by Mr. Davis, my memoranda upon such matters having been made as full as possible.

His self-control was the feature of his character, knowing that his X temper had been high and proud, which most struck me during my attendance. His reticence was remarked on subjects where he knew we must differ; and though occasionally speaking with freedom of slavery, it was as a philosopher rather than as a politician—rather as a friend to the negro, and one sorry for his inevitable fate in the future, than with rancor or acrimony against those opponents of the institution whom he persisted in regarding as responsible for the war, with all its attendant horrors and sacrifices. Of the "abolitionists," as such, he never spoke, though often of the anti-slavery sentiment; and he impressed me as having in good faith accepted the new order of things which the late struggle and its suppression have made necessary.

The Southern states have been essentially conquered by military force, and now—taking the worst view of the case—await such terms as the conqueror may see fit to impose. The problem before all good men in the country—that for which our soldiers and sailors poured out their blood, and all loyal men labored and made sacrifices in their respective spheres—is the restoration of the Union as it existed in harmony, glory, and prosperity before the recent war, with, of course, such changes and modifications as the rebellion may have proved necessary. The writer believes it will be found that the men who were chief actors in the late rebellion, are now the promptest and most clear-headed in accepting its results; are not only willing but solicitous to accept and forward all such changes as the new order of things may render requisite; passing a sponge over the political errors of the past, and now only aiming to direct their people in the road by which the material prosperity and glory of the Union, one and undivisible, may be most quickly secured for the benefit of all interests and sections.

Mr. Davis is remarkable for the kindliness of his nature and fidelity to friends. Of none of God's creatures does he seem to wish or speak unkindly; and the same fault found with Mr. Lincoln—unwillingness to sanction the military severities essential to maintain discipline—is the fault I have heard most strongly urged against Mr. Davis.

As for the rest, the character of Mr. Davis, we believe, will receive justice in history. Mistaken in devotion to a theory of State sovereignty, which, before the recent war, was all but universally accepted by the people of both sections, he engaged reluctantly (as he says)

*X not an appropriate expression, and offensive unless excused for ignorance.*

**{(}** in a rebellion **{X}** for the sustainment of his faith. He and those who thought and acted with him have suffered terribly for that error; but it can be neither magnanimity nor wisdom to slander or oppress them in their moment of misfortune. It is by the conciliatory and generous policy of President Andrew Johnson that the bleeding gashes of the body politic are to be bound up and healed; and in a restoration of the Union as it existed before the late sad conflict—with only slavery abolished, the rebel debt repudiated, and the national debt accepted in good faith—the aspirations of those who served in our army and navy will be most happily realized. If Mr. Davis has been guilty of any private crime, such as connivance with the assassination of Mr. Lincoln or unauthorized cruelties to our prisoners, no punishment can be too heavy for him; but let the fact of his guilt be established in fair and open trial. If on the other hand, his only guilt

*true faith & allegiance as a citizen of a sovereign state*

has been **{(}** rebellion, **{?}** let a great nation show the truest quality of greatness—magnanimity—by including him in the wide folds of that act of amnesty and oblivion, in which all his minor partners, civil and military, in the late Confederacy are now so wisely enveloped. Make him a martyr and his memory is dangerous; treat him with the generosity of liberation, and he both can and, we think, will be a power for good in the future of peace and restored prosperity which we hope for the Southern States.

Believing that the views of Mr. Davis may throw important light on the true policy to be pursued, the author noted down all such as he could remember, or has had made notes of, as faithfully and as conscientiously as if giving his evidence under oath in a court of justice.

*X* Nowhere has he sought to better by concealment or misrepresentation the actual character or views of the person for whom he confesses that his professional, and finally his personal sympathies, have been warmly enlisted; and the only points he has been led to suppress—and they have been very few—were such merely medical details as neither the public would care for, nor any physician be authorized to expose. "Be just even to your enemies," is not only one of the noblest, but wisest maxims which antiquity has left us; and there is another like unto it: "It is lawful, even from your enemies, to learn wisdom."

And now with some few suggestive questions, this final chapter will be brought to a close.

Has any evidence yet brought before the Reconstruction Committee of our Congress been franker, clearer, more evidently honest, or more heartily aiming to bring before the country the actual needs, wishes, and aspirations of the South than that of such gentlemen as Robert E. Lee, Alexander H. Stephens, and the other late leaders of the rebellion, who have been examined, and whose testimony has been spread before the public? And has there not been manifest in all such testimony yet taken, an unreserved acquiescence in the results of the recent war, and a very earnest desire to restore the relations of the Union on a basis of harmony, good faith, and future complete assimilation of interests and institutions which shall endure for ever? The intelligent of the beaten rebels are to-day, and likely to remain, as faithful supporters of the Union as can be found on the face of the globe—is not this conceded? And while the opinions of the gentlemen examined have been regarded and treated by the highest authority as of deserved importance in aiding us to solve the problem of reconstruction—can it be wise, we ask, that those of Mr. Davis, their confessedly ablest leader in the political field, and the man most powerful over the affections and confidence of the Southern masses, should be now ignored in silence, or for ever suppressed in the silent cell of an untried and unconvicted imprisonment? For the crime of treason, not one of these—not the humblest official under the late rebellion—was one whit more or less guilty than the man whom they elected their titular President; and if any other crimes can be alleged against him, in the name of justice, and for the honor of our whole country, both now and in the hereafter, are not his friends and suffering family entitled to demand that he may have an early and impartial trial as provided by the laws of our country?

# ·APPENDIX·

General Miles was never able to outlive the criticism that he had abused Jefferson Davis. After a long and successful career on the frontier, Miles commanded the army in the Spanish-American War. Following it Miles was mentioned by some as presidential timber, while others rejoined with memories of Davis's imprisonment. In 1902 General Miles visited the Philippines to evaluate the army's headway against the Filipino guerrillas. Miles was shocked by the conditions he found in the American-run prison camps where rebels routinely were tortured to obtain information. Miles returned home and reported his dismay to Congress. "In my judgment," he wrote, "nothing could be more detrimental to the military service of the United States, or more discreditable to American Arms than the commission, or in the slightest degree the justification, of such acts, which belong to a different age and civilization than our own."[1] These remarks prompted a renewed attack on the general for permitting Davis to be "tortured."

Miles permitted his version of the events at Fort Monroe to be told in an anonymous pamphlet published in 1902 and reprinted below. It is not known if Miles himself wrote this work; however, it contained many private letters addressed to him. Even if Miles did not do the actual writing, he must have approved of it and aided whoever prepared it. Along with copies of Miles's correspondence, the account included a small portion of a letter from Mrs. Davis, thanking him for the courtesies extended her while she was at the fort. Other letters from subordinates testified that Miles had not abused Davis. Mrs. Davis attacked Miles's defense. Without actually denying that she had written a letter thanking Miles, she challenged him to produce it.[2] The general responded by placing a signed and condensed version of the anonymous pamphlet in *The Independent.* This exchange was the impetus for the second edition of the *Prison Life,* which appeared in 1905.

---

[1]Nelson A. Miles, "General Miles' Report on the Philippines," *Army and Navy Journal* 40 (2 May 1903): 862.

[2]*New York Times,* 21 February 1905, 3.

# A
## STATEMENT OF THE FACTS
## CONCERNING THE
## IMPRISONMENT AND TREATMENT
### OF
## JEFFERSON DAVIS
## WHILE A MILITARY PRISONER
## AT FORT MONROE, VA.
## IN 1865 AND 1866.*

**Washington, D.C.,
Gibson Bros., Printers and Bookbinders,
1902.**

During the great Civil War from 1861 to 1865 that was waged with greater intensity and ferocity than any other of modern times, it is well known that certain plots were formed against the person or life of President Lincoln. On the night of April 14, 1865, President Lincoln was assassinated and a desperate effort made to take the life of Secretary of State Seward, and the assassination of the Vice-President and General Grant was also contemplated by the conspirators who formed the plot to destroy the heads of the Government. Fortunately, General Grant was absent at Baltimore on that fatal night. The actual assassinations were to be committed by a few insignificant and obscure men who could have had no motive in such a fiendish conspiracy.

On May 2, 1865, the then Chief Magistrate of the United States, Andrew Johnson, who, after the death of Abraham Lincoln, had taken the oath of office as President, issued the following proclamation:

Whereas it appears from evidence in the Bureau of Military Justice that the atrocious murder of the late President, Abraham Lincoln, and the attempted assassination of the Hon. William H. Seward, Secretary of State, were incited, concerted, and procured by and between Jefferson Davis, late of Richmond, Virginia, and Jacob Thompson, Clement C. Clay, Beverly Tucker, George N. Saunders, William C. Cleary, and other rebels and traitors against the Government of the United States, harbored in Canada:

Now, therefore, to the end that justice may be done, I, Andrew Johnson, President of the United States, do offer and promise for the arrest of said persons, or either of them, within the limits of the United States, so that they can be brought to trial the following awards:

One hundred thousand dollars for the arrest of Jefferson Davis;

Twenty-five thousand dollars for the arrest of Clement C. Clay.

Twenty-five thousand dollars for the arrest of Jacob Thompson, late of Mississippi.

Twenty-five thousand dollars for the arrest of George N. Saunders.

Twenty-five thousand dollars for the arrest of Beverly Tucker.

Ten thousand dollars for the arrest of William C. Cleary, late Clerk of Clement C. Clay.

The Provost-Marshall General of the United States is directed to cause a description of said persons, with notice of the above rewards, to be published.

In testimony whereof, I have hereunto set my hand and caused the seal of the United States to be affixed.

---

*Richard Lathers Collection, Manuscripts Division, Library of Congress.

Done at the City of Washington this second day of May, in the year of our Lord one thousand eight hundred and sixty-five, and of the Independence of the United States of America the eighty-ninth.

*Andrew Johnson.*

By the President:

W. Hunter,
*Acting Secretary of State.*

Jefferson Davis did not surrender when the capital of the Confederacy, Richmond, was captured. He did not surrender with his principal armies when they surrendered under Robert E. Lee and Joseph E. Johnston, but it was his intention, as he admits in his own book, "The Rise and Fall of the Confederate Government," to try and escape and cross the Mississippi so that he could join the Confederate army in that section and continue the war.* He was hunted down and caught in the disguise of a woman near Selma, Alabama. The waterproof and shawl which covered his male attire were taken and sent to the War Department at Washington, where they still remain, and he was sent to Fortress Monroe to await trial on the charge of complicity in the assassination of Mr. Lincoln. It was the expectation and purpose of the Government at that time to bring him to trial on that charge as soon as the trials of the assassins then going on were completed.

The proclamation issued by the President was imperative and authoritative to every officer and soldier in the military service of the United States. They could not question the reliability of the statements contained in it, but were bound to accept them as based on facts; in fact, the proclamation itself states:

> *It appears from evidence in the Bureau of Military Justice* that the atrocious murder of the late President Abraham Lincoln, and the attempted assassination of the Hon. William H. Seward, Secretary of State, were incited, concerted, and procured by and between Jefferson Davis * * * and other rebels and traitors against the Government of the United States * * *

The details for the close custody of Mr. Davis were drawn up by Major General Halleck, commanding that Department, in person, and in his own handwriting. The last paragraph of the instruction reads as follows:

* * * * * * * *

7. The Commanding General of the District is authorized to take any additional precautions he may deem necessary for the security of his prisoners.

(Signed) *H. W. Halleck, U.S.V.,*
*Com'd'g.*

To Bvt. Maj. Gen'l Miles,
*Com'd'g, &c.*

Fort Monroe, *May 22, 1865.*

The Assistant Secretary of War, Charles A. Dana, went to Fortress Monroe, by direction of the Secretary of War, to also see that every detail was properly arranged for the safe custody of the prisoner, and, in his own handwriting, he wrote the following order as an additional precaution against the possibility of any escape, or attempt to escape, and also against the possibility of the prisoner doing any violence to himself or to any member of the guard.

---

*In the signed version, published in *The Independent* (23 February 1905), the following two sentences were changed to read: "He was hunted down and caught near Irwinville, Ga. He was sent to Fortress Monroe to await trial on the charge of complicity in the assasination [*sic*] of Mr. Lincoln."

Fortress Monroe, *May 22, 1865.*

Brevet Major-General Miles is hereby authorized and directed to place manacles and fetters upon the hands and feet of Jefferson Davis and Clement C. Clay whenever he may think it advisable in order to render their imprisonment more secure.

By order of the Secretary of War:

*C. A. Dana,*

*Assistant Secretary of War.*

Mr. Dana in his official report to the Secretary of War, described the appearance and condition of Jefferson Davis at that time in the following language:

Davis bore himself with a haughty attitude. His face was somewhat flushed, but his features were composed, and his step firm. In Clay's manner there was less expression of bravado and dramatic determination.

Notification was sent to the officials at Fortress Monroe of several plots which were formed to effect the escape or rescue of Davis, and they were directed to take every precaution to prevent it. The place selected for his confinement was one of the casemates of the fort then occupied by one of the officers of the fort with his family. The officer and his family were moved out of the rooms and Mr. Davis placed in them.

To comply with what was authorized and, in fact, suggested by the orders of both Assistant Secretary Dana and Major-General Halleck, light anklets were placed upon the ankles of Jefferson Davis in order to prevent the possibility of his attempting to jump past the guard or commit any act of violence while the wooden doors were being removed from the room which he occupied and grated doors substituted. These did not prevent his walking about the room, but would have prevented him from running, if, by any chance, an opportunity had occurred. The change of doors was completed in five days and the anklets were then removed. During this time mechanics were constantly going in and out of the rooms. It will be remembered that Louis Napoleon escaped through the connivance of a physician and mechanics who were employed in his prison.

Mr. Davis's physical condition at that time has been misrepresented. He was as strong and agile as other men of his age—56. According to his own account on page 702 of his book, "The Rise and Fall of the Confederate Government," he was confident, at the time of his capture, of his ability to single-handed and alone tumble a mounted soldier from his horse and then spring into the saddle and escape.

He was, however, prevented from making the attempt. At the time the anklets were placed on his ankles, he knocked down one powerful man and it took four strong men to hold him.

There was not the least desire or purpose on the part of any official of the Government to place any indignities upon Mr. Davis, or to in any way humiliate him. This is shown by a letter written long afterwards by Assistant Secretary of War Dana, from which the following is an extract:

The Sun

New York,

*September 3, 1895.*

Dear Sir:

\* \* \* \* \* \* \* \*

When the War Department was advised that Jefferson Davis would be landed at Fortress Monroe, Mr. Stanton appointed General Miles, then a colonel, to the command of the Fortress, and sent General Halleck, then Chief of Staff, to the Army, and myself to supervise the landing and see that everything that could look toward the safety of the prisoner should be carefully attended to. * * *

The disposition of his guards about the casemate, and of the sentry who was kept constantly within it, were under the orders of General Halleck; while I, on my part, executed the instructions I had received from the Secretary by directing Colonel Miles to see that the prisoner was prevented from doing violence to himself, or from forcing the guard within the casemate to do violence to him, by the application of handcuffs, if he (Colonel Miles) should think that application to be prudent. This order was of a purely precautionary nature, and was not founded at all upon any wish to humiliate the prisoner.

> I am, dear sir,
> Very truly yours,
> (Signed) C. A. Dana

Mr. Leslie J. Perry.

The insinuations that discourtesies were shown Mr. Davis or his people are best answered by the following extracts from letters written during his confinement by Mrs. Davis and Mrs. V. C. Clay to General Miles, thanking him for courtesies extended:

> Fort Monroe, Va.,
> [May 23, 1865.]

Please receive my thanks for your courtesy and kind answers to my questions of this morning [May 23]. I cannot quit the harbor without begging you again to look after my husband's health for me. * * * *

> Yours very respectfully,
> *Varina Davis.*

---

> July 27, 1865.

Your very kind and comforting letter reached me two days after dispatching a second to you. * * * Accept my heartfelt gratitude for your response with the hope that I may soon welcome a second note from you. * * *

I thank you for mentioning Mr. D. in your letter and the assurance of his "improved health." Please do me the favor to tender to him my deepest sympathy and most affectionate remembrance. * * *

Again begging your kind offices for your prisoners and thanking you for your letter, I remain,

> Respectfully, &c.,
> *V. C. Clay.*

---

> September 4, 1865.

Accept my heartfelt thanks for your great kindness in forwarding my dear husband's letter. May you never be placed in a condition to realize the mingled joy and sorrow its reception gave me. * * *

With grateful appreciation of your courtesies to Mr. Clay and myself, I am,

> Respectfully, your obedient servant,
> *V. C. Clay*

It is a fact that every precaution was taken to prevent the possibility of Mr. Davis's health being impaired by his confinement. General Miles gave positive orders to the surgeon to attend carefully to his physical condition, giving him anything that would tempt his appetite, and furnishing everything that was needed to preserve him in health and strength. This order was given in the presence of General Miles' Adjutant General, Captain John S. McEwan, A.D.C. and A.A.A.G., who made the following affidavit:

Fort Monroe, Va., *May 31, 1866.*

Personally appearing before me the subscriber, Captain John S. McEwan, 7th N.Y. Artillery, A.D.C. and A.A.A.G., who, being duly sworn, deposeth and says, that one day in the month of May or June, 1865, Maj.-Gen. Nelson A. Miles, commanding "Military District of Fort Monroe, Va.," did in his (deponent's) presence, say to Surg. J.J. Craven, U.S.V., "I want you to take charge of the health of the State prisoners"—Jefferson Davis and Clement C. Clay, Jun'r, being at that time in prison in the fort. "I do not wish they should suffer in health on account of treatment or fare; I would not for a great deal have either of them die while at this post; I want you to make any suggestions or recommendations that you think will benefit their health."

*JOHN S. McEWAN,*
*Captain, A.D.C. and A.A.A.G.*

Sworn to and subscribed before me this 31st day of May 1866, at Fort Monroe, Va.

*H. S. GANSEVOORT,*
*1st Lt. 5th U.S. Artillery,*
*Judge Advocate.*

Sensational statements were made in certain papers of that period, intended to excite sympathy for Mr. Davis, and a book entitled, "The Prison Life of Jefferson Davis," purporting to have been written by Mr. Craven, but which was really written by Charles G. Halpin in twelve days, was also published for the same purpose.

All the principal officers who were on duty at Fortress Monroe at the time made written official statements, as follows:

Fort Monroe, Va.,
*September 2, 1866.*

Maj.-Gen'l N. A. Miles, U.S.V.,
*Com'd'g Dist. Fort Monroe,*
*Fort Monroe, Va.*

GENERAL: In view of the distorted statements of a portion of the press, and especially of Surgeon Craven's book regarding the imprisonment of Jefferson Davis at this Post, the undersigned officers of the Government are unwilling such representations should go into history unanswered, on the statement of one individual, and we deem it due you to say that in your course as Commandant of this district, we are satisfied that you have practised all the leniency to Mr. Davis your duty to the Government required.

Mr. Jefferson Davis was not only a State prisoner, but came here under the charge of complicity in the assassination of President Lincoln, added to that of treason. His safekeeping—under the plots formed for his rescue—was a matter of necessity, and the utmost vigilance was required to be observed in preventing any attempt to effect it.

His treatment—so far as physical necessities are concerned—was all that humanity demanded under the circumstances.

We feel it is due you to say that the confinement of Mr. Davis has been as comfortable as it could be made while he was kept in safe custody.

With sentiments of esteem and respect for yourself, and a desire for your prosperity, we are, General,

Very respectfully,

JAMES CURRY,
*Col. & C.S.V.*

THOMAS G. WHYTAL,
*Bvt. Lt. Col. & A.Q.M.*

---

I coincide with the views expressed in the foregoing letter, my opinion having been formed from personal observations since my arrival at this Post, viz., Dec. 12, 1865.

H. S. BURTON,
*Bvt. Brig. Gen., U.S.A.*

Jas. W. Piper,
*1st Lt., 5th Arty., Regt. & Post Adjt.*

---

Since my arrival at this Post, February 15, 1866, so far as my observation goes, the treatment of Mr. Davis by General Miles has been as humane and considerate as the circumstances would justify.

*WILLIAM HAYS,*

*Maj. 5th Art., Bvt. Brig. Gen.*

---

The undersigned officers, on duty at this Post, have no hesitation in endorsing the action of General Miles towards Mr. Davis, as expressed in the foregoing letter.

*VAL. H. STONE,*

*1st Lieut. 5th Regt. Art., Bvt. Major, U.S.A.*

*H. S. GANSEVOORT,*

*Bvt. Major, U.S.A.*

*JAS. P. PRINCE,*

*Surg. & Bvt. Lt. Col., U.S.V.*

*T. P. McELRATH,*

*1st Lt., R.Q.M., 5th U.S. Arty., Bvt. Maj., U.S.A.*

---

Washington, D.C.,
*Feb. 15, 1867.*

Maj. Gen. Nelson A. Miles, U.S.A.,
*Late C.O., District of Ft. Monroe, Va.*

GENERAL: I was on duty at Ft. Monroe during the first six months of the imprisonment of Jefferson Davis, being in command of the regiment (3d Pa. Heavy Artillery) which guarded him during that period. I had a good opportunity from personal observation and frequent conversation with officers of my regiment of knowing of your treatment of him, and it was my impression, as well as that of my officers, that it was strictly in accordance with instructions from superior authority. His physical comforts were all that could be expected or desired, his meals having been sent to him, after the first few days of his imprisonment, from Dr. Craven's own table.

Not having read Dr. Craven's book, I do not know what statements he has made respecting you.

I am, General,
Very respectfully,
Your obedient servant,
JOSEPH ROBERTS,
*Lt. Col. 4th U.S. Art.,*
*Bvt. Colonel U.S. Army,*
*Late Col. 3d Pa. Heavy Art'y, and*
*Bvt. Brig. Gen. Vols.*

All the changes that were made from time to time by which Mr. Davis was allowed greater liberty and additional comforts—in fact, luxuries—were made by General Miles or upon his recommendation, and he also recommended that he either be brought to trial or released. He was finally released in May, 1867, and left Fortress Monroe in better condition than when he entered. He lived for 24 years after he was first imprisoned, and died of old age at the age of 81, and the statements to the effect that he was maltreated or that his physical condition was impaired as a result of his imprisonment, were utterly untrue.*

Since that terrible war the spirit of magnanimity and friendship has been manifested by many millions of people, and is described by General Miles in his book, "Personal Recollections." Speaking of the closing scenes at Appomattox Court-House, he says (pages 43 and 44):

\* \* \* \* \* \* \* \*

It is utterly impossible to adequately describe the scene or the feelings that swelled the souls of that army. Thankfulness, joy, generosity, magnanimity, patriotism, were all mingled in the feelings of the hour. The exultation of victory and the joyous anticipation of returning to our homes, were tempered by sympathy and respect for a vanquished but valiant foe.

\* \* \* \* \* \* \* \*

The black-mouthed cannon at last parked in silence, and the long commissary trains of the victorious army passed through the surrendered lines to supply alike both armies. The magnanimity and generosity of the silent commander touched the hearts of all with respect and admiration, and all realized that the cause that divided the two forces had at last disappeared, and that friendship and confidence must be restored.

The great-hearted leader and beloved President was soon to fall, but his wise and generous words expressed the spirit of the million of armed veteran soldiers who put off the habiliments of war and resumed the responsibilities and duties of American citizens. They represent the earnest appeal and wise council contained in his first inaugural: "We are not enemies, but friends. We must not be enemies. Though passion may have strained, it must not break our bonds of affection. The mystic chords of memory stretching from every battlefield and every patriot grave to every living heart and hearthstone all over this broad land may yet swell the chorus of the Union, when touched again, as surely they will be, by the better angels of our nature," and his words at Gettysburg, "With charity for all, with malice towards none, let us bind up our nation's wounds."

The same spirit is also evidenced in the following letters:

Selma, Alabama, *March 4,* 1898.

General Nelson A. Miles,

      *Washington, D.C.*

SIR: I was a Lieut. in the Confederate Army at the age of eighteen, and have seen some service. I am a member of the United Confederate Veterans, and belong to Camp Catesby Ap. R. Jones, of Selma, Ala. My son, John W. Craig, is a Lieut. in the 5th U.S. Cavalry at San Antonio, Texas, and another son is the 1st sergeant of the Dallas County Dragoons, of this city, and another is a sergeant of Infantry at the University of Alabama. Our fathers fought for the old flag. We are ready to follow the same in your hands; and I offer my services, and can muster you three thousand stalwart fighting Southern men at the tap of the drum, headed by the Old Confederate Veterans, to defend the Stars and Stripes and the honor of our country. We honor and trust you, as the able and fearless leader of our Army, and respect you as a man and citizen.

---

*The signed version ends here.

Yours with respect,
*GEO. H. CRAIG.*

P.S.—The man who intimates that the Southern men would *hesitate* to fight under you is simply ignorant of the state of feeling in this "neck of the woods." I know the above offer should go through or to our Governor, but I want you to know how our people here feel *"your ownself"* and from an old Confederate.

———————————

Headquarters of the Army,

Washington, *March* 11, 1898.

My Dear Sir:

Thirty-three years ago, the war drums ceased to beat; the bugles sounded the last charge, and the last tattoo was heard over the graves of heroic sacrifice; and as the veterans partook of the soldiers' fare from the same wagon train, it was there determined that—

> Henceforth and forever one nation we'd be,
> From ocean to ocean, from the lakes to the sea,
> And o'er all our land one flag shall float,
> One song ascend from every throat,
> That flag, the banner of the free,
> That song, the song of liberty.

Ever after that time the earnest, patriotic effort was to be exerted in building up the waste places of our land and developing its untold resources, strengthening the moral, political, and material elements of our nation, so that whether dangers came from within or without, all true Americans would stand shoulder to shoulder in maintaining our glorious institutions, our liberties and our sacred honor. Such was the spirit; and at this hour I rejoice to witness such a grand and noble manifestation of it throughout our wonderful country as that of which your much appreciated letter is typical; a sentiment finding unequivocal expression in every quarter of the great Republic—North, South, East, and West.

Yours very truly,
NELSON A. MILES.

Honorable Geo. H. Craig,
*Selma, Alabama.*

# •BIBLIOGRAPHY•

## MANUSCRIPT SOURCES

Barbee, David Rankin. Manuscripts Division. Library of Congress. Washington D.C.

Bayard Family Papers. The Historical Society of Delaware. Wilmington.

Beer, William. The Manuscripts Section. The Special Collections Division. Tulane University Library. New Orleans LA.

Blair, Francis P. (Family). Manuscripts Division. Library of Congress. Washington D.C.

Bradley, Chester D. Correspondence between Dr. Bradley and Professor William Hanchett; copies sent by Dr. Bradley to the author. 17 June 1982 to 11 April 1983.

Braly, William C. United States Army Military History Institute. Carlisle Barracks PA.

Clay, Clement Claiborne, Jr. Manuscripts Department. William P. Perkins Library. Duke University. Durham NC.

Craven, John J. Manuscripts Division. Library of Congress. Washington D.C.

Curry, Jabez Lamar Munroe. Manuscripts Division. Library of Congress. Washington D.C.

Davis Family Papers, 1868-1906. The Historic New Orleans Collection. New Orleans LA.

Davis, Jefferson. Jefferson Davis Collection. Transylvania University Library. Lexington KY.

——————. Louisiana Historical Museum. New Orleans LA.

——————. Manuscripts Division. Library of Congress. Washington D.C.

——————. The Manuscripts Section. The Special Collections Division. Tulane University Library. New Orleans LA.

Davis, Jefferson—J. Addison Hayes, Jr. Papers. The Mississippi Valley Collection. John Willard Brister Library. Memphis State University. Memphis TN.

Early, Jubal Anderson. Manuscripts Division. Library of Congress. Washington D.C.

Fort Monroe. Letters Sent from Post and the Artillery School, 1855-1863. Old Army Records. Record Group 393. The National Archives. Washington D.C.

Halbert, Henry Sale. State of Alabama. Department of Archives and History. Montgomery.

Harrison, Burton N. (Family). Manuscripts Division. Library of Congress. Washington D.C.

Johnson, Andrew. Manuscripts Division. Library of Congress. Washington D.C.

Johnston, William Preston. The Manuscripts Section. The Special Collections Division. Tulane University Library. New Orleans LA.

Lathers, Richard. Manuscripts Division. Library of Congress. Washington D.C.

Letters Sent by the Secretary of War Relating to Military Affairs, 1800-1889. Microfilm. Group M-6. The National Archives. Washington D.C.

Louisiana Historical Association Collections.
    Administrative Records.
    Jefferson Davis Papers.
    Joseph Chalaron Papers.
        The Manuscripts Section. The Special Collections Division.
        Tulane University Library. New Orleans LA.

Mercier, Alfred. The Manuscripts Section. The Special Collections Division. Tulane University Library. New Orleans LA.

Mitchell, Lise. The Manuscripts Section. The Special Collections Division. Tulane University Library. New Orleans LA.

Pettus, Edmund Winston. State of Alabama. Department of Archives and History. Montgomery.

Phillips, Philip (Family). Manuscripts Division. Library of Congress. Washington D.C.

Pierce, Franklin. Manuscripts Division. Library of Congress. Washington D.C.

Redpath, James. Rosemonde and Emile Kuntz Collection. The Manuscripts Section. The Special Collections Division. Tulane University Library. New Orleans LA.

Returns from United States Military Posts, 1800-1916. Microfilm. Group M-617. Reels 793-94. The National Archives. Washington D.C.

Sage, Bernard Janin. Louisiana Historical Museum. New Orleans LA.

Samuel Richey Collection of the Southern Confederacy. The Walter Havighurst Special Collections Library. Miami University. Oxford OH.

Titlow, Jerome. Manuscripts Division. Library of Congress. Washington D.C.

Watts, Thomas Hill. State of Alabama. Department of Archives and History. Montgomery.

Wheeler, John Hill. Manuscripts Division. Library of Congress. Washington D.C.

Wright, Marcus. Old Army Records Division. The National Archives. Washington D.C.

Yancey, Benjamin Cudworth. State of Alabama. Department of Archives and History. Montgomery.

## NEWSPAPERS

*Daily National Intelligencer* (Washington D.C.)

*Evening Star* (Washington D.C.)

*Evening Telegraph* (Philadelphia)

*New York Citizen*

*New York Herald*

*New York Times*

*Philadelphia Inquirer*

## PUBLISHED PRIMARY SOURCES

Akin, Warren. "The Letters of Warren Akin, Confederate Congressman." Edited by Bell Irvin Wiley. *Georgia Historical Quarterly* 42 (March 1958): 70-92; (June 1958): 193-214; (September 1958): 294-313; (December 1958): 408-27; 43 (March 1959): 74-90.

Burchenal, Mary Day. "A Yankee Girl Meets Jefferson Davis." *Holland's, The Magazine of the South* 50 (October 1931): 17-18, 43, 45.

Clay-Clopton, Virginia. *A Belle of the Fifties; Memories of Mrs. Clay of Alabama Covering Social and Political Life in Washington and the South, 1853-1866.* Edited by Ada Sterling. New York: Doubleday, Page & Co., 1905.

Craven, Bvt. Lieut.-Col. John J., M.D. *Prison Life of Jefferson Davis. Embracing Details and Incidents of His Captivity, Particulars Concerning His Health and Habits, Together with Many Conversations on Topics of Great Public Interest.* New York: Carleton, Publisher, 1866.

_____. Second edition. New York: G. W. Dillingham Co., 1905.

_____. Third edition. Beauvoir MS: The Jefferson Davis Shrine, 1960.

_____. Fourth edition. Beauvoir MS: The Jefferson Davis Shrine, 1979.

Dana, Charles A. *Recollections of the Civil War; with the Leaders at Washington and in the Field in the Sixties.* New York: D. Appleton and Co., 1902.

Davis, Jefferson. "Andersonville and Other War Prisons." *Belford's Magazine* 4 (January 1890): 161-78; (February 1890): 337-53.

_____. "Autobiography of Jefferson Davis." *Belford's Magazine* 4 (January 1890): 255-66.

_____. "The Doctrine of State Rights." *The North American Review* 150 (February 1890): 205-19.

_____. *Jefferson Davis, Constitutionalist: His Letters, Papers, and Speeches.* Ten vols. Edited by Dunbar Rowland. Jackson MS: Department of Archives and History, 1923.

_____. *Jefferson Davis, Private Letters, 1823-1889.* Edited by Hudson Strode. New York: Harcourt, Brace & World, Inc., 1966.

_____. *The Papers of Jefferson Davis.*

Vol. one, *1808-1840.* Edited by Haskell M. Monroe, Jr. and James T. McIntosh. Baton Rouge: Louisiana State University Press, 1971.

Vol. two, *June 1841-July 1846.* Edited by James T. McIntosh. Baton Rouge: Louisiana State University Press, 1974.

Vol. three, *July 1846-December 1848.* Edited by James T. McIntosh, Lynda L. Crist, and Mary S. Dix. Baton Rouge: Louisiana State University Press, 1981.

Vol. four, *1849-1852.* Edited by Lynda Lasswell Crist, Mary Seaton Dix, and Richard E. Berringer. Baton Rouge: Louisiana State University Press, 1983.

Vol. five, *1853-1855.* Edited by Lynda Lasswell Crist and Mary Seaton Dix. Baton Rouge: Louisiana State University Press, 1985.

_____. *The Rise and Fall of the Confederate Government.* Two vols. New York: D. Appleton and Co., 1881.

_____. *A Short History of the Confederate States of America.* New York: Belford Co., 1890.

_____. "Robert E. Lee." *The North American Review* 150 (January 1890): 55-66.

Davis, Varina [Howell] Jefferson. *Jefferson Davis, Ex-President of the Confederate States of America: a Memoir by His Wife.* Two vols. New York: Belford Co., 1890.

Davis, Varina Anne. "Jefferson Davis in Private Life." *New York Herald,* 11 August 1895.

"Debate on Pensioning Jefferson Davis," condensed from the *Proceedings of the U.S. Senate,* 3 March 1879.

Fleming, Walter L. *Documentary History of Reconstruction.* Two vols. Cleveland: A. H. Clark Co., 1906-1907.

Glenn, William Wilkins. *Between North and South: a Maryland Journalist Views the Civil War.* Edited by Bayly Ellen Marks and Mark Norton Schatz. Rutherford NJ: Fairleigh Dickinson University Press, 1976.

Halpine, Charles G. *Baked Meats of the Funeral. A Collection of Essays, Poems, Speeches, Histories and Banquets. By Private Miles O'Reilly* . . . New York: Carleton, 1866.

_____. *The Life and Adventures, Songs, Services, and Speeches of Private Miles O'Reilly* . . . New York: Carleton, 1864.

_____. *The Poetical Works of Charles G. Halpine (Miles O'Reilly).* Edited by Robert B. Roosevelt. New York: Harper & Brothers, 1869.

_____. *Prison Life of Jefferson Davis* . . . See entries under Craven, John J.

Harrison, Constance Cary. *Recollections Grave and Gay.* New York: Charles Scribner's Sons, 1916.

Heth, Henry. "The Memoirs of Henry Heth." Edited by James L. Morrison, Jr. *Civil War History* 8 (March 1962): 5-24; (September 1962): 300-26.

Johnson, Andrew. *The Papers of Andrew Johnson.* Six vols. Edited by Leroy P. Graf, Ralph W. Haskins, et al. Knoxville: University of Tennessee Press, 1967-1983.

Johnston, William Preston. "Jefferson Davis Recalls the Past: Notes of a Wartime Aide, William Preston Johnston." Edited by Marilyn McAdams Sibley. *Journal of Mississippi History* 33 (May 1971): 167-78.

Jones, John B. *A Rebel War Clerk's Diary at the Confederate States Capital.* Two vols. Philadelphia: J. B. Lippincott & Co., 1866.

Kean, Robert Garlick Hill. *Inside the Confederate Government: the Diary of Robert Garlick Hill Kean.* Edited by Edward Younger. New York: Oxford University Press, 1957.

Keckley, Mrs. Elizabeth. *Behind the Scenes: Thirty Years a Slave and Four Years in the White House.* New York: G. W. Carleton & Co., 1868.

McClure, Alexander K. "My Recollections of Jefferson Davis." *World's Events Magazine* 7 (December 1906): 7, 34-35.

MacCulloch, Campbell. "The Last Days of the Confederacy." *Spare Moments* 2 (October 1906): 3-4; (November 1906): 4, 18-19; (December 1906): 5-6, 18-21; (January 1907): 6, 20-21; (February 1907): 7, 14; (March 1907): 7, 19.

Mann, A. Dudley. *"My Ever Dearest Friend": the Letters of A. Dudley Mann to Jefferson Davis, 1868-1889.* Edited by John Preston Moore. *Confederate Centennial Studies,* no. 14. Tuscaloosa AL: Confederate Publishing Co., Inc., 1960.

Miles, Nelson A. "General Miles' Report on the Philippines." *Army and Navy Journal* 40 (2 May 1903): 860-62.

_____. "My Treatment of Jefferson Davis." *The Independent* 58 (23 February 1905): 413-17.

_____. *Personal Recollections and Observations.* Chicago: The Werner Co., 1896.

_____. *Serving the Republic: Memoirs of the Civil and Military Life of Nelson A. Miles, Lieutenant-General, United States Army.* New York: Harper & Brothers, 1911.

[_____]. *A Statement of the Facts Concerning the Imprisonment and Treatment of Jefferson Davis While a Military Prisoner at Fort Monroe, Va. in 1865 and 1866.* Washington D.C.: Gibson Brothers, 1902.

Rawick, George P. et al., eds. *The American Slave: a Composite Autobiography.* Supplement, series 1, vol. 8, Mississippi Narratives. Westport CT: Greenwood Press, 1977.

Richardson, James D., ed. *A Compilation of the Messages and Papers of the Presidents, 1789-1904.* Ten volumes. Washington D.C.: Bureau of National Literature and Art, 1904.

Russell, William Howard. *My Diary North and South.* Edited by Fletcher Pratt. New York: Harper & Row, 1954.

Sherman, William T. *Memoirs of William T. Sherman, Written by Himself.* Two vols. New York: D. Appleton, 1891.

Strode, Hudson, ed. "The Prison Letters of Jefferson and Varina Davis." *Comment* 2 (Spring 1966): 5-18.

Taylor, Richard. *Destruction and Reconstruction: Personal Experiences of the Late War.* New York: D. Appleton and Company, 1879.

United States War Dept. *The War of the Rebellion: a Compilation of the Official Records of the Union and Confederate Armies.* Seventy vols. Washington D.C.: Government Printing Office, 1880-1901.

Woodward, C. Vann, ed. *Mary Chesnut's Civil War.* New Haven: Yale University Press, 1981.

## SECONDARY SOURCES

### Books

[Addey, Markinfield.] *Life and Imprisonment of Jefferson Davis Together with the Life and Military Career of Stonewall Jackson, from Authentic Sources.* New York: M. Doolady Publisher, 1866.

Ambrose, Stephen E. *Halleck; Lincoln's Chief of Staff.* Baton Rouge: Louisiana State University Press, 1962.

Arthur, Robert. *History of Fort Monroe.* Fort Monroe VA: Printing Plant, The Coast Artillery School, 1930.

Bancroft, A. C., ed. *The Life and Death of Jefferson Davis.* New York: J. S. Ogilvie, 1889.

Bennett, Walter H. *American Theories of Federalism.* University AL: University of Alabama Press, 1964.

Burkert, Walter. *Structure and History in Greek Mythology and Ritual.* Berkeley: University of California Press, 1979.

*Calendar of the Jefferson Davis Postwar Manuscripts in the Louisiana Historical Association Collection, Confederate Memorial Hall.* New Orleans LA, 1943.

Cassirer, Ernst. *The Philosophy of Symbolic Form.* Three vols. Translated by Ralph Manheim. New Haven: Yale University Press, 1955.

Connelly, Thomas L. *Will Success Spoil Jeff Davis?* New York: McGraw-Hill Book Co., 1963.

_____ and Bellows, Barbara L. *God and General Longstreet: The Lost Cause and the Southern Mind.* Baton Rouge: Louisiana State University Press, 1982.

Conrad, Glenn R. *Inventory of the Louisiana Historical Association on Deposit in the Howard-Tilton Memorial Library, Tulane University, New Orleans, Louisiana.* New Orleans LA: Louisiana Historical Association, 1983.

Cutting, Elisabeth B. *Jefferson Davis, Political Soldier.* New York: Dodd, Mead and Co., 1930.

Dalby, J. Arnold. *A History of Old Point Comfort and Fortress Monroe, Va., from 1608 to January 1st, 1881.* Norfolk VA: Landmark Steam Book and Job Presses, 1881.

Davis, Burke. *The Long Surrender.* New York: Random House, 1985.

Davis, Henry Alexander. *The Davis Family (Davies and David) in Wales and America: Genealogy of Morgan David of Pennsylvania.* Washington D.C.: Henry Alexander Davis, 1927.

Davis, Varina Anne Jefferson. *A Romance of the Summer Seas.* New York: Harper & Bros., 1898.

_____. *The Veiled Doctor.* New York: Harper & Bros., 1895.

Degler, Carl N. *Out of Our Past.* New York: Harper & Row, 1970.

Dixon, Thomas. *The Victim: a Romance of the Real Jefferson Davis.* New York: D. Appleton and Co., 1914.

Dodd, William E. *Statesmen of the Old South, or from Radicalism to Conservative Revolt.* New York: The Macmillan Co., 1911.

Duffy, John. *The Healers: A History of American Medicine.* Second ed. Urbana: University of Illinois Press, 1979.

Eaton, Clement. *Jefferson Davis.* New York: Free Press, 1977.

Escott, Paul D. *After Secession: Jefferson Davis and the Failure of Confederate Nationalism.* Baton Rouge: Louisiana State University Press, 1978.

Everett, Frank E., Jr. *Brierfield: Plantation Home of Jefferson Davis.* Hattiesburg: University and College Press of Mississippi, 1971.

Faulkner, William. *Absalom, Absalom!* New York: Modern Library Edition, 1964.

Feinstein, Howard M. *Becoming William James*. Ithaca NY: Cornell University Press, 1984.

Ferrell, Chiles Clifton. *"The Daughter of the Confederacy": Her Life, Character, and Writings*. Jackson MS: Historical Society, 1899.

_____. *Varina Anne Jefferson Davis*. Volume eight of *Library of Southern Literature*. Atlanta: Martin and Hoyt Co., 1917.

*First Circular and Catalogue of the Louisiana Historical Association*. New Orleans LA: Hopkins Printing Office, 1891.

Fleming, Donald. *William H. Welch and the Rise of Modern Medicine*. Boston: Little, Brown and Co., 1954.

Flood, Charles Bracelen. *Lee, the Last Years*. Boston: Houghton Mifflin Co., 1981.

Foote, Shelby. *The Civil War, a Narrative*. Three vols. New York: Random House, 1958-1974.

Frazer, Sir James George. *The Golden Bough: A Study in Magic and Religion*. New York: Macmillan Co., 1922.

Freeman, Douglas Southall. *The South to Posterity: an Introduction to the Writings of Confederate History*. New York: Charles Scribner's Sons, 1939.

Gaston, Paul M. *The New South Creed: A Study in Southern Mythmaking*. New York: Alfred A. Knopf, 1970.

Grantham, Dewey W., Jr., ed. *The South and the Sectional Image: The Sectional Theme since Reconstruction*. New York: Harper & Row, 1967.

Green, Margaret. *President of the Confederacy: Jefferson Davis*. New York: Julian Messner, 1963.

Hanchett, William. *Irish: Charles G. Halpine in Civil War America*. Syracuse NY: Syracuse University Press, 1970.

_____. *The Lincoln Murder Conspiracies*. Urbana: University of Illinois Press, 1983.

Hermann, Janet Sharp. *The Pursuit of a Dream*. New York: Oxford University Press, 1981.

Hesseltine, William B. *Confederate Leaders in the New South*. Baton Rouge: Louisiana State University Press, 1950.

Jones, J. William, ed. *The Davis Memorial Volume; or Our Dead President Jefferson Davis, and the World's Tribute to His Memory*. Richmond: B. F. Johnson and Co., 1890.

Kane, Harnett T. *Bride of Fortune: a Novel Based on the Life of Mrs. Jefferson Davis*. Garden City NY: Doubleday & Co., Inc., 1948.

Kirk, G. S. *Myth, Its Meaning and Functions in Ancient and Other Cultures*. Cambridge: Cambridge University Press, 1970.

Lanier, Sidney. *Tiger-Lillies*. Volume five of *The Centennial Edition of the Works of Sidney Lanier*. Edited by Garland Greever, assisted by Cecil Abernethy. Baltimore: Johns Hopkins University Press, 1945.

Lévi-Strauss, Claude. *Myth and Meaning*. New York: Schocken Books, 1978.

Louisiana Historical Association. *Calendar of the Jefferson Davis Postwar Manuscripts*. New York: Burt Franklin, 1970.

McElroy, Robert. *Jefferson Davis: the Unreal and the Real*. Two vols. New York: Harper & Brothers, 1937.

McKitrick, Eric L. *Andrew Johnson and Reconstruction*. Chicago: University of Chicago Press, 1960.

Nichols, Roy Franklin. *Franklin Pierce: Young Hickory of the Granite Hills*. Philadelphia: University of Pennsylvania Press, 1931.

Nowell, Edward P. *Ballad of Jefferson D*. Portsmouth NH: Brewster & Son, 1865.

Oglesby, T. K. *Captor and Captive: the Shackler and the Shackled, the Truth of History as to the Shackling of Jefferson Davis.* Atlanta: The Franklin Printing and Publishing Co., 1899.

Olsen, Theodore V. *There Was a Season: a Biographical Novel of Jefferson Davis.* Garden City NY: Doubleday & Co., Inc., 1972.

Osterweis, Rollin G. *The Myth of the Lost Cause, 1865-1900.* Hamden CT: Archon Books, 1973.

Patrick, Rembert W. *Jefferson Davis and His Cabinet.* Baton Rouge: Louisiana State University Press, 1944.

Pollard, Edward A. *The Life of Jefferson Davis with a Secret History of the Southern Confederacy Gathered "Behind the Scenes in Richmond."* Philadelphia: National Publishing Co., 1869.

_____. *The Lost Cause; a New Southern History of the War of the Confederates.* New York: E. B. Treat & Co., 1866.

*Portrait and Biographical Record of Suffolk County (Long Island).* New York: Chapman, 1896.

Ranck, James B. *Albert Gallatin Brown, Radical Southern Nationalist.* New York: Appleton-Century Co., 1937.

Randall, Ruth Painter. *I Varina: a Biography of the Girl Who Married Jefferson Davis and Became the First Lady of the South.* Boston: Little, Brown and Co., 1962.

*Reviews of* Jefferson Davis, Constitutionalist: His Letters, Papers, and Speeches. Jackson: Mississippi Department of Archives and History, 1924.

Ross, Ishbel. *First Lady of the South: the Life of Mrs. Jefferson Davis.* New York: Harper & Bros., 1958.

Rowland, Dunbar. *History of Mississippi, the Heart of the South.* Two vols. Chicago & Jackson MS: S. J. Clarke Publishing Co., 1925.

_____. *Jefferson Davis's Place in History as Revealed in His Letters, Papers, and Speeches.* Jackson: Mississippi Historical Dept., 1923.

Rowland, Eron Opha Moore. *Varina Howell, Wife of Jefferson Davis.* Two vols. New York: Macmillan Co., 1927-1931.

Shea, George. *Jefferson Davis: a Statement Concerning the Imputed Special Causes of His Long Imprisonment by the Government of the United States and of His Tardy Release by Due Process of Law.* London: Edward Stanford, 1877.

Shenton, James P. *Robert John Walker: a Politician from Jackson to Lincoln.* New York: Columbia University Press, 1961.

Shingleton, Royce Gordon. *John Taylor Wood: Sea Ghost of the Confederacy.* Athens: University of Georgia Press, 1979.

Shryock, Richard Harrison. *Medicine and Society in America, 1660-1860.* New York: New York University Press, 1960.

Simkins, Francis Butler and James W. Patton. *The Women of the Confederacy.* Richmond: Garrett and Massie, 1936.

Stampp, Kenneth M. *The Era of Reconstruction, 1865-1877.* New York: Alfred A. Knopf, 1966.

Strode, Hudson. *Jefferson Davis, American Patriot, 1808-1861.* New York: Harcourt, Brace & World, Inc., 1955.

_____. *Jefferson Davis, Confederate President.* New York: Harcourt, Brace & World, Inc., 1959.

_____. *Jefferson Davis, Tragic Hero: the Last Twenty-Five Years, 1864-1889.* New York: Harcourt, Brace & World, Inc., 1964.

Tate, Allen. *Jefferson Davis: His Rise and Fall; a Biographical Narrative.* New York: Minton Balch & Co., 1929.

Taylor, William R. *Cavalier and Yankee.* New York: George Braziller, Inc., 1957.

Thomas, Emory. *The Confederacy as a Revolutionary Experience.* Englewood Cliffs NJ: Prentice-Hall, Inc., 1971.

Thompson, Ray M. *The Confederate Shrine of Beauvoir, the Last Home of Jefferson Davis.* Biloxi MS: C. C. Hamill & Assoc., 1957.

Tolman, Newton F. *The Search for General Miles.* New York: G. P. Putnam's Sons, 1968.

Vandiver, Frank E., ed. *The Idea of the South: Pursuit of a Central Theme.* Chicago: University of Chicago Press, 1964.

_____. *Jefferson Davis and the Confederate State: an Inaugural Lecture Delivered before the University of Oxford on 26 February 1964 by Frank E. Vandiver.* Oxford: Clarendon Press, 1964.

Wagers, Margaret Newnan. *The Education of a Gentleman: Jefferson Davis at Transylvania, 1821-1824.* Lexington KY: Buckley & Reading, 1943.

Warren, Robert Penn. *Jefferson Davis Gets His Citizenship Back.* Lexington: University Press of Kentucky, 1980.

_____. *The Legacy of the Civil War: Meditations on the Centennial.* New York: Random House, 1961.

Werstein, Irving. *Abraham Lincoln versus Jefferson Davis.* New York: Thomas Y. Crowell Co., 1959.

Whitsitt, William H. *Genealogy of Jefferson Davis.* Richmond: Everett Waddey Co., 1908.

Wiley, Bell Irvin. *The Road to Appomattox.* New York: Atheneum, 1973.

Wilson, Edmund. *Patriotic Gore: Studies in the Literature of the American Civil War.* New York: Oxford University Press, 1966.

Winston, Robert W. *High Stakes and Hair Trigger.* New York: Henry Holt and Co., 1930.

Wyatt-Brown, Bertram. *Southern Honor, Ethics, and Behavior in the Old South.* New York: Oxford University Press, 1982.

## SECONDARY SOURCES

### Articles

ANCHOR. "Disputed Authorship." *The Historical Magazine,* 2d series, 5 (March 1869): 210-11.

Arnold, William E. "An Analysis of Some Speeches of Jefferson Davis." *Journal of Mississippi History* 33 (November 1971): 351-55.

Ballard, Michael B. "Breakdown in Macon." *Civil War Times Illustrated* 19 (October 1980): 31-33.

_____. "Cheers for Jefferson Davis." *American History Illustrated* 27 (May 1981): 9-15.

Barbee, David R. "Dr. Craven's 'Prison Life of Jefferson Davis'—an Exposé." *Tyler's Quarterly Historical and Genealogical Magazine* 32 (April 1951): 282-95.

Bigelow, Martha Mitchell. "Vicksburg: Experiment in Freedom." *Journal of Mississippi History* 26 (February 1964): 28-44.

Birrer, Ivan J. "Letter of Introductions." *Military Review* 45 (August 1965): 59-62.

Bleser, Carol K. and Frederick M. Heath. "The Impact of the Civil War on a Southern Marriage: Clement and Virginia Tunstall Clay of Alabama." *Civil War History* 30 (September 1984): 197-220.

Boyle, Virginia Frazier. "Jefferson Davis in Canada." *Confederate Veteran* 37 (5 March 1929): 89-93.

Bradford, Gamaliel, Jr. "Lee and Davis." *Atlantic Monthly* 107 (January 1911): 62-72.

Bradley, Chester D. "Dr. Craven and the *Prison Life of Jefferson Davis.*" *Virginia Magazine of History and Biography* 62 (January 1954): 50-94.

_____. "Was Jefferson Davis Disguised as a Woman When Captured?" *Journal of Mississippi History* 36 (August 1974): 243-68.

Brent, Robert A. "Mississippi and the Mexican War." *Journal of Mississippi History* 31 (August 1969): 202-14.

Brough, Charles Hillman. "The History of Banking in Mississippi." *Publications of the Mississippi Historical Society* 3 (1900): 317-40.

Brumgardt, John R. "The Confederate Career of Alexander H. Stephens: the Case Reopened." *Civil War History* 27 (March 1981): 64-81.

Bryson, Thomas A. "A Lawsuit Concerning the Publication of Jefferson Davis's *The Rise and Fall of the Confederate Government*." *Georgia Historical Quarterly* 54 (Winter 1970): 540-52.

_____. "A Note on Jefferson Davis's Lawsuit against Appleton Publishing Company." *Journal of Mississippi History* 33 (May 1971): 149-65.

Burr, Frank A. "Jefferson Davis, the Ex-Confederate President at Home." *Tyler's Quarterly Historical and Genealogical Magazine* 32 (January 1951): 163-80.

"The Capture of President Jefferson Davis." *The Register of the Kentucky Historical Society* 64 (October 1966): 270-76.

Carter, George E. "A Note on Jefferson Davis in Canada—His Stay in Lennoxville, Quebec." *Journal of Mississippi History* 33 (May 1971): 133-39.

C. C. W. "The Prison Life of Jefferson Davis." Review of *Prison Life of Jefferson Davis*, 2d ed. *Current Literature* 38 (June 1905): 500-502.

Chaille, Stanford E. "The Professional Services of Dr. Richardson, with Appendices." *In Memory of Prof. T. G. Richardson, M.D.* New Orleans: Faculty of the Medical Department of Tulane University, 1893.

Collins, Bruce. "The Making of Jefferson Davis." Review of *The Papers of Jefferson Davis*, vols. three and four. *Journal of American Studies* 18 (December 1984): 437-42.

Cooper, William J., Jr. "A Reassessment of Jefferson Davis as War Leader: the Case from Atlanta to Nashville." *Journal of Southern History* 36 (May 1970): 189-204.

Cotterill, Robert S. "The Old South to the New." *Journal of Southern History* 15 (February 1949): 3-8.

Coulter, E. Merton. "Jefferson Davis and the Northeast Georgia Fair." *Georgia Historical Quarterly* 50 (September 1966): 253-75.

Crellin, J. K. "Robert King Stone, M.D., Physician to Abraham Lincoln." *Illinois Medical Journal* 155 (February 1979): 97-99.

Crist, Lynda Lasswell. "A Bibliographical Note: Jefferson Davis's Personal Library: All Lost, Some Found." *Journal of Mississippi History* 45 (August 1983): 186-93.

Currie, James T. "Benjamin Montgomery and the Davis Bend Colony." *Prologue* 10 (Spring 1978): 5-21.

Daniel, John W. "Life, Services, and Character of Jefferson Davis." *Southern Historical Society Papers* 17 (1889): 113-59.

Deutsch, Eberhard P. "*United States v. Jefferson Davis:* Constitutional Issues in the Trial for Treason." *American Bar Association Journal* 52 (February 1966): 139-45; (March 1966): 263-68.

Dimick, Howard T. "The Capture of Jefferson Davis." *Journal of Mississippi History* 9 (October 1947): 238-54.

Dolensky, Suzanne T. "Varina Howell Davis, 1889-1906: The Years Alone." *Journal of Mississippi History* 47 (May 1985): 90-109.

Donald, David. "Very Symbol of the South." Review of *Jefferson Davis, Tragic Hero: the Last Twenty-Five Years, 1864-1899* by Hudson Strode. *New York Times Book Review,* 27 September 1964, 6, 30.

Dorris, Jonathan T. "Pardoning the Leaders of the Confederacy." *Mississippi Valley Historical Review* 15 (June 1928): 3-21.

Dufour, Charles L. "The Night the War Was Lost, the Fall of New Orleans: Causes, Consequences, Culpability." *Louisiana History* 2 (Spring 1961): 157-74.

Escott, Paul D. "Jefferson Davis and Slavery in the Territories." *Journal of Mississippi History* 39 (May 1977): 97-116.

_____. "Joseph E. Brown, Jefferson Davis, and the Problem of Poverty in the Confederacy." *Georgia Historical Quarterly* 61 (Spring 1977): 59-71.

Evans, W. A. "Jefferson Davis, His Diseases and His Doctors, and a Biographical Sketch of Dr. Ewing Fox Howard." *The Mississippi Doctor* 20 (June 1942): 14-26.

_____. "Jefferson Davis Shrine—Beauvoir House." *Journal of Mississippi History* 2 (October 1940): 206-11.

Ezell, John. "Jefferson Davis and the Blair Bill." *Journal of Mississippi History* 31 (May 1969): 121-26.

_____. "Jefferson Davis Seeks Political Vindication, 1851-1857." *Journal of Mississippi History* 26 (November 1964): 307-21.

Falk, Stanley L. "Jefferson Davis and Josiah Gorgas: an Appointment of Necessity." *Journal of Southern History* 28 (February 1962): 84-86.

Felt, Jeremy P. "Lucius B. Northrop and the Confederacy's Subsistence Department." *The Virginia Magazine of History and Biography* 69 (April 1961): 181-93.

Ferrell, Charles Clifton. "The Daughter of the Confederacy." *Publications of the Mississippi Historical Society* 1 (1898): 69-84.

Fleming, Walter L. "Concerning Jefferson Davis." *Bookman* 59 (March 1924): 82-85.

_____. "Early Life of Jefferson Davis." *Proceedings of the Mississippi Valley Historical Association* 9 (1917): 151-76.

_____. "Jefferson Davis's Camel Experiment." *Popular Science Monthly* (February 1909): 141-52.

_____. "Jefferson Davis's First Marriage." *Publications of the Mississippi Historical Society* 12 (1912): 21-36.

_____. "Jefferson Davis, the Negroes and the Negro Problem." *Sewanee Review* 16 (October 1908): 407-27.

_____. "Jefferson Davis at West Point." *Publications of the Mississippi Historical Society* 10 (1909): 247-67.

_____. "The Religious Life of Jefferson Davis." *The Methodist Quarterly Review* 49 (April 1910): 325-42.

Fulgham, Matt. "Research Brings Evidence to End Long Dispute on Craven's Book." *Daily Press* (Newport News VA), 23 March 1952, D-1.

Gaston, Paul M. "The 'New South.'" In *Writing Southern History.* Edited by Arthur S. Link and Rembert W. Patrick. Baton Rouge: Louisiana State University Press, 1965.

Gonzales, John E. "Henry Stuart Foote: Confederate Congressman and Exile." *Civil War History* 11 (December 1965): 384-95.

Gray, Frederic W., M.D. and Chester D. Bradley, M.D. "The Medical History of Jefferson Davis." *Virginia Medical Monthly* 94 (January 1967): 19-23.

Gray, Virginia and Rudolph Matas. "Richardson, Tobias Gibson." *Dictionary of American Biography,* rev. ed., 1963.

Green, Arthur S. "Beauvoir, the Beautiful View." *American Mercury* 91 (December 1960): 114-16.

Hall, Mark. "Alexander H. Stephens and Joseph E. Brown and the Georgia Resolutions for Peace." *Georgia Historical Quarterly* 64 (Spring 1980): 50-63.

Halsell, Willie D. "The Friendship of L. Q. C. Lamar and Jefferson Davis." *Journal of Mississippi History* 6 (July 1944): 131-44.

Hanchett, William. "Reconstruction and the Rehabilitation of Jefferson Davis: Charles G. Halpine's *Prison Life*." *Journal of American History* 56 (September 1969): 280-89.

Hansen, Vagn K. "Jefferson Davis and the Repudiation of Mississippi Bonds: the Development of a Political Myth." *Journal of Mississippi History* 33 (May 1971): 105-32.

Hatcher, William H. "Some Mississippi Views of American Federalism, 1817-1900." *The Southern Quarterly* 6 (October 1967): 117-41.

Hattaway, Herman. "A Note on Jefferson Davis as an Inspiring Speaker." *Mississippi Quarterly* 22 (Spring 1969): 147-49.

Hayes, John D. and Doris Maguire. "Charles Graham Halpine: Life and Adventures of Miles O'Reilly." *New York Historical Society Quarterly* 51 (October 1967): 326-44.

"Jefferson Davis and the Lost Cause." *Public Opinion* 1 (8 May 1886): 61-67.

Johnson, Ludwell H. "Jefferson Davis and Abraham Lincoln as War Presidents: Nothing Succeeds like Success." *Civil War History* 27 (March 1981): 49-63.

Jones, Archer. "The Gettysburg Decision." *The Virginia Magazine of History and Biography* 68 (July 1960): 331-43.

_____. "The Vicksburg Campaign." *Journal of Mississippi History* 29 (February 1967): 12-27.

Jones, James P., ed. " 'Your Left Arm': James H. Wilson's Letters to Adam Badeau." *Civil War History* 12 (September 1966): 230-45.

Joyner, Fred B., ed. "A Brief Calendar of Jefferson Davis Papers in the Samuel Richey Confederate Collection of the Miami University Library, Oxford, Ohio." *Journal of Mississippi History* 25 (January 1963): 15-32.

Jurney, Chesley W. "Defense of the South by Northern Democrats, as Portrayed in the Trial of Jefferson Davis, 1865-1868." U.S. *Congressional Record,* 70th Cong., 1st sess., 1928, 10105-109.

Kimball, William J. "The Bread Riot in Richmond, 1863." *Civil War History* 7 (June 1961): 149-54.

McKitrick, Eric. "Party Politics and the Union and Confederate War Efforts." In *The American Party Systems: Stages of Development*. Edited by William N. Chambers and W. Dean Burnham. New York: Oxford University Press, 1967.

McMurray, Richard M. " 'The Enemy at Richmond': Joseph E. Johnston and the Confederate Government." *Civil War History* 27 (March 1981): 5-31.

_____. "The Mackall Journal and Its Antecedents." *Civil War History* 20 (December 1974): 311-28.

McWhiney, Grady. "The Confederacy's First Shot." *Civil War History* 14 (March 1968): 5-14.

_____. "Controversy in Kentucky: Braxton Bragg's Campaign of 1862." *Civil War History* 6 (March 1960): 5-42.

_____. "Jefferson Davis and the Art of War." *Civil War History* 21 (June 1975): 101-12.

_____. "Jefferson Davis: the Unforgiven." *Journal of Mississippi History* 42 (May 1980): 113-27.

M[onaghan], F[rank]. "Halpine, Charles Graham." *Dictionary of American Biography,* 1932.

Monroe, Haskell M., Jr. "The Papers of Jefferson Davis." *Manuscripts* 19 (Fall 1967): 28-32.

Moore, J. Preston. "Jefferson Davis and Ambrose Dudley Mann." *Journal of Mississippi History* 19 (July 1957): 137-53.

Morse, William Eugene. "The Fight of Jefferson Davis over the Will of His Brother, Joseph E. Davis, for His Home, 'Brièrfield.' " *Journal of Mississippi History* 33 (May 1971): 141-48.

Morton, C. Brinkley. "The Later Life of Jefferson Davis." *Journal of Mississippi History* 8 (July 1946): 129-35.

Muldowny, John. "Jefferson Davis: the Postwar Years." *Mississippi Quarterly* 23 (Winter 1969-1970): 17-33.

Murphree, Dennis. "Hurricane and Brierfield: the Davis Plantations." *Journal of Mississippi History* 9 (April 1947): 98-107.

Nichols, Roy Franklin. "United States *vs.* Jefferson Davis, 1865-1869." *American Historical Review* 31 (January 1926): 266-84.

Niven, Alexander C. "Joseph E. Brown, Confederate Obstructionist." *Georgia Historical Quarterly* 42 (September 1958): 233-57.

Nuermberger, Ruth Ketring. "Clay-Clopton, Virginia Caroline Tunstall." *Notable American Women, 1607-1950,* 3 vols. (Cambridge: Belknap Press, 1971) 1:348-49.

Palmer, B. M. "The Representative Life and Character of Dr. Richardson." *In Memory of Prof. T. G. Richardson, M.D.* New Orleans: Faculty of the Medical Department of Tulane University, 1893.

Parks, Joseph S. "State Rights in a Crisis: Governor Joseph E. Brown versus President Jefferson Davis." *Journal of Southern History* 32 (February 1966): 3-24.

Parrish, William E. "Jefferson Davis Comes to Missouri." *Missouri Historical Review* 57 (July 1963): 344-56.

Poe, Clarence H. "The Tragedy of Jefferson Davis." *The Outlook* 89 (13 June 1908): 333-36.

Potter, David M. "Jefferson Davis and the Political Factors in Confederate Defeat." In *Why the North Won the Civil War.* Edited by David Donald. Baton Rouge: Louisiana State University Press, 1960.

Rabun, James Z. "Alexander Stephens and Jefferson Davis." *American Historical Review* 58 (January 1953): 290-321.

Rainwater, Perez L. "An Analysis of the Secession Controversy in Mississippi, 1854-1861." *Mississippi Valley Historical Review* 24 (June 1937): 35-42.

Rawson, Donald M. "Democratic Resurgence in Mississippi, 1852-1853." *Journal of Mississippi History* 26 (February 1964): 1-27.

Reston, James, Jr. "A Reporter at Large: You Cannot Refine It." *The New Yorker* (28 January 1985): 35-71.

Review of *The Rise and Fall of the Confederate Government* by Jefferson Davis. *The Atlantic Monthly* 48 (September 1881): 405-11.

R[hodes], C[harles] D[udley]. "Miles, Nelson Appleton." *Dictionary of American Biography,* 1933.

Richardson, Ralph. "The Choice of Jefferson Davis as Confederate President." *Journal of Mississippi History* 17 (July 1955): 161-76.

Robbins, Peggy. "Beauvoir, Last Home of Jefferson Davis." *Early American Life* 5 (August 1974): 30-33.

Ross, Steven Joseph. "Freed Soil, Freed Labor, Freed Men: John Eaton and the Davis Bend Experiment." *Journal of Southern History* 44 (May 1978): 213-32.

Shaw, Arthur Marvin. "The Family Sorrows of Jefferson Davis." *Alabama Historical Quarterly* 9 (Fall 1947): 400-403.

Shofner, Jerrell H. and William Warren Rogers. "Montgomery to Richmond: the Confederacy Selects a Capital." *Civil War History* 10 (June 1964): 155-66.

Stennis, John. "The Image of Jefferson Davis." *Journal of Mississippi History* 22 (April 1962): 123-27.

Stephenson, Nathaniel W. "A Theory of Jefferson Davis." *American Historical Review* 21 (October 1915): 73-90.

Strode, Hudson. "Judah P. Benjamin's Loyalty to Jefferson Davis." *The Georgia Review* 20 (Fall 1966): 251-60.

Sutton, Horace C. "How Wide the Gulf." *Saturday Review* 41 (1 February 1948): 29-30.

Thompson, James W. "Jefferson Davis at Beauvoir." *Confederate Historical Institute Journal* 1 (Winter 1980): 19-33.

Tindall, George B. "Mythology: A New Frontier in Southern History." In *Myth and Southern History.* Edited by Patrick Gerster and Nicholas Cords. Chicago: Rand-McNally, 1974.

Tingley, Donald Fred. "The Jefferson Davis-William H. Bissell Duel." *Mid-America* 38 (July 1956): 146-55.

Vandiver, Frank E. "The Confederacy and the American Tradition." *Journal of Southern History* 28 (August 1962): 277-86.

_____. "Jefferson Davis and Confederate Strategy." In *The American Tragedy: the Civil War in Retrospect.* Edited by Avery O. Craven and Frank E. Vandiver. Hampden-Sydney VA: Hampden-Sydney College, 1959.

_____. "Jefferson Davis—Leader without a Legend." *Journal of Southern History* 43 (February 1977): 3-18.

_____. "Jefferson Davis and Unified Army Command." *Louisiana Historical Quarterly* 38 (January 1955): 26-28.

_____. "The Shifting Roles of Jefferson Davis." In *Essays on Southern History, Written in Honor of Barnes F. Lathrop.* Edited by Gary W. Gallagher. Austin: University of Texas Press, 1980.

von Abele, Rudolph. "Jefferson Davis, Nationalist." *The American Mercury* 64 (March 1947): 313-19.

Wallis, S. Teackle. "Imprisonment of Davis." (Bledsoe's) *Southern Review* 1 (January 1867): 233-55.

Warren, Robert Penn. "A Reporter at Large: Jefferson Davis Gets His Citizenship Back." *The New Yorker* (25 February 1980): 44-99.

Weisberger, Bernard A. "Horace Greeley: Reformer as Republican." *Civil War History* 23 (March 1977): 5-25.

Wharton, Vernon L. "Reconstruction." In *Writing Southern History.* Edited by Arthur S. Link and Rembert W. Patrick. Baton Rouge: Louisiana State University Press, 1965.

Whitridge, Arnold. "Jefferson Davis and the Collapse of the Confederacy." *History Today* 11 (February 1961): 79-89.

Wiley, Bell Irvin. Foreword to *The Rise and Fall of the Confederate Government* by Jefferson Davis. New York: Thomas Yoseloff, 1958.

_____. "Jefferson Davis: an Appraisal." *Civil War Times Illustrated* 6 (April 1967): 4-11, 44-49.

Williams, T. Harry and James S. Ferguson, eds. " 'The Life of Jefferson Davis' by M'Arone." *Journal of Mississippi History* 5 (October 1943): 197-203.

Williams, Wirt A. "Jefferson Davis' Lawsuit for Brierfield." *Journal of Mississippi History* 9 (July 1947): 152-65.

Winstead, Arthur. "Jefferson Davis." *Vital Speeches* 16 (15 August 1950): 670-72.

Yearns, Wilfred B. "The Peace Movement in the Confederate Congress." *Georgia Historical Quarterly* 41 (March 1957): 1-18.

## OTHER

*Arthur M. Eastman* v. *Western Union Telegraph Co.* Circuit Court, Southern District of New York (November 1874).

Ballard, Michael B. "A Long Shadow: Jefferson Davis and the Final Days of the Confederacy." Ph.D. dissertation, Mississippi State University, 1983.

Bassett, Martha B. "The History of Beauvoir—Jefferson Davis Shrine." M.A. thesis, University of Southern Mississippi, 1970.

DeMontravel, Peter R. "The Career of Lieutenant General Nelson A. Miles from the Civil War through the Indian Wars." Ph.D. dissertation, St. John's University, 1983.

Escott, Paul D. "Jefferson Davis and the Failure of Confederate Nationalism." Ph.D. dissertation, Duke University, 1974.

*Jefferson Davis* v. *J. H. D. Bowman, Executor et al.* Decision of the Supreme Court of Mississippi (April 1878). 55 *Mississippi Reports* 671-814.

Jones, John J. "A Historiographical Study of Jefferson Davis." Ph.D. dissertation, University of Missouri, Columbia, 1970.

Mallonee, Frank Buckner, Jr. "The Political Thought of Jefferson Davis." Ph.D. dissertation, Emory University, 1966.

Morgan, James Frederick. "Jefferson Davis: the Military Man and the Politician." M.A. thesis, California State University, Fullerton, 1974.

# •INDEX•